THE TELL-TALE HEART

A JOAN KAHN BOOK

Other Books by Julian Symons

THE
TELL-TALE
HEART

The Life and Works of Edgar Allan Poe

JULIAN SYMONS

HARPER & ROW, PUBLISHERS

NEW YORK, HAGERSTOWN

SAN FRANCISCO

LONDON

FIRST EDITION

Designed by Sidney Feinberg

Library of Congress Cataloging in Publication Data

Symons, Julian, 1912–
    The tell-tale heart.
    "A Joan Kahn book."
    Bibliography: p.
    Includes index.
    1. Poe, Edgar Allan, 1809–1849. 2. Authors, American—19th century—Biography.
I. Title. PS2631.S95   818'.3'09 [B]   77–15881

ISBN 0-06-014208-1

78 79 80 81 82 10 9 8 7 6 5 4 3 2 1

To Bill and Marietta Pritchard

CONTENTS

PART TWO: THE WORK

INTRODUCTION

This book springs from a dissatisfaction with existing biographies of Poe. In almost all of them the life is fused with the work, so that an account of what he was doing in a given year will be interrupted by long analyses and discussions of poems and stories. This procedure, acceptable enough in many literary biographies, can be positively misleading in relation to Poe. It tends to conceal or soften the miserable realities of his life, the constant struggle for money, the pride and the drinking, the extent to which criticism and fiction were his occupation although poetry was his ideal, the fact that the constant purpose of his last decade was to edit his own magazine. This was Poe's life, these were his purposes. The stories, whatever later generations have thought about them, were for him at the time primarily a means of making money. Even though he revised them with each new publication, he attached much less importance to them than to his poems, and to the prospect of the magazine.

For the sake of showing Poe's life as it was actually lived, I have separated it as much as possible from the work. Complete separation is not possible and would not be desirable, but I have confined comment in the biographical part of the book to a necessary minimum. An account of the publication and reception of *The Narrative of Arthur Gordon Pym* properly belongs to the biography, a consideration of its character and quality to the critical section—or so it seems to me.

I hope that the book makes a new approach to Poe, but it is not a work of original scholarship. Indeed, a book about him meant for general readers could hardly be so today. Research into Poe's

life has been carried on in his own country with immense thoroughness. It is difficult to think of any further important biographical
contributions that could possibly be made—even the discovery of
an unknown collection of letters would not be likely to add more
than details to our knowledge of his life and character. Recent critical
studies have certainly offered new views of Poe's work, but about
the value of these, as will be seen, I am skeptical. While working
on the book I avoided discussion with Poe scholars, foreseeing that
I should differ from most of them strongly, and on the point of
resolving differences fruitlessly, in my interpretations. I owe a debt
of gratitude to the staff of the Robert Frost Library at Amherst
College, where much of the book was written. They dealt courte-
ously with my endless and sometimes ignorant queries, and showed
unwearying patience in obtaining out-of-the-way books, pamphlets,
and magazines for me.

JULIAN SYMONS

PART ONE

THE LIFE

CHAPTER I

THE ORPHAN

She never came on the Stage, but a general murmur ran through the house, "What an enchanting Creature! Heavens, what a form!— What an animated and expressive countenance!—and how well she performs! Her voice too! sure never anything was half so sweet!"
—Letter in Southern newspaper about Elizabeth Poe

IN 1841 Edgar Allan Poe set down a brief account of his life in the form of a memorandum, and sent it to the man he later chose as his literary executor, Rufus Wilmot Griswold. He had been born, Poe told Griswold, in January 1811, to a "family one of the oldest and most respectable in Baltimore." His father and mother had both died of consumption when he was two years old, and then "Mr. John Allan, a very wealthy gentleman of Richmond, Va., took a fancy to me, and persuaded my grandfather, Gen. Poe, to suffer him to adopt me." He had been brought up in Mr. Allan's family, "and regarded always as his son and heir—he having no other children," and "in 1825 went to the Jefferson University at Charlottesville, Va., where for 3 years I led a very dissipated life—the college at that period being shamefully dissolute." He came home from the university greatly in debt. "Mr. A. refused to pay some of the debts of *honor*, and I ran away from home without a dollar on a quixotic expedition to join the Greeks, then struggling for liberty."

He failed to reach Greece, the memorandum went on, but made his way to St. Petersburg, where he got into difficulties from which he was extricated by the American consul there. In 1829 he came home safe, found Mrs. Allan dead, "and immediately went to West Point as a cadet." About eighteen months later, Mr. Allan married again, "he being then 65 years of age." Poe quarreled with the new wife, and so with Allan. "Soon afterwards he died, having had a son by Mrs. A., and, although leaving a vast property, bequeathed me nothing. The army does not suit a poor man—so I left W. Point abruptly, and threw myself upon literature as a resource." When a Baltimore paper offered prizes for a story and a poem, "the Committee awarded both to me," and "soon after this I was invited by Mr. T. W. White, proprietor of the South. Lit. Messenger, to edit it . . . lately have written articles continuously for two British journals whose names I am not permitted to mention."

Most of these statements were inaccurate, and some were positively untrue. Poe made himself two years younger than he was (and so sent himself to the University of Virginia at the age of fourteen). The Poe family came from Baltimore, but they were hardly one of the city's oldest families, since his paternal grandfather David Poe had been born in Ireland. His grandfather, a spinning wheel maker, took part in the American War of Independence; but although he was commissioned Assistant Deputy Quartermaster General for the city of Baltimore in 1779 and was popularly known as "General" Poe, his rank was that of Major. John Allan was not a very wealthy gentleman but a comfortably situated businessman, and David Poe needed no persuasion to accept him as Edgar's foster father. Allan never adopted him, did not regard him as son and heir, and kept him at the university for only a single year. The journey to Greece and the visit to St. Petersburg were inventions, and when Allan married for the second time he was no more than fifty years old. He had three sons, not one, by his second marriage, and Poe's abrupt departure from West Point took place after a court-martial which the cadet had deliberately engineered. He was never the editor of the *Southern Literary Messenger* in the sense of having full editorial control over the paper, and research has not revealed the two British journals for which he claimed to have written.

Other writers have made inaccurate statements of their year of birth, have given themselves grander backgrounds than they possessed, and have improved upon their careers. The curious thing in Poe's case is that his life was just as romantic as his fictions. It lacked, however, the aristocratic grandeur and the histrionic value demanded equally by his vanity and his dramatic sense. His father and mother were both actors, and his life can best be understood as a play in which he half consciously cast himself as a tragic hero.

The life itself has a strangely circular pattern, with certain places—
Boston, Richmond, Baltimore—assuming an importance that it is
tempting to regard as symbolic. He was born in Boston, and it was
the scene of his most disastrous public appearance. The years of
childhood and adolescence spent in Richmond were those of the
strongest hopes in his life, and it was to Richmond that he returned
in the despairing search for happiness of his last months. It was in
Baltimore, from which came the side of the family in which he
took pride, that he died. And other echoes can be heard. A public
appeal was made for his mother when she lay dying, and one was
made on Poe's behalf during one of his periods of financial need.
The only letter known to have been written by his father oddly
prefigures in its subject and its tone some of those written by Poe
himself. In his own life he acted out a distorted, horrific version
of the kind of melodrama played by his parents on the stage.

Edgar Allan Poe was born in Boston in January 1809, probably
on the 19th of that month. His father, David, was the fourth son
of the "General" Poe already mentioned, and Edgar's great-great-
grandfather was a tenant farmer in Ireland. Of his mother's ancestry
little is known. An actress named Elizabeth Arnold came to America
from England in 1796, bringing with her a nine-year-old daughter
of the same name who was to become Elizabeth Poe. Mr. Arnold
had presumably died before the actress came to America, because
either soon after her arrival or before leaving England she married
a man named Tubbs. In April 1796, Mrs. Tubbs put her daughter
on the stage for the first time, as a singer. The play was a Gothic
melodrama called *The Mysteries of the Castle,* the place the Boston
Theatre.

Elizabeth Poe, or Elizabeth Arnold as she always called herself
on the stage, died at the age of twenty-one; but in her short life
she married twice, bore three children, and made a considerable
reputation as an actress. A couple of years after that first appearance
her mother disappears from theatrical records. Presumably she died,
although it is possible that she left Tubbs and gave up the stage.
Within another year Tubbs too vanished from the scene, and Elizabeth Arnold as a girl of twelve or thirteen was left alone, although
the comradeship of the theatre and her growing reputation made
her position less wretched than it might appear. She sang, she played
Prince John in *Henry IV,* Part One, she danced in ballet. At fourteen

she graduated from supporting roles, or those of children like Little
Pickle in the afterpiece *The Spoiled Child,* to a major part when
she played Ophelia in Philadelphia. There is no doubt that she was
a spirited actress and an attractive personality. She was small, with
a round rosy face, short dark curls, beautiful eyes, and a gay, saucy
manner. In 1802 she married a young actor named Charles Hopkins,
and the two appeared together in many plays until, late in December
1805, Hopkins and two other members of the company died. Within
a few months she was married again to David Poe, an actor with
the company, who had played Joseph Surface opposite Hopkins's
Sir Peter Teazle. No unfaithfulness to Hopkins's memory need be
implied. In the circumstances of the American, or indeed of the
British, theatre at that time it was important for a woman to be
known as under a man's protection.

David Poe is no less shadowy than some other figures in the
background of his son's life. He was a well-set-up and handsome
young man, but evidently not in his wife's class as an actor. "General"
Poe seems to have washed his hands of the son who had done something so rash and disreputable as go on the stage. There is a suggestion that David was a heavy drinker ("indisposition," a euphemism
for being drunk, caused his sudden absence from one play), and
the one letter of his that survives is marked by a sort of disdainful
quarrelsomeness that upon occasion marked his son. The letter, to
his first cousin, reads:

> *You* promised *me* on your honor to meet me at the Mansion House
> on the 23d—*I* promise *you* on *my* word of honor that if you will
> lend me 30, 20, 15 or even 10 $ I will *remit* it to you *immediately*
> on my arrival in Baltimore. . . . Your answer by the bearer will
> prove whether I yet have "favor in your eyes" or whether I am to
> be despised by (as I understand) a rich relation because when a *wild
> boy* I join'd a profession which I then thought and now think an
> honorable one. But which I would most willingly quit if it gave satis-
> faction to your family provided I could do *any thing* else that would
> give bread to mine.

The Poes were valued members of the Boston company, and
were regularly in work except during Elizabeth's confinements; but
they were far from prosperous. One benefit performance in 1808
resulted in "severe losses." The public was encouraged to support
them in a second by a magazine editorial which said that Mrs. Poe

had "maintained a course of characters, more numerous and arduous than can be paralleled on our boards, during any one season," and that she had always been word-perfect in spite of being obliged at times to perform three characters on the same evening.

William Henry, the Poes' first child, had been born in January 1807, and Edgar Allan came two years later. The couple's last child, Rosalie, was born late in 1810. Before that the family had made what proved an unfortunate move to New York. There David Poe's acting was severely criticized, and there on October 18, 1809, he made his last known appearance on the stage, in a play called *Grieving's a Folly*. After that, anything said about him is speculation. Whether he accompanied his wife when she turned from New York to a tour of the South in July 1810 is not known. If he came with her, they soon parted. By one account he died in October 1810, but no record of his death has been found; nor, if he lived, is anything known of how he maintained himself, except that it was apparently not as an actor. It is appropriate to the life of Edgar Allan Poe that his father should have been a man who vanished.

Elizabeth Poe struggled to maintain both her position as an actress and her precarious health. She went from Richmond to Charleston, then to Norfolk and back again to Richmond. "General" Poe had taken charge of the first child, William Henry, but business was generally poor, and Elizabeth's situation after the birth of Rosalie must have been desperate. In August 1811 she was still playing parts in light comedy and melodrama at Richmond, but after October 11 she was too ill to appear. A letter from a Richmond resident, dated November 2, says that the actress is destitute and that "the most fashionable place of resort, now is—her chamber," where "the skill of cooks and nurses is exerted to procure her delicacies." On the 29th of the month she was given a benefit, and a newspaper notice addressed "To the Humane Heart" said that *"Mrs. Poe, lingering on the bed of disease and surrounded by her children, asks your assistance and asks it perhaps for the last time."* The response is not known, but the last phrase was accurate. On December 8, 1811, Elizabeth Poe died.

This is all that we certainly know about the lives and personalities of Edgar Allan Poe's father and mother. It seems at first surprising that American literary scholarship, which is probably the most thorough in the world, has discovered nothing more by way of anecdote and reminiscence. American theatrical life at the time, however, was fugitive, quarrelsome, and erratic. There were only four important centers of theatrical production—New York, Philadelphia, Boston, and Charleston—with Baltimore, Washington, Richmond, and Savannah as places of secondary importance. An actor's life was often short, and almost always financially hazardous. In the East theatrical performances of any kind were strongly opposed, by the Quakers in Philadelphia and by a number of Puritan groups in Boston. Even though the first theatre built in Boston was tactfully called the New Exhibition Room, the co-manager was arrested and the place closed. That was in 1792. Within a few years, however, two theatres had been established and the drama had become popular.

In spite of this popularity, in the East and the South the lives of stage players remained hard. There were fierce quarrels between managers, many actors drank too much, some theatres burned down. The famous Mrs. Hallam was for some time not permitted to act because she was so likely to be drunk, until one night she walked on stage, made her protest to a sympathetic audience, and was reinstated. One of the fiercest arguments of the time, in which Tubbs and his wife were involved, affected the life of their daughter, and was indirectly responsible for her eventual isolation. This was a rebellion in the Charleston theatre run by John Sollee, by which several actors defected from the company. Tubbs may have been the least of them in talent, but he was the most militant of the group, distributing handbills in the streets and shops, and sending children out to tell passers-by that "there is no play this night, the best performers don't play any more." Sollee described Tubbs as "a *vermin* and for that reason I did not wish to have him arrested and put in prison which I could have done for his having taken away from the wardrobe of the theatre the Harlequin dress and some boy's clothes made for Miss Arnold." Acknowledging what was due "to the performers who have dismissed themselves," Sollee said that the $43 he owed the Tubbses and Miss Arnold was overbalanced by money that they owed him for fares and expenses.

The upshot of this battle, which was conducted largely by correspondence in the Charleston press, was that the dissidents set up as the "Charleston Comedians," and played a season which included a benefit for Mrs. Tubbs. Not long after this, however, the Tubbses went their ways, leaving the young Elizabeth on her own.

Such quarrels and divisions were typical in the American theatre of the time. The lives of actors were made more hazardous from the fires caused by the smoking habits of enthusiastic playgoers. The Richmond Theatre was built of brick and not, like many others, of wood, but less than three weeks after Elizabeth Poe's death it was burned down. Seventy-two people died inside it. Before that time, however, Edgar and Rosalie had been taken into care. Edgar had gone to the home of a merchant named John Allan, and Rosalie to a Mrs. Mackenzie. William Henry Poe stayed with his grandfather in Baltimore.

It is sometimes said that Poe can have remembered nothing of his mother. In fact, he was nearly three years old when she died, and he had shared her life up to that time. Vestigial remembrances of that life, poverty-stricken, often wretchedly unhappy but never dull, must have remained with him, and it was a way of living that— of course without intention—he later reproduced in some respects as his own. If he seems sometimes not so much a strongly marked personality as an actor, trying on parts and attitudes to see how they fitted, that was surely not only the effect of heredity but also of the glimpses retained in an extraordinarily retentive mind of what his life had been like before his mother died.

CHAPTER II

FROM EDGAR ALLAN—

Edgar is growing wonderfully and enjoys a good reputation as both able and willing to receive instruction.
—John Allan in a letter, September 28, 1818.

JOHN ALLAN, although he was not very wealthy nor in the English sense a gentleman, was a comfortably placed merchant, a partner in the firm of Ellis & Allan, tobacco exporters and general merchants. He had been born in Scotland, and came to Richmond in his early teens to live with and work for his uncle William Galt. In 1800, when he was twenty, he went into business with Charles Ellis, another clerk employed by Galt, and the business prospered. Allan was naturalized in 1804, a year after he had married an American girl, Frances Keeling Valentine. They had no children, and this was an important consideration in their decision to give a home to Edgar Poe. There can be no doubt that Frances Allan was prepared to regard him as her own son.

Her husband's intentions are by no means so clear. He was not an ordinary man, nor an uncultured one. A letter of his to a woman friend in 1811 begins with a quotation from Scott, embodies another from Swift, and is written with easy flippancy in a mildly literary style. Allan, then, was not devoid of literary knowledge and was in the common affairs of life a genial man. There were, however, other sides to him. He had an obstinacy, toughness, and determination to get his own way that many would regard as peculiarly Scottish. He was a man of strong sensual feeling (he had at least two illegitimate children), and was also a hard drinker. We do not know his exact feelings toward Edgar, or why he did not adopt the boy for his son as the Mackenzies adopted Rosalie as their daughter.

Edgar was brought up in childhood as a son, indeed as the son, of the family without ever being given legal status. There was clearly a reservation in Allan's mind about making the boy his legal son, and so his heir.

Yet there is no indication that in these early years Allan was anything but pleased with his foster son. Edgar was an unusually bright, intelligent child. There are stories of him standing on a chair to recite rhymes after dinner in the presence of company, and then being given sweetened wine and water, and that he was dressed on such occasions in baggy trousers of silk pongee, with red silk stockings and a peaked purple velvet cap that had a gold tassel falling over one shoulder. He was sent to school in Richmond and there impressed his master, William Ewing. When, in 1815, Allan visited Britain to open a branch of the firm there, he took his wife, her sister, and Edgar with him. Nearly two years later Ewing wrote to say that he hoped Edgar liked his English school, adding that he was a charming boy, and asking where he had been sent to school and what he was reading. Allan replied that Edgar "is a fine Boy and I have no reason to complain of his progress."

At this time Poe was attending a boarding school in Stoke New-ington, in north London, his second school in Britain. There is no specific record of his achievements there, but he was evidently an intelligent pupil who found it easy to learn anything that interested him. The Reverend John Bransby, the headmaster, is supposed to have said much later that Edgar Allan was quick and clever, "and would have been a very good boy if he had not been spoilt by his parents," who "allowed him an extravagant amount of pocket money, which enabled him to get into all manner of mischief." It should be remembered that this, like many other recollections of Poe in childhood, rests on no certain factual basis. We know that he attended the school for at least two years, and, from one term's bills, that he was taught dancing but at that time apparently neither drawing, music, nor French. We know that he was called Edgar Allan, and that in November 1819 his foster father was still pleased with him, saying that he was a fine boy and a good scholar. We know also that the school made a deep impression upon the child. He had a great feeling for buildings, and in writing *William Wilson* twenty years later, he not only named the schoolmaster Bransby but also described Manor House School in characteristically vivid, visionary terms as "a large, rambling, cottage-built and somewhat decayed building in a misty-looking village of England, where were a vast number of gigantic and gnarled trees, and where all the houses were excessively ancient and inordinately tall." The rest, what he was taught and what he learned, is conjecture.

If Edgar Allan was given an extravagant amount of pocket money, that was one of the few extravagances possible to John Allan at this time. The stay in Britain was a disaster in almost every way. Frances Allan and her sister were very sick during the crossing, and Frances did not fully recover her health. She had a bad cold and sore throat during a visit to Scotland, was "miserably dissatisfied" in London, took the waters at Cheltenham, and seems to have been in poor health for most of the time the family was in England. And the time chosen for setting up Allan & Ellis (as distinct from Ellis & Allan) in London proved badly chosen. The depression that followed the Napoleonic wars affected the firm's trade in Richmond, and eventually made the abandonment of the London enterprise necessary. In November 1819, Allan wrote to his partner that he had only £100 in England, and could not return until he received some money. A few months later he gave up the hopeless enterprise and brought his family home.

The boy had lived in England for five years. Upon the whole the stay seems to have made little direct impression on him. He used the Manor House School as a setting for part of a story, and incidents from the time remained in his mind—the name Dubourg, that of the mistress who owned the first school he attended, appears in another story—but his writings were very little influenced by the scenes and the people he had lived among.

In his maturity Poe yearned for contact with English literature, but had little interest in English life. He was throughout his adult life emphatically an American, concerned to advance and improve the culture of his country. He seems to have made no particular friends at the English school, and because of Frances Allan's illness he can have seen little of her even in the holidays. Perhaps the two things he carried away most clearly were the sense of his isolation from other people, and the sense of his name. There is no reason to think that John Allan was unkind or ungenerous, but he too can have had little time to spare for Edgar, and the question of his adoption remained undecided. But this, of course, was not known to the boy who was called Master Allan.

CHAPTER III

—TO EDGAR POE

> *Mr. John Allan, Dr.*
> *To present quarter's tuition of Master Poe from June*
>   *11th to September 11, 1822*   *$12.50*
> *1 Horace 3.50. Cicero de Offi 62½*   *4.12½*
> *1 copybook—paper, pens & ink*   *87½*
>   *$17.50*

IN a symbolic, and perhaps in a literal sense, the change from Master Allan to Master Poe was a decisive one. In Richmond, of course, the fact that the Allans had taken the orphan of an actress into their home was well known. But when they returned, more than eight years had passed since the boy had become part of the family, and more than five since they had lived in Richmond. During the years in England Edgar had been known as Master Allan. Now he was again Master Poe. The change suggests Allan's determination not to adopt the boy legally, and to Edgar it must have been disturbing and confusing. It must also have brought home to him with a shock the humbleness of his origins.

The Richmond to which he returned at the age of eleven was a charming and elegant small town of wide streets, green gardens, Georgian houses. If Virginia was the most English part of the United States, Richmond was the most English town in Virginia, and in social relations it was snobbish in a way characteristically English rather than American. Its inhabitants were very consciously civilized and aristocratic, and although they had a taste for the arts and in particular for drama, that was a different matter from accepting the child of strolling players as the equal of their own sons. Allan's financial difficulties were not resolved until 1825, when the death of his uncle William Galt made him a rich man. Until that time he was far from rich, and for nearly a year the family lived at the modest home of his partner Charles Ellis. It reflects well on Allan that Edgar was sent to the best local schools and then to the University of Virginia, although it is true that by the time he went to the university Allan had come into his inheritance, and the years of financial stringency were over. At school the boy was made to understand, at least by some of his contemporaries, that he was not the equal of those born into the Virginian aristocracy. "All this had the effect of making the boys decline his leadership; and on looking back on it since, I fancy it gave him a fierceness he would otherwise not have had," wrote one school friend.

These words were written more than half a century after school-days were over. They must be seen as interesting but not necessarily reliable, like the reminiscences of Tom Ellis, son of Allan's partner, which appeared in print as late as 1900, or of Jack Mackenzie, son of the family who had taken responsibility for Rosalie. Tom Ellis worshipped his older friend, and had no doubt of Edgar's being a leader among his playmates. He was

> very beautiful, yet brave and manly for one so young. . . . He taught me to shoot, to swim, to skate, to play bandy; and I ought to mention that he once saved me from drowning—for having thrown me into the falls headlong, that I might "strike out" for myself, he presently found it necessary to come to my help, or it would have been too late!

The Allans, according to Ellis in his old age, lavished affection upon Edgar, sent him to the best schools, and saw that he was "trained to all the habits of the most polished society." He won an elocution prize and showed great facility in rhyming, swam 6 miles up the James River against the tide, joined the Thespian Society and took part in plays, was a good runner and boxer. His head-master Joseph Clarke remembered him as a boy different from others. "He was remarkable for self-respect, without haughtiness, strictly just and correct in his demeanor with his fellow playmates, which rendered him a favorite even with those above his years." John Mackenzie's stories, again told after Poe's death, of his gaiety, liberal supply of pocket money, and enjoyment of practical jokes, help to fill in the picture of an intelligent and lively boy who was more respected than liked.

Much of this is the common coinage of reminiscence about those who have become unexpectedly famous. We do not know very much at first hand about his early adolescence nor his home life, beyond Mackenzie's comment that although Mr. Allan was a good man in his way, Edgar was not fond of him. "I know that often when angry with Edgar he would threaten to turn him adrift, and that he never allowed him to lose sight of his dependence on his charity." Again, we cannot be sure that this is true, for it conflicts with another account that he never asked any school friend to go home with him. Poe himself, writing in 1840, referred to "the sad experience of my schoolboy days," and this is at least a reflection of what he felt himself about his life at school. The picture painted by one biographer of "Edgar Allan Poe, a well-knit, broad-browed, curly-headed lad with astonishing long-lashed deep grey eyes, seated with his best chums Jack Mackenzie, Rob Sully, little Bobby Stanard and Robert Cabell upon a rail fence like so many crows, each munching a tender juicy turnip, or a raw sweet potato with a little salt on it," is largely imaginary. It seems likely that Edgar's assumption of equality with, or even superiority to, boys who regarded themselves as his social betters was not appreciated by them. From his reactions in later life we know that any real or imagined slight would have been deeply resented, particularly if it had been one reflecting on his birth or social position. Among the many parts he was to play in life, that of Southern gentleman was the earliest and the one to which he adhered most consistently.

We get a glimpse of what John Allan felt about Poe from a letter written in November 1824 to William Henry, Edgar's elder brother. Things at this time were going very badly for Allan. The firm had been dissolved by mutual consent, he had been compelled to make a personal assignment of his assets, and financial difficulties had forced a move to a new house, apparently given to Allan by his uncle. All this may have something to do with Allan's explosion of anger:

Dear Henry,

I have just seen your letter of the 25th ult to Edgar and am much afflicted, that he has not written you. He has had little else to do for me he does nothing & seems quite miserable, sulky & ill-tempered to all the Family. How we have acted to produce this is beyond my conception—why I have put up so long with his conduct is little less wonderful. The boy possesses not a Spark of affection for us not a particle of gratitude for all my care and kindness towards him. I have given a much superior Education than ever I received myself. If Rosalie has to relie on any affection from him God in his mercy preserve her. . . .

Henry Poe was regarded, then and for several years to come, as a brilliant young man. Rosalie was a sweet but vague girl, whose intellect failed to develop after the age of twelve. She was cared for by the Mackenzie family during most of her life.

The frantic irritation that shows through in John Allan's letter was caused no doubt partly by his straitened circumstances, to which his foster son apparently paid little attention. At this time Lafayette visited Richmond, and Poe as a lieutenant in the Richmond Junior Volunteers was co-signatory of a letter asking that the Volunteers should be allowed to retain their arms. It is possible also that if he had by now heard of Allan's frequent and casual infidelities, he may have made his disapproval plain.

The young man's attitude to love, or at least to the idea of love, is shown by his relationships with Mrs. Stanard and Elmira Royster. His school friend Rob Stanard took Poe home with him one day, and there he met Rob's mother, Jane Craig Stanard. Many years later Poe told Sarah Helen Whitman of the encounter. Mrs. Stanard greeted him with words which, as Poe told it to Mrs. Whitman, "so penetrated the sensitive heart of the orphan boy as to deprive him of the power of speech, and, for a time, almost of consciousness itself." Mrs. Whitman adds that Jane Stanard later became "the confidant of all his boyish dreams" and the guide of "his turbulent and passionate youth." The dates involved make this unlikely. Poe was a little more than fifteen when Mrs. Stanard died in 1824, and she had been mentally unbalanced for some while before her death, so that he was only fourteen when he visited her. Poe himself asserts that one of his most famous poems, "To Helen," was written at that time "to the first, purely ideal love of my soul," whom he had renamed Helen. This too must be regarded as doubtful, almost as doubtful as the story that he went nightly to visit Mrs. Stanard's grave. His first volume of poems was published in 1827, and it would have been uncharacteristic of him to omit any completed work from it. "To Helen" first appeared in print in 1831, and the odds are that it was written not long before that date. It is an eloquent, extremely literary, evocation of a loved object rather than a person:

> On desperate seas long wont to roam,
>   Thy hyacinth hair, thy classic face,
> Thy Naiad airs have brought me home
>   To the glory that was Greece,
> And the grandeur that was Rome.

Mrs. Stanard was not the only love of Poe's adolescence. He addressed himself more seriously to Elmira Royster, the daughter of a neighbor. The story was told by Elmira in 1875, but in this case there is no reason to doubt its substantial truth. Edgar Poe, Elmira said from that distant vantage point half a century later, was a beautiful boy, devoted to his foster mother as she was to him. He was not very talkative and his general manner was sad, but he was also "warm and zealous in any cause he was interested in, very enthusiastic and impulsive." She was about fifteen or sixteen when "he first addressed me and I engaged myself to him." Then he went off to the university and wrote her letters of which she knew nothing, because they were intercepted by her father on the ground that the couple were too young. There was, she said, no other reason for the interdict.

Again one senses disapproval of Poe's parentage. Mr. Royster was a solid Richmond citizen, and his objections are as likely to have been on this ground as on that of extreme youth. Elmira Royster became Elmira Shelton when she was seventeen, and she did not learn about the letters Poe had addressed to her until after her marriage. By this time he had left the university, and was ready to make a decisive break from the town in which he had been brought up.

What sort of figure did Edgar Allan Poe present when, in February 1826, at the age of seventeen, he went to the university? His appearance was generally pleasing, with a fine forehead, large and beautiful gray eyes, and a musical voice. He hated any coarseness of speech or lack of refinement in appearance, and his evident sensitivity and warmth of feeling made him particularly attractive to women. He had not yet reached his full height of 5 feet 8 inches but, although a certain bandy-leggedness was noticed by some, his bearing was easy and graceful. He had a small reputation as a poet among friends and acquaintances, based upon several satirical pieces of which only one, a lampoon on a clerk in a dry goods store, has been preserved in its entirety. He was physically lithe and active, particularly in such individual sports as boxing, running, and swimming. The 6-mile swim that he made against the tide in the James River was already locally famous.

The picture is that of an accomplished young gentleman, conscious of his superior abilities, and Poe behaved in accordance with it. Yet he was neither a Southerner nor a gentleman. This knowledge had been brought home to him at school, and it was to be reinforced while he was at the university. There were signs also of family instability—something that was already evident in Henry Poe. Henry was in the navy or the merchant service, and had actually made some of the journeys that Edgar later attributed to himself. Henry had also published poems in magazines, so that his literary reputation may well have seemed enviable to his younger brother.

Why, after writing so severely about Edgar, did John Allan send him to the university? To ask the question is to ignore some of the social realities of Richmond. Allan was now a rich man, and he would have earned reproaches which he might have felt were justified if he had in effect discarded his foster son by consigning him to a clerk's job after such an expensive early upbringing. It is possible also that he may have been happy for the openly censorious boy to be out of the way while he was carrying on his several sexual affairs. Yet although Allan apparently behaved generously, there can be no doubt that he was frantically irritated by Edgar's style and attitude. It is likely also that he resented the perfect naturalness with which Edgar fitted himself to the role of Southern gentleman. Allan, therefore, although he did "the right thing," did not do it from the right motives, and was determined from the first to keep Edgar on a tight financial rein. He might have been satisfied with gratitude and submission; but these were denied him, for Edgar believed he was receiving no more than his obvious rights, grudgingly given. The conflict between his own view of himself as a Southern gentleman receiving a proper education, and John Allan's concept of Edgar as an object of charity who should be constantly grateful, was later to prove a receipt for disaster.

CHAPTER IV

FROM THE UNIVERSITY
OF VIRGINIA–

*The result was the beautiful scene that lay below Monticello, the
exquisitely situated mountain-crest towering eight hundred feet in
the air where "The Father of the University of Virginia" had built
himself an eyrie among the century-old trees overlooking a view
of rolling, river-bounded loveliness, where Piedmont hill and sap-
phire Blue Ridge, gaunt Alleghany and solemn Ragged Mountains
blend into a delightful harmony, all gathering round and enshrining
in their bosom the jewel of Jefferson, the white-domed University.*
— *James A. Harrison in 1902*

IN 1800 Thomas Jefferson told a correspondent of his idea for estab-
lishing in Virginia "an university on a plan so broad and liberal
and *modern* as to be worth patronizing with the public support,
and be a temptation to the youth of other States to come and drink
of the cup of knowledge, and fraternize with us. The first step is
to obtain a good plan . . ." Jefferson's plan was for a nondenominational place of education, to which members of all religions would
be admitted. The very best teachers from Europe would be induced
to come there, and under them students would be free to follow
whatever course of study they chose. A governing Board of Visitors
would administer general rules; but since it could hardly be doubted
that students at such an institution would pursue the highest moral
ends, it was right that they should be self-governing. Jefferson tried
during forty years to make these ideals a reality. In March 1825,
when the University of Virginia opened its doors, he succeeded.

The objections to Jefferson's plan were not principally, as one might expect, to the idea of student self-government, but to the nondenominational nature of the proposed university. William and Mary College, which Jefferson himself had attended, was a Church of England establishment, and Presbyterian feeling was strong throughout most of Virginia. The suggested freedom for students was also felt to be undesirable, and for years the project remained little more than a dream, intermittently pursued by Jefferson during a period in which he became President of the United States. The plan for a university was indeed only part of his general view that education should be freely available to all, and his belief that if precisely equal educational opportunities were offered to all men, the result must be beneficial. "Is not education the most effectual means to prevent tyranny?" he asked. The university was to be a place of advanced education, but it was also to be the crowning achievement in a complete public school system, embracing both elementary and grammar schools.

Little of this had been achieved when, at the age of sixty-six, Jefferson retired from public life. He had become the target for many personal attacks, and was happy to return to the house that had been built for him on the height of Monticello. There were no professional architects in the United States, so he had superintended much of the building, rule in pocket and case of surveying instruments in hand, although for twenty-nine years he had lived at Monticello very little. Now he turned his persuasive powers to the establishment of the university.

The campaign was firmly launched in 1814, the cornerstone of the first building laid three years later. Jefferson himself was the architect, designing the pavilions, dormitories, colonnades, and arcades that were constructed on European models. He drew up plans and supervised the actual work during almost daily visits. It is not surprising that the Board of Visitors almost always deferred to his views, not only from the deference they felt for his knowledge and judgment but also because the whole idea was his, and it was therefore thought right that he should execute it in his own way. His energy was unflagging. When the university opened he was eighty-two years old, but that did not stop him from posting up many circulars for it with his own hands. At his death in the following year only the central rotunda, which had been modeled on the

Pantheon at Rome, was left uncompleted. The university was in being.

The European professors had arrived, as the result of a mission to England undertaken by a Jeffersonian disciple named Francis Walker Gilmer. He did not find it easy to find recruits for professorships in a country so far away, and he was not helped by the fact that lack of funds made it necessary in some cases to assign several subjects to the same instructor, so that chemistry and astronomy were added to the chair of natural philosophy. The mathematical sciences were directed by a young medical student named Key, who was persuaded to accept the position by Gilmer's prediction that there would be an immediate influx of five hundred students, of whom at least two hundred would take the mathematical course. Key's salary was to be $1500 a year, but add to that the $25 paid to the instructor by each student taking a course and there was the prospect of comparative riches. Dr. Blaettermann, the professor of modern languages, had a very distinct foreign accent and was extremely irascible; George Long, professor of ancient languages, was a twenty-four-year-old Fellow of Trinity who had not yet taken his M.A. degree. These were perhaps the best teachers who could have been found, but the remark of a Connecticut paper that "Mr. Gilmer could have fully discharged his mission, with half the trouble and expense, by a short trip to New England," does not seem wide of the mark.

That Gilmer, and Jefferson, had been wildly optimistic about the number of students was shown immediately. The enrollment for 1825 was just over 120 students, and it remained under 200 for several years. The students came mostly from old and wealthy Virginian families, so that the university intended as a symbol of freedom in education was attacked as a province of the rich. The idea of self-government had to be abandoned after a single session. The students gambled, drank, and fought. "They flocked to this new institution as to a watering place," one commentator said, noting that some had "elegant equipages," others "a servant, a fowling piece and a pointer or two." The student censors who were supposed to act as guardians of their fellows' conduct did nothing of the kind. In the first months there were no class roll calls and no examinations. It was plain that something had to be done, and discipline was placed in the hands of the "hotel keepers," as the providers of food were called. This, too, proved unsuccessful. Within a few years the whole idea of self-government had been replaced by draconian ordinances, which demanded that students should wear uniforms, rise at dawn and retire when a curfew sounded at nine in the evening, and should work on through the Christmas holidays. All that, however, was after Poe's time. When he came up for the university's second session in February 1826, no real discipline had been established.

He could hardly have found himself in an environment that gave more encouragement to his fantasies. He was among rich young men, and naturally behaved as they did. He played cards, drank, took part in the activities of students whose dash and style he admired. His card playing was reckless, his drinking passionate and obsessive. Another student remembered that "he would always seize the tempting glass, generally unmixed with sugar or water—in fact, perfectly straight,—and without the least apparent pleasure, swallow the contents, never pausing until the last drop had passed his lips." The contents of the glass were most often whiskey or brandy, sometimes mixed with honey. His first letters home to Allan give a graphic picture of the lack of discipline in the university. Some of the "hotel keepers" then in charge had been indicted by a Grand Jury for gambling:

> Soon after you left here the Grand Jury met and put the Students in a terrible fright—so much so that the lectures were unattended— and those whose names were upon the Sheriff's list—travelled off into the woods & mountains—taking their beds & provisions with them—there were about 50 on the list—so you may suppose the College was very well thinn'd—this was the first day of the fright— the second day "A proclamation" was issued by the faculty forbidding "any student under pain of a major punishment to leave his dormitory between the hours of 8 & 10 AM—(at which time the Sheriffs would be about) or in any way to resist the lawful authority of the Sheriffs'— This order however was very little attended to.

His second letter mentions "a great many fights," including a particular one outside his door in which one student bit another's arm so badly that "it is likely that pieces of flesh as large as my hand will be obliged to be cut out."

In such surroundings, was it possible to work? Evidently it was, for Poe read widely in his year at the university. The records show that he was one of the best Latin and French students, and he impressed the irascible Blaettermann by his translation of a passage from Tasso. He learned languages with remarkable speed, or at least gathered enough of them to be able to speak both French and Latin easily. Fellow students observed that he often entered the lecture room unready to recite, but did so successfully if called on, simply by reading ahead during the lecture.

In some respects study was difficult, for extraordinary restrictions were placed upon use of the library. Books could be withdrawn only when a request had been certified by a member of the faculty, and only twenty tickets a day were issued even for admission to the library as a place of reference. We know that Poe read there some American and some ancient history, but the chief testimony to the development of his personality and talent comes in the recollections of students who knew and admired him. He delighted, one friend said, in reading his own poems and quoting other poets; then "suddenly a change would come over him & he would with a piece of charcoal evince his versatile genius by sketching upon the walls of his dormitory, whimsical, fanciful, & grotesque figures, with so much artistic skill, as to leave us in doubt whether Poe in future life would be Painter or Poet." There is general agreement that he was excitable, sometimes gay and occasionally morose, less about his figure, which some remember as short and compact, and others as delicate and slender. There is no unanimity even about the bow legs.

It is odd that although there is considerable documentation of his activities, including occasions when he read his poems aloud, no individual poem is remembered. When, in 1827, *Tamerlane and Other Poems, By a Bostonian* appeared, Poe said in his prefatory note that "the greater part of the Poems which compose this little volume, were written in the year 1821–2, when the author had not completed his fourteenth year." The statement has been derided, and it is true that Poe always wished to make himself appear more of a prodigy than he was; but the collection is still remarkable, even if it was produced at the university. The poems are naturally influenced by the writers he most admired, Tom Moore and Byron, and this is particularly evident in the four hundred-odd lines of "Tamerlane," which actually includes the line "The sound of revelry by night" without acknowledgment. In theme, "Tamerlane" prefig-

ures much of Poe's poetry. It owes nothing to Marlowe, whose play
Poe had certainly not read at this time, and not much to the facts
of history. Tamerlane is the first of many Poe heroes who end heart-
broken through some failure in love. His heart is still with the beloved Ada he has left, and the conclusion of the poem in this first
version (later it was much changed) sees him returning home "in
a peasant's lowly guise," to be told by a mountain hunter that Ada
is dead.

> *There* rose a fountain once, and *there*
> Full many a fair flow'r raised its head:
> But she who rear'd them was long dead,
> And in such follies had no part,
> What was there left me *now?* despair—
> A kingdom for a broken—heart.

The four-stress line was a favorite of Poe's, and the poem is an
impressive performance for a boy who could have been no more,
and perhaps was less, than seventeen. Like the "Song" ("I saw thee
on thy bridal day") that follows it in this volume, "Tamerlane" no
doubt reflects his emotions at the end of the affair with Elmira Royster. The eight other poems show the unexplained melancholy that
is his hallmark as a poet. Happiness is seen as a dream in several
poems:

> In visions of the dark night
>   I have dreamed of joy departed—
> But a waking dream of life and light
>   Hath left me broken-hearted.

It is easy to call this melancholy factitious, and certainly it seems
excessive for its origins in the death of Mrs. Stanard and Elmira
Royster's marriage. Poe's emotions, however, are often excessive
in any rational sense. Although his life was an unhappy one, he
does not react to the wretched events in it so much as he appears
to anticipate and even to provoke them. He carried with him from
early youth onward the burden of an unhappiness that he did not
attempt to explain to himself. At the time these early poems were
written, he was well placed to make a career in the world. Might
he not have considered himself lucky to be sent to the University
of Virginia, and educated among those who would become generals

and judges, congressmen and railroad presidents? But of course to ask such a question is irrelevant to a personality like Poe's.

The months at the university marked the beginning of the long battle with his foster father that was to end in the complete severance of their relations, a battle conducted upon the grounds of money and behavior but obviously having deeper roots. John Allan's actions and reactions are not much more susceptible of logical analysis than those of Poe. His many friends regarded him as a genial and generous man. He was giving Edgar a fine start in life by sending him to the university, and money was no longer in short supply. Why, then, stint the boy of it as Allan unquestionably did? Perhaps jealousy of Edgar's literary ambitions was mixed with the pride that Allan undoubtedly felt in him, and very likely the fact that the boy behaved exactly as if he were the son of a rich man angered his foster father. When Edgar went home for the Christmas vacation of 1826, Allan refused to permit him to return to college. After eight months the university education was at an end.

The immediate reason for this was the gambling debts Poe had run up, which amounted to something like $2000, and which Allan refused to pay. There is no doubt, however, that Allan himself behaved with extraordinary meanness about ordinary living expenses. "The expenses of the institution at the lowest estimate were $350 per annum," Poe wrote some years later.

> You sent me therewith $110. Of this $50 were to be paid immediately for board—$60 for attendance upon 2 professors—and you even then did not miss the opportunity of abusing me because I did not attend 3 . . . then $15 more were to be paid for room-rent—$12 more for a bed—and $12 more for room furniture. I had, of course, the mortification of running in debt for public property—against the known rules of the institution, and was immediately regarded in the light of a beggar.

That he was not exaggerating the costs involved is shown by a request for money from one of the "hotel keepers" to Allan, to pay the servant whose cleaning services were regarded as a necessary expense. The reference to the third professor lends force to the fact that Poe attended only the classes of Long and Blaettermann. He had no scientific or mathematical training, which makes all the

more remarkable his later interest in scientific theory and his skill
in cryptography.

There can be no doubt that Poe's presence at home acted as
an irritant upon his foster father, and a story told by a former school-
mate suggests that the irritation was not without cause. The young
friend had called at the Allan home on Christmas Eve, and was
invited to stay. When he said that he had no suitable clothes, it
was suggested that Edgar could lend him a suit. This was done,
but halfway through the evening Edgar suggested that they should
leave the house and go off on their own. They did so, with what
result is not recorded. If there were many incidents like this, it is
not surprising that relations between Allan and Poe deteriorated.
In any case, Allan refused to pay his foster son's gambling debts
or his further university fees, although a suggestion that he was
put into the firm's countinghouse at this point seems untrue. It is
likely that he remained what Allan would have called idle, reading
books and seeing his friends.

A break was inevitable. It came in March 1827, when after a
quarrel Poe left the house, and wrote a letter expressing the bitter-
ness he felt. "My determination is at length taken," he said, "to
leave your house and indeavor to find some place in this wide world
where I will be treated—not as *you* have treated me—This is not
a hurried determination, but one on which I have long considered—
and having so considered my resolution is unalterable." He went
on to give reasons. "[I] have been taught by *you* to aspire, to eminence in public life," a possibility which he said had been destroyed
by Allan's capriciously cutting short his education. Allan lacked affection for him, and took delight "in exposing me before those whom
you think likely to advance my interest in this world." Poe complained of continual humiliation. "You suffer me to be subjected
to the whims & caprice, not only of your white family, but the
complete authority of the blacks—these grievances I could not sub-
mit to; and I am gone." It is hard to know how seriously he expected
to be taken. In this, and a letter written on the following day, he
asked for his trunk, his clothes, and some money which would get
him to Boston, "and a little to support me there untill I shall be
enabled to engage in some business." He added that he had not
eaten for more than a day, and had "not one cent in the world to
provide any food."

Allan noted upon the verso of this second note, "Pretty Letter," and wrote a savage reply, admitting that he had taught Edgar to aspire to eminence, "but I never expected that Don Quixotte, Gil Blas, Jo: Miller & such works were calculated to promote the end." He ended on an ironical note by saying that "after such a list of Black charges—you Tremble for the consequences unless I send you a supply of money." We do not know whether he did so, but in any case Poe somehow managed to get a ship to Boston, and arrived there early in April.

CHAPTER V

—TO THE END OF WEST POINT

*My desire is for the present to be freed from the Army—since I
have been in it my character is one that will bear scrutiny & has
merited the esteem of my officers—but I have accomplished my own
ends—& I wish to be gone.*
　　　　　—Edgar Allan Poe to John Allan, December 22, 1828

HOW was he to maintain himself in Boston; what business was there
in which he could engage? During the few weeks Poe spent in
the city he must have been employed in some way, but the details
are unknown. He was, quite remarkably, able to persuade a printer
named Calvin Thomas to produce, in an edition of what is said to
have been forty copies, *Tamerlane and Other Poems.* Whether he
had money to pay for this little book or whether Thomas, who was
a boy not much older than Poe, gave him credit is not known.
The book, however, was in hand by the time that Poe enlisted in
the army, on May 26, 1827. Although he had voluntarily taken instruction at the university gymnasium with a military drillmaster,
Poe's entry into the army can only be regarded as a desperate act,
taken partly from lack of money and partly in an attempt to cut
himself off totally from his former life. He gave his name as Edgar
A. Perry, his age as twenty-two instead of the actual eighteen, his
occupation as that of clerk. His height now was 5 feet 8 inches,
his eyes are listed as gray, his hair as brown, and his complexion
as fair.

This was not the first pseudonym he had used. He had already,
it seems from a note made by Allan upon a letter asking him for
money, called himself Henri le Rennet, and he was to use other
names, both in his own person and as a writer, in the next few

years. By adopting another name, does one take on a new personality? Perhaps Poe hoped that this might happen, and that by immersing himself in the army the troublesome identity of Edgar Allan Poe might disappear. Yet it is also true that this identity was what, in many ways, he wished more than anything to preserve.

The next eighteen months of Poe's life are singularly blank in a career that is for the most part very copiously documented. There are no extant letters, and no suggestion that he made any particular friends, except Colonel William Drayton, to whom he later dedicated a collection of stories. We are left with a number of facts. He was immediately assigned to an artillery battery in Boston Harbor, moved six months later to Fort Moultrie on Sullivan's Island in Charleston Harbor (where he met Colonel Drayton), and a year after that was sent to Fortress Monroe in Virginia. In May 1828 he was made an artificer, and in January 1829 was promoted to Sergeant Major. The Charleston surroundings, and particularly Sullivan's Island, which was both desolate and exotic, made a deep impression on him. He was to use the island as a setting for "The Gold-Bug" and as a background in other stories.

The promotion to Sergeant Major should not be taken to imply that he enjoyed army life, although his career might so far as it went be called successful. On December 1, 1828, he wrote to Allan, signing himself "respectfully & affectionately Edgar A. Poe." Allan had apparently written earlier to say that Poe had better remain where he was until the termination of his enlistment, that is, for five years. The prospect horrified Poe. The prime of his life, as he said, would be wasted, and in several letters he tried hard to convince Allan that he had changed and matured, and was now to be trusted. He stressed that if trust was given, Allan would be delighted by the result. But although he admitted, "I feel that within me which will make me fulfil your highest wishes & only beg you to suspend your judgement until you hear of me again," it was plain that what he immediately wanted was help in obtaining his discharge from the army, and that Allan was unwilling to give it.

The story of Poe's life at this time is told in his letters to John Allan, letters which are never less than moving in their appeal for the financial help that was sometimes grudgingly extended, and for the affection which it was not in Allan's nature to give. Poe's life might have been simpler and happier if Allan's temperament had been different. The need for parental love, praise, and guidance was never greater than now, and the long attempt to mend his relations with the man Poe wished to regard as his father went far beyond a mere desire to reestablish himself as a Southern gentleman, although that played its part. In these letters he often signed himself "your affectionate son" and addressed Allan as "dear Pa." Early in the correspondence he expressed contrition for the past, gave assurances about the future, and emphasized that other people took an interest in him, including his regimental commander Colonel House. "It must have been a matter of regret to me, that when those who were strangers took such deep interest in my welfare, you who called me your son should refuse me even the common civility of answering a letter." A couple of months later he was asking Allan's help in procuring a cadet's appointment at the Military Academy. This would, he said, be proof of what form his "future views & expectations" would take, and he pointed out also the "immense advantages" that he would gain from his situation as a man who had passed through the practical part of artillery work in the ranks. "It would be an unprecedented case in the American army."

At the end of February 1829, Frances Allan died and Allan relented toward his foster son, perhaps at the request of his dying wife. Poe was sent money, returned to Richmond, and there was provided with a suit of black clothes. Further, Allan agreed to support his claim for discharge from the army and enlistment as a cadet at West Point. The details of Colonel House's letter asking for permission to discharge Edgar A. Perry, "at present the Sergeant-Major of the 1st Reg't of Artillery, on his procuring a substitute," were clearly derived from Poe. They tell a partly true, partly fictitious story of orphanage ("his unfortunate parents were the victims of the conflagration of the Richmond theatre"), a wealthy patron, a quarrel, and now "an entire reconciliation on the part of Mr. Allen, who reinstates him into his family and favor." Always one to identify his hopes with reality, Poe now viewed the reconciliation as an accomplished fact, and wrote enthusiastically to "My dear Pa" telling him that he was preparing for the West Point tests, and asking his help in obtaining letters of recommendation.

With Allan's assistance he got them, from Colonel Preston who had been a governor of Virginia, and from other family friends, and he received testimonials from his officers, all of them enthusiastic and one mentioning particularly that "his habits are good and in-tirely free from drinking." After his discharge in April 1829, Poe took these papers to Washington for presentation to Major Eaton, the Secretary of War, together with a letter from John Allan himself. The tone of this letter has been called cold, even arctic. Certainly it was not warm, but he did ask Eaton "to aid this youth in the promotion of his future prospects," and add that "it will afford me great pleasure to reciprocate any kindness you can show him." Allan was, however, intent to make it clear that he was under no obligation to Edgar Poe—those letters beginning "dear Pa" must have been a great trial to him. "Frankly, Sir, do I declare that he is no relation to me whatever," he wrote to Eaton. "That I have many [in] whom I have taken an active interest to promote theirs; with no other feeling than that, every man is my care, if he be in distress." In May, he wrote a friendly enough letter advising Edgar to find out details of his grandfather's service during the Revolutionary War, because "it may be of service & cannot do you any harm." He also sent a bank check for $100, with an injunction to "be prudent and careful." In addition he had made a parting gift of $50 when Poe left Richmond and he had honored a draft for another $50. This, the young man must have felt, was the way in which a father should behave toward his son.

In Washington Poe had what seems to have been a friendly inter-view with Eaton. He then went to Baltimore, where he looked up his grandfather's friends, although as he told Allan there was no need to obtain a certificate about his grandfather because it was well known in Washington that he had been "Quarter Master Gen-eral of the whole U.S. Army during the Revolutionary war." In Balti-more he saw his grandfather's widow, who was living on a small pension, and met for the first time two women who were to play major parts in his life. One was his aunt Maria Clemm, whom he came to regard as his own mother, and the other her daughter Virginia, who became his wife.

Maria at this time was thirty-nine years old, and already a widow. Her husband may have been, as Poe said later, "a gentleman of high standing and some property"; but none of the property came to Maria, who was left with two children—a son, who at this time was nine years old, and Virginia, who was just seven. She was also caring for several children from her husband's first marriage. They were evidently living wretchedly, for Poe says in one letter to Allan that his grandmother is "extremely poor & ill (paralytic)," his aunt Maria "if possible still worse," and his brother Henry "entirely given up to drink & unable to help himself, much less me." Mrs. Clemm was supporting herself by teaching, and Poe was of some help to her by selling for $40 a nine-year assignment to a Negro slave who had been in her employ. The accounts of Mrs. Clemm vary a good deal. They combine to show a kindly, vulgar woman, tactless and without personal charm, yet good-hearted and totally devoted to serving "Eddie," who became for her as the years passed a kind of saint with a few unfortunate human failings. She was strong, vigorous, and determined, with a large frame and rather masculine features. Her close relationship with her nephew lay in the future, and there is no suggestion that he took any special interest at this time either in her or in her daughter Virginia. He was much more concerned with writing poems and getting them published.

An approach to William Wirt, who had been offered the presidency of the University of Virginia during Poe's time there, produced a cautious response. Poe had sent him "Al Aaraaf"—a poem of nearly three hundred lines, and except for "Tamerlane" the only long poem he had attempted. Wirt said that the poem would no doubt be popular with "modern readers," although not with old-fashioned ones like himself. He suggested an approach to more up-to-date literary figures. Poe used this polite brush-off with some adroitness. In sending the poem to the publishers Carey, Lea & Carey, his postscript ran: "I cannot refrain from adding that Mr. Wirt's voice is in my favor"; and in sending the letter to Allan, he remarked on "the flattering character" Wirt had given of the work. He added, with what one can only feel to be mock piety, that he had thought it his duty to tell Allan what he was doing and observed also, in an attempt to touch his foster father's sense of the practical, that "at my time of life there is much in being *before the eye of the world*—if once noticed I can easily cut out a path to reputation."

The firm apparently offered to publish only if Poe could produce some financial backing. Two months after sending the manuscript he withdrew it, saying that he had "made a better disposition of my poems than I had any right to expect." This was to a couple of young men in Baltimore named Hatch and Dunning, who near the end of the year brought out *Al Aaraaf, Tamerlane and Minor*

Poems, on what Poe triumphantly told Allan were "terms advantageous to me they printing it & giving me 250 copies of the book."

Like the sonnet "To Science" that preceded it, "Al Aaraaf" shows Poe's interest in scientific ideas, even though its import is that scientific fact is interesting only as it can be turned to fantasy. In sending the poem to Isaac Lea, the author used some explanatory phrases that are worth quoting because of what he said later about the piece. "I have placed this 'Al Aaraaf' in the celebrated star discovered by Tycho Brache which appeared & disappeared so suddenly— it is represented as a messenger star of the Deity, &, at the time of its discovery by Tycho, as on an embassy to our world." A shortened "Tamerlane" and revised versions of some of the poems in the first collection were also included with the six new pieces. The whole made up a book of seventy-two pages, and the considerable hopes Poe had for it are suggested in a spirited letter he wrote when sending advance proofs to the influential critic John Neal:

> I am young—not yet twenty—*am* a poet—if deep worship of all beauty can make me one—and wish to be so in the more common meaning of the word. I would give the world to embody one half the ideas afloat in my imagination . . . I am and have been from my childhood, an idler. It cannot therefore be said that
> "I left a calling for this idle trade
> A duty broke—a father destroyed—"
> for I have no father—or mother.

Neal wrote about the poet and his coming work in a friendly if condescending way in *The Yankee and Boston Literary Gazette,* and on the book's appearance reviewed it rather in the same spirit. Nathaniel Parker Willis, who was to become friendly with Poe later on, mentioned the poems but did not praise them. Apart from this, the book received little attention.

Its publication produced one of the many crises in Poe's relationship with John Allan. The Richmond merchant must have hoped that the erratic Edgar's occupation was at last settled. He had been a soldier for eighteen months, he was apparently ready to take up the army as a way of life, and upon that understanding he had been given money. Now, however, what was he proposing to do but produce more poems! Allan's response to the letter enclosing Wirt's suggestions, which also proposed that Poe should make up any loss incurred by the book's publication, was quick and sharp. On the back of the letter Allan made a note: "Replied to Monday, 8th June 1829 strongly censuring his conduct—& refusing any aid."

But although John Allan's responses were grudging, he was not adamant. In response to letters from Poe which almost always mentioned the projected volume of poems but otherwise breathed a spirit of obedience, letters which said truthfully that he had made every possible effort to get into West Point and inaccurately that he had declared himself to be the grandson of Benedict Arnold, Allan did send some money. It is also possible, although not certain, that he paid part of the cost of the poems' publication. With the money Allan included a reminder that men of genius should not apply for help. Poe in his letter of thanks replied mildly that a little "timely assistance would prevent such applications."

But the relationship was never easy for long. As weeks went by in which there was no news about West Point, and it became inevitable that further supplies of money should be sent, Allan's irritation was always on the edge of something worse. In October, Poe complained of "a tone of anger as if my former errors were not forgiven," and said that he was as certain eventually of getting the West Point cadetship as he was of being alive. There is pathos in several of these letters, like that of November 12 in which he says: "I would not trouble you so often if I was not extremely pinched—I am almost without clothes—and, as I board by the month, the lady with whom I board is anxious for her money." This letter to "Dear Pa" produced within a few days a check for $80, and apparently a request to see the poems, which Poe sent by an acquaintance who was going to Richmond. If Allan expressed an opinion of them, the letter has been destroyed.

A little later, Poe himself went home. Perhaps Allan wanted to see him; perhaps he merely felt that it would cost less to have Edgar at home than in Baltimore. At any rate he returned to Richmond, as it proved for the last time while his foster father was alive. Allan was at this time having an affair with a local woman. Later, in July 1830, she had twins, which, as John Allan put it in his will, "she says are mine," although he did not know their names. No doubt Poe knew of this relationship. He may not have known, however, that at this time Allan was courting Louisa Gabriella Patterson, a lady from New Jersey. It seems certain that Allan's second marriage a few months afterwards came as a shock to him. In the meantime the visit was a friendly one, not least because in March 1830 Poe was formally accepted as a cadet. He left Richmond at some time in May, entered West Point in June, and matriculated there on July 1.

West Point, on the Hudson River in lower New York State, had been America's largest fort during the war with Britain. Dickens in his *American Notes* called it "this beautiful place, the fairest among the fair and lovely Highlands of the North River," and re-marked rather oddly that there could be no more appropriate ground for "the Military School of America." The need for an acad-emy where the science of warfare could be taught had been appar-ent to the founders of the Republic, but it clashed with the Jefferso-nian democratic ideal of a citizen army. Great European states had been built by the use of standing armies of mercenaries and pressed men, with officers drawn from the aristocracy. Such an idea was opposed to the faith of Washington and Jefferson in a citizen army with officers who should not be drawn from, and must never be allowed to become, a ruling caste. West Point, in the conception of those who founded the Republic, should be controlled by civilians, and it should teach the art of war to students who would not be professional military men. They too would be civilians, who returned to their peaceful occupations after being trained. The Republic had no need for a standing army.

An attempt made in 1796 by the officer commanding West Point to instruct both officers and cadets in the art of drawing fortifications made the officers so indignant, by its implication that they needed to go to school, that they burned down the instruction room. How could it be thought that there was anything to learn about the "art" of war? Five years later, however, a rudimentary school had been founded, with a student body of twelve cadets, and as the single instructor an Englishman who had taught mathematics at Woolwich. As there was only one instructor there could be only one subject, mathematics, with military exercises and field sports occupying the rest of the time.

When Poe entered the academy nearly thirty years later, West Point had changed enormously from those unpromising beginnings. Sylvanus Thayer, who ruled the academy from 1817 to 1833, had been from youth passionately interested in military matters. He was a professional soldier, so far as one could exist in America at that time, although necessarily a largely theoretical one. As Superintendent of West Point he was a strict and aloof disciplinarian. He abolished annual vacations, which were replaced by summer camps; banned all supplies of money except the amount paid the cadets by the government, so that there were no special favors for the rich; and imposed in systematic detail attendance at classes and taking of examinations. He established a merit roll, by which each cadet was ranked within his class in every activity, so that at the end of the four-year training his abilities in each subject would be known. Thayer insisted also on a totally democratic system within the academy, so that the freshman class of "plebes" received exactly the same treatment as those in their third or fourth year. The régime that preceded Thayer's had been extremely lax, and there were two rebellions against him in the early days of his rule. Once these had been suppressed, his authority was unquestioned.

Under Thayer West Point had become famous. About 130 cadets entered every year, so that there was great competition for places, and it was often said that in spite of Thayer's democratic principles appointments went to the sons of the rich and famous. Certainly the entrance examination required only the most rudimentary ability in reading, writing, and arithmetic; it had been kept so low, however, not in order to favor the rich but to give a chance to poor boys who lacked formal education. Although most applicants were admitted through recommendation, the cadets in no way formed a social or intellectual élite.

Why then should Poe, who did not care for external discipline, detested democracy, and had no deep interest in the science of war, have wanted to enter this intellectual desert? He was prompted by quite other motives than an admiration for West Point. The first, unquestionably, was the desire to prove himself in John Allan's eyes, so that he would truly be regarded as a son. This longing for affection is never far below the surface of the letters, which frequently repeat such phrases as: "I am conscious of having offended you formerly—greatly—but I thought that had been forgiven" . . . or "I will be much pleased if you will answer this letter" . . . or "Hoping that you will not forget to write as soon as you receive this." These remarks are sometimes accompanied by requests for money, but the need to be accepted on affectionate terms runs through almost all of them. Poe's second, related reason for wanting to enter West Point was that only by becoming a cadet could he free himself from life as an enlisted man while still retaining Allan's approval and support. He may well have thought that a cadet's life would be much easier and more congenial than that of an ordinary soldier. If so, he was soon to be undeceived.

One of Thayer's principal achievements was the West Point curriculum, which placed a strong emphasis on science. The cadets were drilled and given field exercises, but in the classrooms they learned practical science. They began with mathematics and went on to various aspects of civil engineering, combined with topographical drawing, analytical geometry, and physics. French was the only language taught, and literature was ignored. There was, in fact, a regulation forbidding cadets to keep in their rooms any novel, poem, or other book unrelated to their studies. Poe was at West Point for only a few months, but the instruction he received—in their first year cadets studied algebra, geometry, trigonometry, and mensuration—greatly encouraged his interest in science. Apart from that, the life must have been worse than he had expected, worse even than he had feared. The cadets breakfasted at seven, and attended classes or undertook exercises until nine-thirty at night, with breaks for food. Ten o'clock was lights out.

The reminiscences we have of him at the academy come from his colleagues. He was a fascinating figure to many of them, partly because of his literary bent and partly because he was an experienced soldier among raw cadets. He soon became known as a writer of ironic squibs about the officers of the academy, from Thayer down to Joe Locke, the assistant instructor of military tactics, who was a strong upholder of the rules. One of Poe's verses about him ran:

> John Locke was a notable name;
>   Joe Locke is a greater; in short,
> The former was well known to fame,
>   But the latter's well known "to report."

Other cadets were impressed by Poe's aloofness, his air of mystery, his real or invented knowledge of the world. One wrote home to his mother that Poe had run away from his very rich adopted father, had been in South America and England, graduated at an English college, and then returned to America to enlist as a private soldier. "He is thought a fellow of talent here but he is too much a poet to like Mathematics." The Benedict Arnold story also went the rounds. There are more doubtful anecdotes among the reminiscences of those who knew him, to the effect that he utterly ignored his studies, was a constant brandy drinker, would repeat prose and poetry by the hour from memory. No doubt he was dismayed when he discovered that his cadetship was not, as he had assumed, "a necessary form which I am positive I could run through in six months." Yet if he was idle, he still managed to end up third in French and seventeenth in mathematics out of a class of eighty-seven; if he drank, he was never charged with drunkenness; and the literary stories seem to suggest an unlikely degree of sophistication among his fellow cadets as well as an unlikely slackness in the authorities.

These months marked the final break between John Allan and the child to whom he had rashly stood foster father, a break caused partly by Allan's parsimony and partly by Poe's vacillation about a career, but immediately by the disastrous affair of Bully Graves. The first letter Poe wrote from West Point, soon after his arrival, gives thanks for a remittance of $20 (evidently the regulation about receiving no money from home was not invariably observed), flattered Allan's—and his own—snobbery by remarking that "a great many cadets of good family &c have been rejected as deficient," and observed also how few stayed the full course. In the next, written more than four months later—and after Allan's marriage—"Dear Pa" has changed to "Dear Sir." The letter is friendly enough, however. Poe expresses regret that Allan did not visit him while in New York, says that he is doing well, although "the study requisite is incessant, and the discipline exceedingly rigid," and asks that Allan should either send him a Cambridge Mathematics and a box of instruments or let Colonel Thayer have the money for them.

All this exasperated Allan, who regarded his financial responsibility as ended by Poe's admission to West Point. The regulations certainly said that cadets were to live on the $16 a month plus rations that they received, but it was usual for families to supply things like textbooks, writing materials, fuel and clothing. Allan refused to provide any of them. When Poe says that "my more necessary expenditures have run me into debt," the expenditures really were necessary. At West Point Poe was dissatisfied, but he was certainly not extravagant. It is possible that Allan might have seen this in time, and recanted, but for the letter to Bully Graves.

When Poe was discharged from the army in 1829 he had to find a substitute; according to War Department Records, "Sergeant Samuel Graves of Company H" had reenlisted substitute for Sergeant Major Perry. Poe entered into an arrangement with Graves that he would pay him $75 for this service, and according to one of his letters to Allan he had paid the money. Graves, however, had been dunning Poe for $50, which was either a residue of the money to be paid him as substitute or, less probably, another debt. When Poe was at Richmond in May, waiting to go to West Point, he wrote Graves a rash letter in which he said that "Mr. A is not very often sober," and added:

> I have tried to get the money for you from Mr. A a dozen times—but he always shuffles me off—I have been very sorry that I have never had it in my power as yet to pay either you or St. Griffith—but altho' appearances are very much against me, I think you know me sufficiently well to believe that I have no intention of keeping you out of your money. . . .

He mentioned also that he was going to West Point, which must have seemed an added injury to Graves when he did not get his money. In the end he sent Poe's letter to Allan.

It is easy to imagine Allan's reaction. Indeed, it has to be imagined, since out of the whole Poe-Allan correspondence only two letters from Allan have been preserved. Whatever he wrote must surely have been excelled in savagery by Poe's reply, which began:

> Sir,
> I suppose (altho' you desire no further communication with yourself on my part,) that your restriction does not extend to my answering your final letter.
> Did I, when an infant, sollicit your charity and protection, or was it of your own free will, that you volunteered your services in my behalf? It is well known to respectable individuals in Baltimore, and elsewhere, that my Grandfather (my natural protector at the time you interposed) was wealthy, and that I was his favorite grandchild. . . .

Not all of Poe's complaints were as slightly based as this assertion of his grandfather's wealth. He went on to a recitation of injuries that are by now familiar. At the university, "it was wholly and entirely your own mistaken parsimony that caused all the difficulties." He was compelled to associate with students who were in debt like himself, "they from drunkenness and extravagance—I, because it was my crime to have no one on Earth who cared for me, or loved me." Deprived of university education he had waited vainly for Allan to find him employment, and so ran off to join the army. He mentioned reproachfully the fact that, when Allan's wife died, he had been unable to return until the night after the burial. "If she had not died while I was away there would have been nothing for me to regret—*Your* love I never valued—but she I believed loved me as her own child." The Graves letter? He admitted writing it, but brushed it aside. "As to the truth of its contents, I leave it to God, and your own conscience." West Point? Allan had sent him there like a beggar, he lacked the necessities of life, it was the university over again.

He ended by saying that his life, which would not endure long, "must be passed in indigence and sickness." In the meantime, however, he was determined to leave West Point, and to do so must have Allan's written permission. "From the time of writing this I shall neglect my studies and duties at the institution—if I do not receive your answer in 10 days—I will leave the point without—for otherwise I should subject myself to dismission."

So ended what was perhaps the most important emotional relationship of Poe's life. He never again looked for a father who would love, understand and forgive him. The need for love, understanding, and forgiveness nevertheless remained, and was to be fulfilled in his relationships with Maria Clemm and Virginia. Yet these relationships were essentially fantasies. He did not desire a real wife, to whom he would make love and with whom he would quarrel, but rather an ideal image of womanhood, just as Maria Clemm served as a mother-image rather than a mother. Perhaps he desired a truer emotional link with Allan, yet even here it seems that what he wanted was somebody who would behave toward him as a father rather than somebody toward whom he would behave as a son. Allan might have treated him better, but it is not likely that he could ever have resembled the ideal father of Poe's imagination.

John Allan for his part was not the man to forgive what had been said about him in the letter to Graves. As far as we know he never communicated directly with Poe again, although he provided money to pay some of his debts. He made a note on the letter just quoted, saying that he would not reply to it. "He may do or act as he pleases, tho I wd. have saved him but on his own terms & conditions since I cannot believe a word he writes." Poe fulfilled his threat by absenting himself from parades and roll calls, and also from "all his academical duties," including attendance at church. For lack of Allan's written permission he was not allowed to resign, but was duly court-martialed and "dismissed the service of the United States" on March 6, 1831. Immediately afterwards he addressed a highly optimistic letter to Thayer, saying that he intended to proceed to Paris "with the view of obtaining, thro' the interest of the Marquis de la Fayette, an appointment (if possible) in the Polish Army," and asking for any help that Thayer could give him by way of introduction.

Before this he had left West Point, without waiting for the inevitable result of the court-martial. From New York he made an attempt to get on friendly terms with Allan again, and more particularly to obtain money from him. This would, he said, be the last time he ever troubled any human being, because he was on a sickbed from which he would never rise:

> My *ear* has been too shocking for any description . . . I have no money—no friends—I have written to my brother—but he cannot help me—I shall never rise from my bed—besides a most violent cold on my lungs my *ear* discharges blood and matter continuall. . . . Please send me a little money—quickly—and forget what I said about you.

It says something about John Allan's feeling for Poe that he kept all these letters, and at times looked through and brooded on them, not with pleasure. On April 12, 1833, he received one more letter, so far as we know the last, imploring assistance: "For God's sake pity me, and save me from destruction." On the same day he looked again at the letter written from New York, and made a note on it:

> Apl 12, 1833 it is now upwards of 2 years since I received the above precious relict of the Blackest Heart & deepest ingratitude alike destitute of honor & principle every day of his life has only served to confirm his debased nature—Suffice it to say my only regret is in Pity for his failings—his Talents are of an order that can never prove a comfort for their possessor

Less than a year later John Allan was dead.

CHAPTER VI

JOURNALISM AND MARRIAGE

The young fellow is highly imaginative and a little terrific. He is at work upon a tragedy but I have turned him to drudging upon whatever may make money.
    —John P. Kennedy to Thomas W. White, April 13, 1835

IN his later days at West Point Poe had circulated among his fellow students a subscription list for a volume of poems. Many of them had put down their names, in the expectation that the book would contain those lively squibs that they had admired about the instructors and administrators. With this guaranteed subscription a New York publisher, Elam Bliss, agreed to issue the book, which appeared in the spring of 1831.

The cadets who turned the hundred-odd pages may have been gratified to see that it was "respectfully dedicated" to the U.S. Corps of Cadets, but in other respects they were disappointed. There was nothing here about Joe Locke or Sylvanus Thayer, but instead poetry of a much more ethereal kind than many of them appreciated. There may have been some who got no further than the extraordinary introductory letter, addressed to a B—who may have been the publisher Elam Bliss, or Edward Bulwer, or a wholly imaginary character. In this long, rambling piece, which reads as if it had been written during a single feverish night, Poe savagely attacked the ideas that lay behind the early work of Wordsworth and Coleridge, and adumbrated a theory of poetry that he developed, but never materially changed, in later years. It seems worth reproducing a fragment of the attack on Wordsworth, which is very typical of Poe's choplogical reasoning:

He [Wordsworth] seems to think that the end of poetry is, or should be, instruction—yet it is a truism that the end of our existence is happiness; if so, the end of every separate part of our existence—every thing connected with existence should still be happiness. Therefore the end of instruction should be happiness; and happiness is another name for pleasure;—therefore the end of instruction should be pleasure: yet we see the above mentioned opinion implies precisely the reverse.

To proceed: ceteris paribus, he who pleases, is of more importance to his fellow men than he who instructs, since utility is happiness, and pleasure is the end already obtained which instruction is merely the means of obtaining.

This introductory letter, which not only attacks Wordsworth and Coleridge, but looks with glancing hostility also at Johnson as being the very opposite of poetry ("think of his huge bulk, the Elephant!"), expresses feelings that were later refined and rendered more subtle. The poems themselves were called "Second Edition" boldly on the title page. "Al Aaraaf" and "Tamerlane" were rehearsed, and revised again, as were some of the other early poems. The newly printed pieces included what are, by general agreement, three of his finest poems, "To Helen," "Israfel," and "The Doomed City." The two latter pieces were also to undergo considerable revision, and in the case of the last a change of title, to "The City in the Sea." All three suggest Poe's longing for another world of ideal, superhuman beauty. In contrast to the beauty of Helen, or of the angel Israfel's music, is the picture in "The Doomed City" of a world inhabited by the dead. The agonized romanticism that conceived life in such terms can be expressed by putting the most famous verse in "Israfel" beside one of the more vivid pictorial scenes in "The Doomed City":

> If I did dwell where Israfel
> Hath dwelt, and he where I,
> He would not sing one half as well—
> One half as passionately,
> And a sterner note than this would swell
> From my lyre within the sky.
>
> ("Israfel")

> There shrines, and palaces, and towers
> Are—not like any thing of ours—

> O! no—O! no—*ours* never loom
> To heaven with that ungodly gloom!
> Time-eaten towers that tremble not!
> Around, by lifting winds forgot,
> Resignedly beneath the sky
> The melancholy waters lie.
> ("The Doomed City")

This was a collection which included poems remarkable enough to justify all of Poe's ambition, yet it received no more than a couple of friendly notices. If John Allan had seen the book, he might have felt that its tone confirmed his prediction that such talents would not prove a comfort to their possessor. Other poets in the nineteenth century wrote in similar terms, invoking in their work superhuman joys and unearthly sorrows, but for most of them these were only phrases. It was Poe's unhappy distinction to live out the spirit of his poems in his life.

To have published three volumes of poetry by the age of twenty-two was a remarkable achievement when one considers Poe's circumstances, but it was not a way of earning a living. He went to Baltimore, to live with the Clemm family and Henry Poe, whom he had reported eighteen months earlier as given over to drink. Henry, whose future had seemed so bright a few years back when his poems were being published by Baltimore and Philadelphia papers, was by now overwhelmed with drink and debts. In August 1831 he died of tuberculosis at Mrs. Clemm's house, and one can only conjecture about the effect on Edgar of seeing his brother die. Henry had been a seaman, had by his own account visited Russia, and had certainly sent back from Montevideo a report which had appeared in a Baltimore paper. It is likely that his elder brother was to Edgar at one time an impressive and inspiring figure, and that the end of such evident promise in failure and death affected him deeply. He adopted the Russian travels as his own, and some of his narratives of imaginary travel may have owed something to stories told him by Henry Poe.

Things went from bad to worse. In November Poe wrote to John Allan that he had been arrested for a debt which he said had been incurred as much on Henry's account as on his own, and Mrs. Clemm joined in, saying that "I should consider it as one of the greatest obligations to myself and family if you will be so generous as to assist him for this time only." He does not appear to have been arrested, but the debt existed and Allan paid it. It would be wrong to think that Poe was idle, although he does not seem to have tried to get a job that would bring in money regularly to the household. He was writing short stories, and he submitted five of these for a prize contest that was run by a Philadelphia paper. He did not win the $100 prize but the paper printed the stories anonymously, although whether they paid for them is doubtful.

These stories are not in the first or even the second rank of Poe's writings, but the author's attitude toward them is interesting. They were part of a series which was to be called *Tales of the Folio Club*. The Club had eleven members, among them Mr. Solomon Seadrift, "who had every appearance of a fish," Mr. Horribile Dictu, "with white eyelashes, who had graduated at Gottingen," and "Mr. Blackwood Blackwood who had written certain articles for foreign magazines." The remarks made by the Club members upon the stories were intended as "a burlesque upon criticism." Were the stories themselves jokes, parodies, or ironic comments on existing literary styles and established magazines like *Blackwood's?* Upon occasion Poe admitted as much. Or was *Metzengerstein,* at least, a serious study in the horrific, even though not wholly original, as was acknowledged by the subtitle "In Imitation of the German" added on later publication? Perhaps. But perhaps also *Metzengerstein* was thought of by its author as not imitative at all, for on still later publication the subtitle was removed. Poe's attitude toward these stories varied, as it did to much of the rest of his work, and he was capable both of saying that the stories were not to be taken seriously and, with encouragement, of defending them as works of genius.

The two years after he left West Point were among the hardest of Poe's life. So far as is known he stayed in Baltimore, and lived with Mrs. Clemm. He saw occasionally his cousin Neilson Poe, and Rebecca Herring (the daughter of Mrs. Clemm's younger sister Elizabeth), in whose album he wrote two acrostic verses on her name. Possibly he flirted with Rebecca, but somebody so poor was not likely to have received encouragement from her father. He may have found some kind of intermittent journalistic work, but if so it was miserably paid.

Poe's closest friend at this time was a journalist, poet, novelist and playwright named Lambert Wilmer. In 1827 Wilmer had published a play called *Merlin,* which took as its basis Poe's affair with Elmira Royster, even going so far as to call the heroine Elmira. Wilmer was poor during most of his life, and his example in scraping a living by doing hackwork for periodicals while preserving his integrity as a writer of poems and novels was not lost on his friend. Wilmer knew Poe well for several years, and says that at this time in Baltimore he "lived in a very retired way with his aunt Mrs Clemm." She had scolded him once for coming home drunk, although Wilmer in this period "never saw him intoxicated in a single instance." His appearance—remarkably, as Wilmer thought in view of his poverty—was always "fashionably neat with some approximation to elegance," and he was a scrupulously polite and even-tempered but rather characterless figure, whose conduct was decided often by whim and impulse. One must make allowance in this description for the fact that Wilmer himself was a coarsely vigorous man, and one so untidy that he is said never to have done up his shoelaces. His psychological acuity is obvious, however, in remarks like this one in which he defends Poe from the charge of libertinism:

> Of all men that ever I knew, he was the most *passionless;* and I appeal to his writings for a confirmation of this report. . . . Edgar A. Poe never wrote a line that gives expression to a libidinous thought. The female creations of his fancy are all either statues or angels.

In May 1833, just after he had made his last appeal to Allan, Poe sent one of the Folio Club tales to the *New England Magazine,* adding to his brief descriptive letter a P.S. which said: "I am poor." The story was rejected, but a little later he had better luck. The Baltimore *Saturday Visiter* offered a "premium of 50 dollars" for the best tale and $25 "for the best Poem" submitted to them. Poe sent six Folio Club stories, and *MS. Found in a Bottle* won the prize. He also won the poetry award, but the judges felt that two prizes could not go to the same writer.

The money must have been a godsend, but the chief benefit for Poe was that through the award he met John Pendleton Kennedy, one of the judges. In a practical sense he needed a benefactor, in an emotional sense perhaps he still longed for a father; for a short time Kennedy played both parts. He was in his thirties, a handsome, intelligent and cultured lawyer who had become prominent in Baltimore politics as a mouthpiece of the business community. He was also a novelist, one whose first piece of fiction, *Swallow Barn,* is still respected as a clear unromantic portrait of Virginian life in the early nineteenth century. In later years he was to become Secretary of the Navy, and later still president of the Northern Central Railroad Company. At this time, Kennedy was already a celebrated author. His preference was for work written in a clear, direct, and straightforward style, and it was to his credit that he recognized at once a kind of genius uncongenial to him.

Writing in his journal after Poe's death, Kennedy said that at their first meeting the young prizewinner was in a state of starvation. One of the other judges, John Latrobe, recalled on the other hand that the young man who came to thank him was dressed with conspicuous neatness, all in black, with frockcoat buttoned to the neck. His figure was good, and he carried himself erect. The neat clothes were shabby, but "there was something about this man that prevented me from criticizing his garments." Kennedy tried without success to get his own publisher to take the Folio Club stories, although in a tactful letter he did not put the matter in this way, but said that the publisher thought the stories should appear in print elsewhere first. A request for Kennedy's support in getting a teacher's position for Poe in a Baltimore school was answered by an invitation to dinner. It was perhaps when this was declined "for reasons of the most humiliating nature [in] my personal appearance" that Kennedy fully realized Poe's urgent need. He wrote an introductory letter to Thomas Willis White, editor of the *Southern Literary Messenger.* Poe sent some stories to White, among them *Berenice.* The story was accepted.

MS. Found in a Bottle, Berenice, and possibly *Metzengerstein* are the first among Poe's published stories to have what a reader today regards as his characteristic flavors of the grotesque, the adventurous and the horrible. These were all more or less current literary coinage at the time. Interest in exploration was intense, whether it was of unknown parts of the world or of regions above or below the earth, and Poe exploited this in many stories, of which *MS. Found in a Bottle* is the first. What look like absurdities to us seemed possible wonders to the magazine and newspaper readers of the time, and such themes would recur.

The theme of horror first touched on in *Metzengerstein* and the grotesque sensationalism of *Berenice* were also popular modes. The critics who have said that Poe took his poems seriously but wrote his stories for dollars are perhaps basically right, but a statement so simple does not cover the complexity of his intentions. He stated this typically in a letter to White, when the editor complained of the horrors in *Berenice*. He first acknowledged the justice of the criticism, and said that the story had been written to win a bet that such a subject could not be treated seriously; then he went on to say that all successful magazines owed a great deal to similar pieces. "The ludicrous heightened into the grotesque: the fearful colored into the horrible: the witty exaggerated with the burlesque: the singular wrought out into the strange and mystical." Poe referred White to stories found in *Blackwood's* and the *New Monthly Magazine* in response to the suggestion that such stories were in bad taste. The letter is a brilliant piece of special pleading for the stories he had written and was to write, and at the same time reflects his dual attitude toward them. They were written to make his always cool pot boil, yet many of them were expressions of his deepest and most intense feelings.

With Kennedy's encouragement White printed a story by Poe each month, gave him reviewing to do, and eventually suggested that the young man might come to work for him. Nothing, Poe replied, would give him greater pleasure. He wanted to settle in Richmond, where the periodical was published, and would accept any position with the magazine or elsewhere, even though the salary were "the merest trifle." In August 1835 he left Baltimore to work for the paper, apparently on a trial basis.

Like many magazine owners of the time, White was a printer. He seems to have been a genial, ebullient man, and in founding the *Southern Literary Messenger* he demonstrated that he was also an optimistic one. The South was well known to be a graveyard for literary magazines, and at the time the *Messenger* came on the scene in August 1834, it had no Southern rival. The first editor, James E. Heath, did the work for nothing, but gave up after a few months; he was succeeded by Edward Vernon Sparhawk, who lasted only three months before leaving. The position of editor was not an easy one, for White regarded the magazine as his own, and although it was Heath who remarked of *Berenice* that in spite of being marked by "too much German horror," it showed "a superior capacity and a highly cultivated taste in composition," White's was the directing hand. It was not a particularly successful hand. The paper's circulation was already dwindling, and he must have looked forward to the arrival of a young and enthusiastic assistant.

Poe was, however, a difficult man to employ. He had many virtues, prime among them the ability to do an enormous amount of work efficiently and skillfully. Above all he was a brilliant journalist, with a strong intuitive sense of what the American magazine public would appreciate. He knew little about the technical details of preparing a magazine for the press when he went to Richmond, but learned them with remarkable speed, as he did almost anything to which he set his mind. The most constant desire of his life was to possess his own magazine, and he had already drafted the prospectus of a periodical to be edited jointly with Wilmer. The project had no hope of fulfillment, because Wilmer was almost as poor as Poe, but the latter must immediately have regarded the *Southern Literary Messenger* as his own.

Even before coming to Richmond, Poe had begun both to criticize the periodical's contents and to make suggestions about the type used. In these trial weeks it must have become apparent to White that Poe, if employed permanently, would be in effect the editor, whatever he might be called in name. It also became clear in these weeks that he was at least an occasional heavy drinker, and one not able to hold his liquor. After Poe had returned to Baltimore, White wrote him a reproachful but affectionate letter. Among the moralistic good advice ("Look to your Maker for help, and you are safe! . . . Learn to respect youself, and you will very soon find that you are respected. Separate yourself from the bottle, and bottle companions, for ever!") is a passage that strikes a different note, one suggesting a real liking for the odd, reserved young man whose devotion to literature was so evidently of a kind beyond White's own grasp:

> How much I regretted parting with you, is unknown to anyone on this earth, except myself. I was attached to you—and am still,— and willingly would I say return, if I did not dread the hour of separation very shortly again.

And in this letter he did in effect say return, with the condition that if Poe were again "an assistant in my office," the arrangement

would end "the moment you get drunk." The offer was not likely
to be refused. A few weeks later Poe was back in Richmond.

His drinking—and it should be emphasized that this was his first
known bout of real drunkenness—had its roots in an almost intolerable emotional disturbance. The return to Richmond must itself
have been distressing, even though Poe longed for it. Here he met
again old acquaintances whom he had known before on terms of
equality; here he passed the house in which he had lived. He was
no longer welcome there, for the second Mrs. Allan disliked and
distrusted him, and although some of the old friends were friends
still, both he and they must have been aware that their futures
were firmly and prosperously settled while his was utterly uncertain.
As he went up the stairs to the little magazine office on the corner
of Main and Fifteenth Streets—there was a shoe shop on the ground
floor and Ellis & Allan's office had been next door—and sat there
with White preparing the magazine, he must have compared the
carefree past with his present drudgery. The crucial blow to his
mental balance, however, came in the form of a letter from Mrs.
Clemm in which she told him that his cousin Neilson Poe, who
had married Virginia's half sister, had offered to give a home to
Virginia and to pay for her education. Old Mrs. Poe had died a
month earlier, and her pension had died with her.

In Poe's reaction to this news we see for the first time his total
emotional reliance on the relationship he had established with Maria
Clemm and her daughter. The suggestion drove him into a frenzy
of despair. The three closely written pages sent to "My dearest
Aunty" show the stress under which they were written in the occasional omission of letters and even words. He is driven to declare
his love for Virginia, and this becomes the letter's theme:

> I love, *you know* I love Virginia passionately devotedly. I cannot
> express in words the fervent devotion I feel towards my dear little
> cousin—my own darling. . . . Can I, in honour & in truth say—Vir-
> ginia! do not go!—do not go where you can be comfortable & perhaps
> happy—and on the other hand can I calmly resign my—life itself.
> If she had truly loved me would she not have rejected th(e) offer
> with scorn? . . . The tone of your letter wounds me to the soul—
> Oh Aunty, Aunty you loved me once—how can you be so cruel now?
> You speak of Virginia acquiring accomplishments, and entering into
> society—you speak in so *worldly* a tone. . . . Adieu my dear Aunty.

I cannot advise you. Ask Virginia. Leave it to her. Let me have, under her own hand, a letter, bidding me *good bye*—forever—and I (m)ay die—my Heart will break—but I will say no more.

There was a postscript for Virginia: "My love, my own sweetest Sissy, my darling little wifey, thi(nk) (w)ell before you break the heart of your cousin. Eddy." And there was also a touch of the fanciful optimism with which he was capable of viewing any situation. He had found "a sweet little house . . . newly done up and with a large garden and (ev)ery convenience," which would only cost $5 a month. Since White would pay him $60 a month, he would be able to support them all. And then Virginia would have a far better chance of entering society in Richmond, where Edgar had been received "with open arms," than with Neilson . . .

If one remembers that the suggestion was no more than that Virginia should be looked after and educated, Poe's reaction shows how intense was his emotional involvement. If she went with Neilson Poe, he said, he would "never behold her again—that is absolutely sure," and it may well be that Neilson, at this time a successful journalist, disapproved of Edgar. It is too simple to say that Poe was, in the ordinary sense of the word, in love with his young cousin. He was endlessly susceptible to women, and is said to have fallen in love with two girls while in Baltimore, to one of whom Virginia carried messages. He had also cast an appreciative eye on White's daughter Eliza. To be in love meant, for him, to take a particular woman as an ideal, and an ideal woman is by definition one as far as possible removed from reality. The discussion about Poe's possible impotence cannot be resolved, but it is clear that when he wrote of loving Virginia "passionately devotedly," he did not mean physical love. His anguish at the thought of losing her sprang partly from the breaking up of what he thought of as his family, partly from the loss of an ideal woman.

It was under such pressures that Poe drank. Accounts of his drinking vary, but it does seem that he was one of those unlucky people who are quickly affected by small amounts of alcohol. This may have been a family weakness, for Rosalie slept for hours after taking a single glass of wine. It seems also that he was unable to stop drinking once he had started. A couple of weeks after the hysterical letter to Mrs. Clemm he wrote a gloomy one to Kennedy, expressing gratitude for past kindness, but touching the note of desperation that will by now have become familiar. "Convince me that it is worth while—that it is at all necessary to live, and you will prove yourself indeed my friend." When Poe was unhappy, he often hinted at the possibility of suicide; the fact that he never attempted it did not lessen the genuine nature of his anguish. Nor was it lessened by a long postscript in which he went into details about the possible printing of the Folio Club stories. But Kennedy was hardly to be blamed for taking this part of the letter seriously, and attributing the rest to what he called the blue devils. Kennedy was generous and kindly, but he was a man of affairs, incapable of comprehending a nature like Poe's. His reply, with its injunctions to rise early, live generously, and make cheerful acquaintances, and his advice that Poe should try his hand at "some farces after the manner of the French Vaudevilles," can hardly have seemed helpful.

Soon after this exchange of letters with Kennedy, Poe visited Baltimore. It is likely, although there is no legal proof, that he was secretly married to Virginia there on September 22, 1835. An open, officially acknowledged marriage took place at Richmond in the following May, when the bride was stated to be "of the full age of twenty-one years," although in fact she was not quite fourteen. Whether or not a secret marriage took place, there was no further question of Virginia going to live with Neilson Poe; early in October 1836 what may be called the Poe family was back in Richmond in a boarding house, where full board for the three of them cost $9 a week.

The extraordinary nature of this marriage has been little commented on by Poe's biographers. It was not positively illegal in the United States for a girl of thirteen to be married, as it would have been in England, but the fact that Virginia's age was concealed shows the disfavor with which marriage to a child bride would have been regarded. Did Virginia love her Eddy, in any sense of the word that can be regarded as meaningful, or was Mrs. Clemm the prime mover in the affair? It is hard to associate intense emotion of any sort with Virginia. She was a plump little creature, sweet, shy, and easily amused. She had the chalk-white complexion of Poe's bloodless heroines, black hair, a round face, a full figure, and a soft delicacy of speech emphasized by a slight lisp. Few stranger households can ever have been set up than that of the erratic, neatly dressed, precise man who went each morning to work in the small office above the shoe shop and came home in the evening to write visionary or horrific tales about emotionally tortured lovers; the strong-featured woman, who was now no longer "My dear Aunty" but "Muddie" or mother; and the shy girl, "Sissy," who is never known to have expressed any opinion or made any decision, but simply did what she was told by Muddie or Eddy. Virginia may well have adored Eddy, although she rarely read what he wrote and understood only part of what she read. There is no doubt that Eddy loved his Sissy as an otherwise deprived child values something that is truly his own. Brooding over their lives was Muddie, a benevolent but enigmatic presence, who as the years passed was to become cook and housekeeper and gardener, act as intermediary between Eddy and demanding editors, listen to his work and comment on it, and even compose and write letters on his behalf.

This was to be the way of things in the thirteen years of life that remained to Edgar Allan Poe after his official marriage ceremony. Everything of decisive emotional importance in his life had now happened: the death of his mother, the separation from the foster father who had never returned his love, the painful construction of a family life. Now he had a family, and he also had a purpose. He would become editor of his own magazine, and through it would raise the level of American literature—partly by the example of his own imaginative writings, and partly by adherence to unsparing critical standards. Americans should be taught to distinguish genuine from gimcrack, the serious from the trivial. As an editor he would be a stern but generous oracle, from whose verdict there would be no appeal. All this was in his mind when he came again to work on the *Southern Literary Messenger.* Now and in the future he hoped to make his readers aware of true critical standards, and by encouraging such awareness to revolutionize American literature.

CHAPTER VII

THE ASPIRING EDITOR

No man is safe who drinks before breakfast.
—Thomas Willis White to Edgar Allan Poe, September 29, 1835

THE American literary world into which Poe now entered as a critic
was one upon the whole deeply antipathetic to him. He thought
little of Fenimore Cooper and Washington Irving, two of the galaxy
of writers now living in New England and based generally around
Boston. They had added a dash of native Puritanism to respect for
an English tradition. Writers like William Ellery Channing, John
Neal (who had praised his poems), and Catharine Maria Sedgwick
wrote thin and thought high. Emerson, Bryant, Longfellow were
all in their different ways poets of everyday life rather than visionary
writers, and they shared a democratic view of society and a moral
earnestness that Poe found detestable or absurd. He cared even
less for Fitz-Greene Halleck, Lewis Gaylord Clark, and a dozen
others famous in their time, all of them grouped round the literary
power center of New York.

Poe opposed them, as much in the name of the South as because
he thought little of their writings. From the first critical pieces he
wrote until the end of his life he was consciously a propagandist
for the morality and style, as well as for the literature, of the South.
The brash literary manners of the New York writers were as little
to his taste as the democratic priggishness of the Bostonians. He
looked instead for an aristocratic tone, a romantic style, an idealistic
approach. Perhaps these did not mark Southern writers any more
than Eastern ones—Kennedy's *Swallow Barn* is no more romantic
or nostalgic than some of Washington Irving's work—but for Poe

[54]

the fact that Kennedy's book was set in a vanished Virginia was itself a recommendation; he would praise a Southern poet like Philip Pendleton Cooke and a novelist like William Gilmore Simms, who might have had short shrift if they had been Easterners. This partisanship had its ambiguities, like so many of Poe's attitudes. He himself had been born in Boston, and it was as the work of "a Bostonian" that his first collection of poems had been published.

The period of Poe's connection with the *Southern Literary Messenger,* from October 1835 until the end of the following year, must have been among the happiest of his life. His position on the paper was never exactly defined. Soon after his return to Richmond, White wrote to a friend about the paper and said that he could mention Poe's name "as amongst those engaged to contribute to its columns—taking care not to say as editor." Many pieces were accepted by White on the advice of Southern friends, without reference to Poe. The new contributor, however, wrote a great deal of the paper; he wrote almost all of the critical notices, produced new stories, and reprinted some of his own poems. He was paid a salary of about $15 a week.

Poe's industry was astonishing. He contributed more than a dozen stories, as well as a large part of his longest prose work, *The Narrative of Arthur Gordon Pym,* plus *Scenes from an Unpublished Drama* which later appeared as *Politian,* and an article on "Autography." In addition he wrote reviews for every issue, and it was the character of these reviews, even more than the stories and poems, that put up the paper's circulation from something like 700 to a figure approaching 5,000 during his association with it.

Poe's reading was extensive, and his ability to assimilate what he read remarkable. He greatly admired the important British literary magazines, in particular *Fraser's* and *Blackwood's,* and was especially fascinated by the savagely comic caricatural talent of *Blackwood's* John Wilson, under the pseudonym of Christopher North. There can be no doubt that *Blackwood's* was one of those British journals "whose names I am not permitted to mention" for which Poe later imagined himself writing; Christopher North, with his sarcasm, joviality, and arrogance about "Cockney" literature, was probably at this time his ideal critic. The note of social superiority struck by Christopher North in dealing with Leigh Hunt and Hazlitt must have been deeply congenial to his American admirer.

But if Poe's approach to the books he received was often Black-woodian, the point of view from which he dealt with them was wholly his own. In reading these early reviews one catches two notes: first, of a man exultant at being given space in which to make known his ideas; and second, of a critic determined to raise the standards by which American literature should be judged. When the Southern writer J. K. Paulding told White that his periodical was the best in the United States, and Poe "decidedly the best of all our young writers," it was the criticism as much as the stories that he had in mind.

The books that Poe received were the heterogeneous collection that lands on any editor's desk, science and romance, poetry and novels, gift annuals and miscellanies, lives of necromancers, a Virginia gazetteer, *Tales of the Peerage and the Peasantry.* He reviewed them all, and about all of them found something distinctive to say. It was often said with an acerbity marked even in a period when criticism was aggressively phrased, although when accused of "regular cutting and slashing" he protested that of the ninety-four reviews he had contributed in a little less than a year, only eight books had been severely treated. This depends on what one calls severity. When Poe in a review of new volumes by three lady poetasters—Mrs. Sigourney, Miss Gould, and Mrs. Ellet—remarks that Mrs. Sigourney has acquired the name of the American Hemans "solely by imitation," and adds of one of Mrs. Ellet's translations that not the slightest conception of the original can be obtained from it, this might perhaps be thought severe.

But Poe did not regard it so, and it is true that this was a mild piece by his own standards. One review that made him celebrated was that of a novel, published anonymously, called *Norman Leslie.* The review began:

> Well!—here we have it! This is *the* book—*the* book *par excellence*—the book bepuffed, beplastered, and be-*Mirrored:* the book "attributed to" Mr. Blank, and "said to be from the pen" of Mr. Asterisk: the book which has been "about to appear"—"in press"—"in progress"—"in preparation"—and "forthcoming": the book "graphic" in anticipation—"talented" *a priori*—and God knows what *in perspectu.* For the sake of everything puff, puffing and puffable, let us take a peep at its contents!

The whole of the long review was written in this savagely jocose strain, and in the course of it Poe revealed that the author was Theodore S. Fay, an editor of the *New York Mirror*. Southerners, or some Southerners, were delighted, but New York critics and writers were naturally annoyed. This was the first shot in a ten-year war that ended disastrously for Poe. A few months later he attacked with equal zest another anonymous novel, *Ups and Downs in the Life of a Distressed Gentleman*, actually written by Colonel William L. Stone of the *New York Commercial Advertiser*. "This book is a public imposition," the review begins, and it ends by identifying Stone as the author, and saying that the work "should have been printed among the quack advertisements in a spare corner of his paper." Such reviews made Poe some unforgiving enemies.

"The general merit of our whole national Muse has been estimated too highly," he was to comment later in writing about the poems of J. G. Brainard, and concern for a standard of criticism is evident in these early pieces, an awareness that the best of American verse is infinitely inferior to what was being produced in England. In dealing at great length with the poetry of Joseph Rodman Drake and Fitz-Greene Halleck ("perhaps at this particular moment there are no American poems held in so high estimation by our countrymen"), Poe prefaced his generally derogatory remarks by a picture of American attitudes:

> We get up a hue and cry about the necessity of encouraging native writers of merit—we blindly fancy that we can accomplish this by indiscriminate puffing of good, bad, and indifferent, without taking the trouble to consider that what we choose to denominate encouragement is thus, by its general application, rendered precisely the reverse. In a word, so far from being ashamed of the many disgraceful literary failures to which our own inordinate vanities and misapplied patriotism have lately given birth, and so far from deeply lamenting that these daily puerilities are of home manufacture, we adhere pertinaciously to our original blindly conceived idea, and thus often find ourselves involved in the gross paradox of liking a stupid book the better, because, sure enough, its stupidity is American.

Poe himself, as we shall see, was not immune from the charge of puffing, but in these early reviews even a benefactor like Kennedy came in for a rap over the knuckles. His *Horse-Shoe Robinson* was praised for its adventurous and picturesque quality and its rich and forcible style ("with the exception of now and then a careless, or inadvertent, expression"), but he was rebuked for faulty punctuation. Almost all of the books Poe reviewed in these months were eminently forgettable, yet behind the harsh words there was always concern for a native literature that might be considered on equal terms with that of Britain. A definable aesthetic was also apparent— a theory of the nature of art and the character of the artist that was later to be embodied fully in *The Poetic Principle* and *The Rationale of Verse.*

It would be wrong to think that readers of the periodical understood much of this. What they found was criticism of an acuity and a vividness far beyond anything they commonly read. Poe had the journalist's gift of writing in a way that compelled attention, and knew instinctively the kind of subjects that would appeal to his readers. In two issues he ran articles on "Autography," in which he used the device of a series of imaginary letters with actual facsimile signatures of well-known people appended to them, to discuss their handwriting. Fenimore Cooper's hand is said to be "bad— very bad. There is no distinctive character about it, and it appears to be *unformed.*" Washington Irving's calligraphy was "commonplace . . . nothing indicative of genius about it." Kennedy's, as might perhaps have been expected, was "our *beau ideal* of penmanship." Several of the stories Poe published were not only remarkable pieces of writing, but also dealt with matters frequently discussed in the press, like ballooning, pestilence, voyages to distant places where extraordinary things happened. The favorable accounts of each issue given by other papers, which he triumphantly printed as supplements each quarter, were chiefly concerned with the critical pieces and the spirit behind them.

With so great an increase in circulation, and so much praise showered on the periodical, it might be supposed that White would be delighted with Poe. But although indeed pleased, he was also uneasy. "No man is safe who drinks before breakfast," as he had warned the young man. Poe had so far stayed sober, yet White feared always that he would not remain so. White also felt at times that the magazine was no longer quite his own. He wrote to one correspondent that since he employed Poe as editor, everything was submitted to him and "I abide by his dicta"; but this was no doubt only a way of shifting responsibility, for White still selected much of the material. It was, however, never the stories and essays White had selected that came in for praise, but only Poe's contributions. The relations of the owner and his assistant were friendly, yet they contained an element of strain.

In the meantime, several ideas were afloat for helping Mrs. Clemm and improving the family fortunes. A letter was written to George Poe, a first cousin of Mrs. Clemm and a second cousin of Edgar, asking for help so that she could open a boarding house. Capital would be necessary, and Edgar was prepared to advance $100. Another cousin, William Poe, had already given some financial help, as well as finding subscribers for the magazine. Possibly William's brother Robert would join him in lending a further $100. If George would lend Edgar the same amount ("I will be responsible for the repayment of this sum, in a year from this date"), the boarding house scheme would be under way. George Poe sent the money, but no boarding house was opened.

And then, as it seemed to Poe, Virginia and her brother Henry should receive some money from an inheritance. In a letter to Kennedy, he went into great mathematical detail. "Each, then, is entitled to $\frac{1}{7}$ of $\frac{1}{5}$th of $\frac{1}{3}$ = $\frac{1}{105}$th of the whole lot." Kennedy patiently investigated, and reported that debts and advances had wiped out the inheritance, so that there was no claim to anything. What about "General" Poe's claim against the government for his outlays of money during the war? Poe wrote an eloquent letter to a Washington attorney suggesting that this could easily be substantiated, but nothing came of it. Then the boarding house scheme was revived, with the refinement that White would participate in it. He would buy a house, rent it to Mrs. Clemm, and board there himself with his family. When the house was bought, however, it proved to be large enough only for a single family. Poe, in the meantime, had optimistically obtained $200 worth of furniture on credit. Could Kennedy (to whom all this was told) possibly lend him $100 for six months?

The tale told by these abortive ideas is of a man always urgently in need of money. One can feel much sympathy for him. He not only wrote brilliantly but also worked extraordinarily hard. He was left with no more than $6 a week after expenses had been paid, and his bitter statement after he had left the magazine that the drudgery was excessive and the salary contemptible was not unjust.

Yet White had sunk a good deal of his own money into it, and could not afford even what he paid to Poe.

White from his own point of view had just cause for grievance, apart from worry about the savagery of Poe's criticism and the feeling that he was losing control over his own magazine. After several months, what White had feared happened. Poe sometimes drank too much, and was then confined to bed for days afterwards, so that two numbers of the magazine were delayed. When White made a trip to New York, he found the office in confusion on his return. In September 1836 he warned Poe about the drinking, and at the end of December he dismissed him. "I am once more at the head of affairs," he wrote happily to a friend. Perhaps Poe was not sorry to go. He had worked very hard, and had made a reputation as a critic. If he was unappreciated and underpaid in Richmond, things would surely go better elsewhere. And where better than in New York?

CHAPTER VIII

NEW YORK AND PHILADELPHIA

In regard to Burton . . . My situation is embarrassing. It is impossible, as you say, to notice a buffoon and a felon, as one gentleman would notice another.
  —Edgar Allan Poe to Dr. Joseph E. Snodgrass, April 1, 1841

IN fact the chances of making a living at this time by serious criticism—even if it was spiced with squibs like the "Autography" article—were poor, in New York or anywhere else. Magazines proliferated, but they paid contributors very badly. No copyright act existed, and when it was possible to pirate good English work for nothing, why should editors pay native writers handsomely for stories and poems, let alone reviews? The *North American Review* paid $1 for a page of around six hundred words, the *Democratic Review* $2 for a much larger page; these rates were typical rather than exceptional. The *Southern Literary Messenger* paid nothing at all to the well-to-do Southern gentlemen who wrote for it.

Stories and poems did not offer much better prospects. In his time at the *Messenger,* Poe had sent to Harper's a collection of tales, including horror stories and pieces intended, as he told Kennedy, as "half banter, half satire." They were rejected with a long, reasoned explanation. Most of the pieces had appeared before, they were separate stories instead of the connected tale most readers preferred, and they were "too learned and mystical," so that few people would understand them. There were friendly words about Poe's quality as a critic in the letter. Encouraged by the hint about readers' "decided and strong preference for works . . . in which a single and connected story occupies the whole volume," he wrote

The Narrative of Arthur Gordon Pym. This was accepted by Harper's, and although it did not appear until the autumn of 1838, its reception may be mentioned here.

Poe had done his best to meet the publisher's suggestions by offering a realistically written, single, and connected story of the most bloodthirsty kind. The title page, which says that the narrative comprises "the details of a mutiny and atrocious butchery on board the American brig Grampus," plus a shipwreck, famine, a cruise in the Antarctic, and another massacre, was an attempt to catch the current taste for adventure blended with horror. Poe's touch for sensational journalism had deserted him here or, to put it differently, he was simply not capable of producing the kind of adventure story that might have been popular. Those who took the book to be meant as the account of a real voyage complained that it was outrageously improbable, and those who might have appreciated it as fiction found the horrors distasteful. In England it had much more success, and actually went into a second edition, although it seems unlikely that this brought Poe any money.

In New York he found it almost impossible to get reviewing work or to sell stories. The country was in a state of financial panic, and magazines on which he had expected to get work either suspended publication for a time or closed their doors against new contributors. Several of them would, in any case, not have opened them to Poe. The New York editors and writers that he had offended seem minuscule figures now, especially in relation to the Boston-based group, which included Emerson and James Russell Lowell; but at the time men like Lewis Gaylord Clark, editor of the *Knickerbocker* (which boasted that it paid $5 a page to some contributors), and Theodore S. Fay were influential and powerful. During several months in the city Poe sold only two stories. The family lived in an old frame house at 113 ½ Carmine Street in what was later Greenwich Village. They survived through the lodgers taken in by the indomitable Maria Clemm. One of these, a bookseller named William Gowans, left an over-lyrical but still interesting account of the household. He called Poe one of the most courteous, gentlemanly and intelligent companions he had ever met, and said that he was a man never in the least affected by liquor. Virginia's beauty and liveliness were matchless, her disposition sweet, her devotion total. Maria stays unmentioned, but she said later that the three of them lived for each other, and there is no reason to doubt that this is true. Poe's stability of mind, even his ability to write, were linked with his reliance on his substitute mother and his girl wife. During this time in New York he completed *Arthur Gordon Pym,* of which two installments had appeared in the *Messenger.* The terms given to him by Harper's for the book are not likely to have been particularly generous, nor materially to have eased the family poverty. After a year or a little more Poe gave up the struggle to make a living in New York, and they moved again, this time to Philadelphia.

Here things went better. Philadelphia was second only to New York as a publishing center of weekly and monthly journals, with new magazines appearing almost monthly, most of them trying to capture the market of middle-class women readers now recognized to exist. These readers wanted pretty pictures to look at, sentimental stories and poems to weep over. Poe was not ideally fitted to meet such requirements, but his talents were known, there was little enmity toward him of the kind that existed in New York, and a dash of horror, a touch of sensationalism were acceptable enough provided that they did not go too far. He sold what he afterwards called his finest story, *Ligeia,* to a new magazine in Baltimore, and although he got only $10 for it, that must have been manna in the desert. He wrote other poems for the magazine, and in the winter of 1838 put his name to a piece of hackwork called *The Conchologist's First Book.* This textbook for schools was taken complete from a book published five years earlier. Poe added an introduction, and may have translated descriptions of the animals, "which . . . according to Cuvier, are given with the shells." When accused of plagiarism, he retorted angrily that all school books were made in the same way, and threatened legal action. The most interesting thing about the publication is that his name was well enough known to be of value on the title page.

In July 1839 Poe joined *Burton's Gentleman's Magazine,* run by William E. Burton. He was to be paid $10 a week for two hours' work a day, "except occasionally," so that it would be easy for him to follow "any other light avocation." Burton's letter making this offer ended: "I shall dine at home today at 3. If you will cut your mutton with me, good. If not, write or see me at your leisure."

Two men less likely to agree, either personally or in their views

of literature, could not easily have been found. Burton was an Englishman intended for the Church, who had become an actor in 1820
when he was eighteen years old. He was well known on the English
stage, but true success came to him when, in 1834, he visited the
United States, and made his home there. His activities were protean.
His powerful voice and extravagant use of gesture and facial expression made him, as was later said, the leader of the dramatic profession
in the country. He also wrote plays and leased theatres, one of which
he renamed Burton's Theatre. At his death in 1860 he left a large
library, rich in Shakespearean and other drama. In 1839 he was
already a celebrated man, a hearty and genial vulgarian. His idea
of a lively magazine was like his idea of a good play—that it should
be a vehicle for undemanding entertainment. Poe's fastidiousness
of speech, dress and style were something quite alien to him, and
so, too, was the idea that criticism might at times be profound in
content and severe in tone. On Poe's side Burton's fame as an actor
must have roused dormant feelings, never far below the surface,
about his own ancestry.

Poe was prepared to do dubious hackwork like *The Conchologist's
First Book,* but not to compromise about matters of critical principle.
He did not at once accept Burton's offer, but wrote a letter that
was evidently gloomy in tone, and that commented on the magazine's lack of any critical standard. Burton's answer was not angry
but candid. He said that he had been "as severely handled in the
world as you can possibly have been" (although that was not so),
but he did not for that reason take a harsh view of other writers.
"We shall agree very well, but you must get rid of your avowed
ill-feelings towards your brother authors—you see that I speak
plainly." Several friends had warned him about Poe's critical fierceness, and although "the independence of my book reviews has been
noticed throughout the Union . . . there is no necessity for undue
severity." The tone of the letter is generous and friendly, but it
suggests the irreconcilable differences between the two men.

However, Poe went to work, and as always he worked hard. In
the July 1839 issue his name appeared as editor, and he wrote all
of the reviews. They were short notices, including one that recommended a book by Thomas Wyatt as "the author of an exceedingly
well arranged, accurate, and beautifully illustrated 'Conchology.'"
He shared the reviews in the next issue with Burton, and his dislike

of the owner and of what he was doing is shown in a letter to the Southern poet Philip Pendleton Cooke. Poe sent Cooke a copy of the magazine but told him not to think of subscribing:

> The criticisms are not worth your notice. Of course I pay no attention to them—for there are two of us. It is not pleasant to be taxed with the twaddle of other people, or to let other people be taxed with ours. Therefore for the present I remain upon my oars— merely penning an occasional paragraph, without care.

Poe wrote more serious criticism in the magazine than he suggests here, including a long piece about the Baron de la Motte Fouque's German romance *Undine*. He also contributed his own stories, including *The Fall of the House of Usher,* which is perhaps his most famous piece of fiction, and *William Wilson,* which he reprinted from one of the annuals of the period, *The Gift.* And each month from January 1840 until June, he published *The Journal of Julius Rodman,* the installments of which were presumably written month by month, since after his break with Burton the story was left uncompleted. *Julius Rodman,* like *Pym,* makes the pretense of being a genuine document, and was no doubt an attempt to produce the kind of light adventure story in which the magazine specialized. Poe was paid $3 a page for these pieces, which was better than his usual rate, although it hardly justifies Burton's remark that "my contributors cost me something handsome."

Poe had also found a local publisher, Lea & Blanchard, who were ready to publish a collection of his stories. The terms were hardly what he could have hoped—the publishers "at their own risque and expense" printed an edition of 750 copies, from which they took the profit. The author was given a few copies for his friends. This collection of twenty-five stories included almost everything he had published in prose. The book was called *Tales of the Grotesque and Arabesque,* the "grotesques" being mostly the Folio Club tales, and the "arabesques" the tales of horror. In his brief preface Poe denied the Germanic nature of his horror stories, saying that "If in many of my productions terror has been the thesis, I maintain that terror is not of Germany but of the soul." He had revised the stories carefully, and must have had great hopes for them. Like so many of his hopes, these were disappointed. "The Philadelphians have given me the *very highest possible* praise," he wrote; but the belief expressed to a correspondent that the edition had been almost exhausted within a few days of publication was far from the truth.

It is clear from the volume of work he produced at this time that Burton's two hours a day suggestion was not very wide of the mark. As always when things were going well, Poe began to entertain extravagant literary hopes and to make elaborate plans. To one correspondent he mentioned a fictitious "profitable engagement with Blackwood's Mag," and said that he had been promised a very commendatory review there by Christopher North himself. A Baltimore journalist who said that Poe had enemies was asked to name them, because "it is always desirable to know *who are* our enemies." In an attempt to promote sales Poe asked Joseph Evans Snodgrass, a Baltimore doctor and minor man of letters, to write a notice about the most recent issue of the *Gentleman's Magazine,* embodying a very friendly view of his talents that had appeared in a St. Louis paper. He suggested that when the piece had been written, Snodgrass should give it to Neilson Poe, who was editing a Baltimore daily paper. When this devious piece of puffing was rejected by his cousin on the ground of their relationship, Poe was angry:

> I *felt* that N. Poe would not insert the article editorially. In your private ear, I believe him to be the bitterest enemy I have in the world. Was it "relationship &c" which prevented him from saying *any thing at all* of the 2 or 3 last Nos. of the Gents' Mag?

In Poe's world, friendship could change in a moment to evident enmity. Neilson Poe had wanted to take Virginia away from him, and had objected to the marriage, but Poe had been prepared to forget or ignore this in his eagerness to see a friendly notice in the paper. If it is suggested that this hardly accords with his concern for critical principles, the answer would be that a puff in a newspaper was not in his eyes the same thing as a long article in a serious magazine. So, when he received a letter from Washington Irving "abounding in high passages of compliment in regard to my Tales," and saying that it might be publicly used, Poe told Snodgrass that this was indeed a duty he owed himself which it would be foolish to neglect through false modesty. Words of praise were better than gold to him. If his eagerness to use them seems sometimes distasteful, it should be remembered that he was conscious of tremendous talent, acknowledged only in a way that placed him on a level with those whom he knew to be infinitely his inferiors. There were people who liked Edgar Allan Poe, and many more people who admired him, but in the ordinary sense of the word he had few friends. Friendship implies a kind of equality, and perhaps he did not truly feel that he had any equals. He had his family, and that was enough.

He would soon, he had no doubt, also have his own magazine. Much of his leisure time was spent in planning it, although it does not seem that he neglected his work for Burton. Nor did his occasional drinking bouts interfere with the magazine's regular appearance, although his own statement at this time that it was four years since he had taken any kind of alcohol was untrue. It would be surprising, however, if Poe had not made known at times to Burton his intention of starting a magazine, and his certainty that it would be infinitely superior to the one for which he was now working. Burton was a generous but not a patient man, and he was much more interested in theatrical management than in publishing. It may be true, as Poe told Snodgrass, that he had stopped paying contributors. In the spring of 1840, in any case, Burton decided to sell the magazine, and advertised it for sale apparently without telling Poe. George R. Graham, already an editor and publisher, bought the list of 3500 subscribers for as many dollars, merged the magazine with his already existing *Casket,* and called the result *Graham's Magazine.*

Before the sale Poe had resigned—or perhaps been sacked. In an exchange of furious letters (Poe's reply to Burton, of which we have what is probably a draft, is certainly furious, and it would be surprising if Burton's letter were less so), Poe complained that Burton had tried to bully him, and advised him to "preserve, if you can, the dignity of a gentleman." He attributed what he called Burton's hostility toward him to the fact that the actor had written a very harsh review of *Pym,* which Poe himself calls "a very silly book":

> Had I written a similar criticism upon a book of yours, you feel that you would have been my enemy for life, and you therefore imagine in my bosom a latent hostility towards yourself. This has been a mainspring in your whole conduct towards me since our first acquaintance. It has acted to prevent all cordiality.

It is likely that Poe was here attributing his own feeling to Burton, a kind of transference that was not at all beyond him. He went on to give a detailed mathematical calculation of their accounts which suggested that he owed Burton nothing at all, and (this was perhaps the touchiest point) said that he would never have dreamed of starting his own magazine if he had not known that Burton was giving up the *Gentleman's*. Within a few days Poe was writing to Snodgrass calling Burton a scoundrel, and suggesting means by which he might be shown as such. Snodgrass, however, did not act on these suggestions. Burton on his side felt no lasting anger; his last words to Graham were a request to look after his young editor.

CHAPTER IX

"THE PENN"

*The magazine will be issued on the first of March, and, I believe,
under the best auspices.*
— Edgar Allan Poe to John P. Kennedy, December 31, 1840

IT is worth trying to envisage Poe as his colleagues and rivals in
journalism saw him at this time. He seemed to them an extraordinary
figure—not, as to us, for his saintly or psychopathic personality, but
in his appearance, style, and habits. There were odd characters
enough among American journalists of the period, but most of them
were bluff extroverts, a little larger and louder than life. Among
them Poe was an oddity. His pale, delicate, intellectual face, with
its curling, disdainful lips, his evident poverty and elaborate neatness, his foible of dressing almost always in black, would have been
enough by themselves to mark him out. His voice was low where
most of those around him were raucous, and it was thought by some
to be deliberately cultivated, pitched as though for an elocution
lesson. When sober, his punctuality was invariable, his courtesy
hardly less so; yet the courtesy had in it an undertone of irony
which must have been an irritant. And then his interests were so
different from those among whom his life was cast, he was so deadly
serious about what for them was just a way of making a living,
that he appeared a man apart.

Even Poe's trivial interests were not like those of others. Early
in 1840, before going to work for Burton, he had contributed to a
local paper called *Alexander's Weekly Messenger.* He wrote short
pieces about the cultivation of beetroot and the invention of the
daguerrotype, as well as a collection of puns of which the first went:

"Why are the Thugs like crack omnibuses?" to which the answer was: "Because they are Phansigars—*fancy cars,* "and the last: "Why ought the author of the 'Grotesques and Arabesques' to be a good writer of verses?" "Because he's a poet to a *t.* Add *t* to Poe makes it Poet." These were probably too obscure for the popular taste, but his offer to solve cryptograms brought considerable response. Poe's ability to solve ciphers is remarkable when his lack of mathematical education is remembered. His interest in ciphers sprang from a fascination about what the human mind could do purely by logical reasoning. He regarded phrenology and the reading of character by handwriting as logical also in a different way, a proof of the form in which science operated in nature. "A set of rules might absolutely be given by which almost any enigma in the world could be solved instantaneously," he claimed, excluding puzzles which were nonsense and so could have no logical answer. He said that he solved all the ciphers sent in to him, and although they were simple substitution ciphers, on the lines of Conan Doyle's "Dancing Men," the achievement is still notable.

With the cryptograms in mind, one could divide Poe's activities between those of a conscious and a hidden self. The conscious self did all the work involved in editing periodicals, soliciting contributions, reading proofs, supervising the layout of pages, and did it well. The conscious self also wrote criticism of a rational and closely analytic kind—it was Poe's lengthy analyses of texts that disturbed Burton and White as much as his critical severity. The conscious self delighted in logical puzzles, and was responsible not only for the cryptograms but also for what Poe named his tales of ratiocination and we call the first short detective stories. The unconscious self, on the other hand, was subject to drives and passions such as the need for a family, and the impulse to write stories expressing the terror that was not of Germany but of the soul—a terror merging into overwhelming horror and disgust. It is the unconscious Poe who chiefly interests the twentieth century, but this was not the man his contemporaries saw. And whatever he may unconsciously have desired or needed, his greatest conscious desire was to own and edit a magazine.

We have several glimpses of the Poe family life during the six years spent at one home and another in Philadelphia. He was poor and proud, but he liked to bring visitors home and show them his

Sissy, whom some found ethereal and others plump, and the aunt whom he now always called Muddie. One journalist companion who saw the family at home, probably in Coates Street, near Fairmount Park, wrote of "the little garden in summer, and the house in winter overflowing with luxuriant grape and other vines, and liberally ornamented with choice flowers of the poet's selection." Poe, he said, was a pattern of social and domestic worth, and Virginia "an exquisite picture of patient loveliness, always wearing upon her beautiful countenance the smile of resignation, and the warm, ever-cheerful look with which she ever greeted her friends." The picture may seem to be painted in sickly colors, but other visitors tell what is essentially the same story. In the good times, when Eddie was in regular work, Maria and Virginia would go out shopping in the morning, and then do housework or gardening. Maria did the cooking, by all accounts in a good plain manner. Eddie would sit at home writing after he returned from work. Caterina, a tortoiseshell cat, completed the household. An acquaintance in the South offered Virginia a fawn as a pet, but the difficulty of sending it to Philadelphia was insuperable, although Poe acknowledged it with thanks, "precisely as if the little fellow were nibbling the grass before our windows." There is no doubt that it was a happy household, and since lodgers are not mentioned it seems that Poe was able to support them all.

That is, of course, while he worked for Burton. But would he be able to do so when the new magazine, which was to be called *The Penn*, appeared? Most purely literary magazines of the time had fluttered and failed after a bright start, but Poe was relying on the flair that had enabled him to achieve success with the *Messenger*. He ignored such practical questions as his total lack of capital, and issued a prospectus announcing that the first number would appear on January 1, 1841. The prospectus is too long to be printed in full, but it is important in its general statement of principle, its indication of what the editor conceived as an ideal literary magazine. After two paragraphs about his work on the *Messenger*, and an acknowledgment that his critical writing there had been at times unnecessarily severe, Poe continues:

> It shall be the first and chief purpose of the Magazine now proposed to become known as one where may be found at all times, and upon all subjects, an honest and a fearless opinion. It shall be

a leading object to assert in precept, and to maintain in practice the rights, while in effect it demonstrates the advantages, of an absolutely independent criticism—a criticism self-sustained; guiding itself only by the purest rules of Art; analyzing and urging these rules as it applies them; holding itself aloof from all personal bias; acknowledging no fear save that of outraging the right; yielding no point either to the vanity of the author, or to the assumptions of antique prejudice, or to the involute and anonymous cant of the Quarterlies, or to the arrogance of those organized *cliques* which, hanging like nightmares upon American literature, manufacture, at the nod of our principal booksellers, a pseudo-public-opinion by wholesale. These are objects of which no man need be ashamed.

The critical and literary nature of the enterprise is stressed throughout. Nothing is said about stories or poems, although Poe meant to include them. Political and social affairs, "matters of *very* grave moment," would be left to other periodicals. A handsome production was promised, one which would "surpass, by very much, the ordinary Magazine style." There would be illustrations by leading artists, introduced to accompany the text. Each issue would be about eighty pages long, and the magazine would cost $5 a year.

On the face of it *The Penn* had no chance at all of success. It was to cost a good deal more than most of its rivals, and the tone of the prospectus almost deliberately avoided the idea of popularity. And then, where was the money to come from? The assured tone of the prospectus suggested powerful financial support, but in fact there were no backers and the prospectus was issued partly in hope of finding them. Poe responded to one man who wrote asking for employment by suggesting that he might care to advance $500, which would "defray the expences of visiting the chief northern cities, of printing and distributing circulars, of advertising, &c &c."

Nevertheless Poe remained euphoric, writing letters on the back of prospectuses to old acquaintances in the South, potential contributors, anybody who might be likely to help. His old patron Kennedy was asked for an article of any kind or length, because his name would add "caste"—"I need the countenance of those who stand well in the social not less than in the literary world." He wrote at least one similar letter, and it is clear that the truly important factor for him at the inception of the magazine was the ability to express his own opinions freely and at length rather than the nature of other contributions. A postmaster in Tennessee sent the names of nine subscribers, a Pennsylvania physician was told that his beautiful lines, "By an Octogenarian," would certainly appear in the first number. At least two distant relatives, William and Washington Poe, were approached, and asked to act as agents in the Southern cities where they lived. They were told, with more candor than was used to others, that to produce the first number he must have five hundred subscribers by December 1. He expected most of the subscriptions to come from Southern men of letters, and some of them were indeed enthusiastic, but he did not get the necessary number. In December Poe was taken ill, and although in the New Year 1841 he told Snodgrass that the prospects for *The Penn* were glorious, publication was postponed until March. In April he was saying that *The Penn* was scotched, not killed. In the meantime, however, he bowed to economic necessity, and accepted the offer made by George Rex Graham to work for his magazine.

Graham's Magazine took up very much where the *Gentleman's* had left off, with a collection of mostly lighthearted literary all sorts, and a good deal of poetry. Graham added features especially attractive to women, including colored fashion plates, mezzotints, and engraved plates. He also paid what were by the standards of the time extremely handsome rates: $4 to $12 a page for prose, and between $10 and $50 for a poem. (Longfellow got $50.) Poe was at the bottom end of this scale, but even so he was paid $20 or $25 for a five-thousand-word article, which was something like a living wage. For his editorial work—he called himself the editor in writing to contributors, but seems in fact to have been the literary editor—he received $15 a week.

The stories Poe wrote for *Graham's* included the first of the "tales of ratiocination," *The Murders in the Rue Morgue,* and among the most notable of his lengthy critical essays were those on Bulwer and Dickens. He also exploited his cryptographic skill, offering the same kind of challenge to readers that he had issued earlier. He was, typically, much annoyed when a reader sent in a correct solution to one cryptogram. His slightly contemptuous astonishment was expressed to the solver ("Your solution *astonished* me. You will accuse me of vanity in so saying—but truth is truth"), and to another correspondent he made an ungrounded suggestion that cheating had occurred.

Graham, a young publicist with no particular opinions of his own, allowed him a free rein, and made no complaint about asperous reviews. Poe appreciated the tolerance, yet he was not satisfied. *Graham's* was all very well but it was hardly *The Penn*. For the first time in his life, however, he had enough to live on, even though an attempt to publish his fiction under the title *The Prose Romance of Edgar A. Poe* ended after the publication of a single pamphlet containing two stories. If to his salary is added the money he made from writing in the magazine, he must have made at least $1200 a year. In this unaccustomed flush of what was for him prosperity, he bought a harp and a piano for Virginia, and Mrs. Clemm acquired fourposter beds, thick red carpets, a tea set, and white curtains. Their sitting room was still a long way from the ideal room of which he had written in an article on *The Philosophy of Furniture*, with its curtains "of an exceedingly rich crimson silk, fringed with a deep gold, and lined with the silver tissue, which is the material of the exterior blind," its glossy silver-gray walls, Sèvres vases, magnificently bound books, sofas in rosewood and crimson silk, and octagonal table "of the richest gold-threaded marble." A long way indeed. Yet this must have been one of the happy periods in Poe's life. In Graham's office he ruled the roost, dealing with the artists who produced illustrations for the paper, as well as with other contributors.

His comparative contentment ended in January 1842, when Virginia ruptured a blood vessel in her throat while singing. For two weeks it seemed likely that she would die, and afterwards her condition fluctuated, so that although in May she seemed much better she had another hemorrhage in June. "It is folly to hope," Poe wrote to a friend, and in truth Virginia never recovered fully, although she lived for another five years. From this time onward she was an invalid, cheerful but never well, always liable to suffer a hemorrhage from the tuberculosis that was killing her.

Her illness left Poe in despair. His thoughts turned again, by a contrast that is by no means a contradiction, to the magazine. Perhaps Graham would join him and become his backer? This was not quite such a pipedream as it may appear, for the idea of having both a popular magazine (if Poe is to be believed, forty thousand copies were being printed early in 1842) and another designed for an intellectual audience flattered Graham's vanity. He seems to have given it a provisional blessing, and Poe began writing letters saying: "Mr. George R. Graham, of this city, and myself, design to establish a Monthly Magazine upon certain conditions—one of which is the procuring your assistance in the enterprise." These were sent to several of America's best-known writers, Washington Irving, Kennedy, Longfellow, Fitz-Greene Halleck, and Fenimore Cooper among them. All except Kennedy had been roughly handled by Poe at some time. In spite of an assurance that "the amplest funds" would be available, and the promise of fine paper, a broad margin, and stitching done in the French style, the replies were unencouraging. It may be that Graham thought again about backing the paper. In any case, this second attempt to launch *The Penn* foundered more quickly than the first.

If *The Penn* was to exist, it seemed that Poe would have to provide money for it himself. He could do so only if he had a job that was more or less a sinecure, giving him time for literary work. Now it looked as if this job might be offered to him. The prospect opened through the agency of a lawyer, minor politician, and novelist named Frederick W. Thomas, whose *Clinton Bradshaw* had been said by Poe to be a sort of pendant to Bulwer's *Pelham,* and to belong to "that very worst species of imitation, the *paraphrasical."* Thomas, a fervent admirer of Poe, took no offense, and after a meeting did his best to use his political influence to find a comfortable job for his new friend.

A more practical man than Poe might have had doubts about Thomas when he suggested that a one-legged man with a crutch should act as agent for *The Penn* in St. Louis, and have been skeptical when he wrote from Washington asking:

> How would you like to be an office holder here at $1500 per year payable monthly by Uncle Sam who, however slack he may be to his general creditors, pays his officials with due punctuality. How would you like it? You stroll to your office a little after nine in the morning leisurely, and you stroll from it a little after two in the afternoon homeward to dinner, and return no more that day. . . . Come on and apply for a clerkship, you can follow literature here as well as where you are.

It sounded simple enough. Thomas himself had a temporary clerkship to the Treasury, which he had obtained just by asking for it.

Could not Poe slip down to Washington and see President Tyler?—
or Thomas would see him—or perhaps something could be managed
through Kennedy. When Poe replied that he had no money to get
to Washington, Thomas began to back away a little. In May he had
been confident, but by the end of August 1842, he was saying that
although President Tyler's sons (with whom he was in touch) were
sure that Poe would eventually be given something, it was no use
applying to the President at present.

Poe had no particular political feelings beyond an aversion to
any kind of democratic rule, but on reading a poem written by
Robert Tyler, one of the President's sons, he was struck by the notion
that *The Penn* might after all play a part in national politics, rather
as *Blackwood's* did in England. Perhaps Robert Tyler would back
it, giving Poe some sort of proprietary right? But he was spinning
all this out of a cloth of fantasy, for young Tyler had no money
except his comparatively small salary. The prospect of getting a
job in the Custom House haunted Poe for months.

In *Graham's* he reviewed *The Old Curiosity Shop* in admiring
terms, and he met Dickens when the novelist came to Philadelphia.
One would like very much to know what impression each made
on the other, and what they talked about, but neither writer left
a record of the occasion. Dickens must have admired Poe's work,
for he took away a copy of the *Tales of the Grotesque and Arabesque*
to try to find an English publisher for them. He failed in this, which
must have disappointed Poe, and he was disappointed too by Lea
& Blanchard's brisk rejection of a suggestion that they should publish
a new collection of stories, including *The Murders in the Rue Morgue*,
together with a second edition of *Tales*. Poe asked for no more
than the wretched terms he had received before, but the publishers
pointed out that they had not yet "got through the edition of the
other work & up to this time it has not returned to us the expense
of its publication."

Yet in spite of these troubles and setbacks, Poe was, during these
years in Philadelphia, at the height of his energy and power as short
story writer and critic. The exact dates at which some of his stories
were written remain uncertain, but between 1841 and 1843 he published fifteen stories, in addition to a number of long critical pieces.
When it is remembered that he was also working for Graham, writing letters about *The Penn,* and looking after Virginia, his productive
power was remarkable.

In a letter written in June 1842 he said that his ill-health, lack of money, and "the renewed and hopeless illness of my wife" had forced him to abandon "all mental exertion," and that his only hope lay in bankruptcy. No doubt he believed what he was saying, but in fact he wrote some reviews during this time, and possibly also some stories. Two of the reviews, which ran to something like five thousand words each, have particular biographical interest. He greeted Rufus Wilmot Griswold's five-hundred-page anthology, *The Poets and Poetry of America*, with praise of the editor's "taste, talent and *tact*," and said that it was "the most important addition which our literature has for many years received." The review of *The Quacks of Helicon* by his old friend Lambert Wilmer made many general observations about the state of American literature and said rather little about the poem; but Wilmer was praised for his energy, although censured as too severe. The manner of the censure would hardly have pleased those defended, however: "It will not do in a civilized land to run a-muck like a Malay. . . . Mr. Bryant is not *all* a fool. Mr. Willis is not *quite* an ass. Mr. Longfellow *will* steal, but, perhaps, he cannot help it."

It is much to the credit of William Cullen Bryant, Nathaniel Parker Willis, and Henry Wadsworth Longfellow that they took little offense at such phrases. Poe himself was no longer able to endure even mild criticism of his work or personality. He recommended *The Quacks of Helicon* to Snodgrass as "really good—good in the old-fashioned Dryden style," but when two years later he learned that Wilmer had said unfriendly things about his drinking habits, he reversed this verdict, saying that he had "rendered myself liable to some censure by writing a review of his filthy pamphlet." Within a few months he had changed his mind also about Griswold's anthology, commenting: "I shall make war to the knife against the New-England assumption of 'all the decency and all the talent' which has been so disgustingly manifested in the Rev. Rufus W. Griswold's 'Poets & Poetry of America.'" The reason for this particular change of tune was that Griswold had become editor of *Graham's*.

There was no obvious cause for Poe to leave the periodical. It is true that, as literary editor and contributor, he was not treated very handsomely. His salary was $800 a year, and he was on the bottom end of the contributors' pay scale. On the other hand he found Graham personally congenial—gentlemanly but weak was the worst he had to say of the publisher—and he had freedom to write at whatever length and in whatever way he liked. In the end, though, this was not enough to reconcile him to working for a magazine which he described as filled with "contemptible pictures, fashion-plates, music, and love-tales." Although he chose to resign, it was not in his nature to look kindly on his successor, and the fact that Griswold was a younger man and that he was paid $200 a year more for the same work cannot have pleased him.

But basically the trouble was that *Graham's* was not *The Penn*. In Graham's tribute to Poe after his death, the publisher said that Poe's only financial concern was to protect his wife and his mother-in-law:

> Except for their happiness—and the natural ambition of having a magazine of his own—I never heard him deplore the want of wealth. The truth is, he cared little for money, and knew less of its value. . . . What he received from me in regular monthly instalments, went directly into the hands of his mother-in-law for family comforts.

Letters and reminiscences can convey only external circumstances. It might be said that Poe reduced his family to poverty by giving up his job, but this is to ignore the intensity of the emotional pressures that moved him. Some were unconscious, connected with the sexual life whose unfulfillment is plain in many of the stories. These were the terrors of the soul. But his daytime anguish, his awareness of talents not fully used or appreciated, was just as terrible. To say that Poe was egotistical is a true but altogether inadequate statement of his character. If he could have achieved something of what he wanted in the visible world, those terrors of the soul might not have haunted him so powerfully. In the end he failed, and in the process was destroyed.

CHAPTER X

"THE STYLUS"

On the first of July next I hope to issue the first number of "The Stylus" a new monthly with some novel features. I send you, also, a paper containing the Prospectus. In a few weeks I hope to forward you a specimen sheet.
—Edgar Allan Poe to James Russell Lowell, March 27, 1843

THERE are times in Poe's life when it is hard to see how he maintained himself and his family, and the months after he left *Graham's* were such a time. He remained a contributor, did some other journalism, and published several stories, but the money he got cannot have paid for food and lodging. The indefatigable Maria did a lot of donkey work. She took articles to magazines and sometimes brought back rejections, kept the house clean, encouraged Eddie to write, did the shopping, sometimes in Virginia's company but often alone. They moved from Coates Street by the river to a less pleasant but more central house in Spring Garden Street. It was prettily furnished, with white curtains, painted chairs, and flowering plants for decoration, but in the two years that they lived there most of the furniture was pawned, together with Virginia's piano. The good times in Philadelphia had gone.

Stories were not easy to sell. *The Murders in the Rue Morgue* had made a considerable stir, but the tale he called a sequel to it, *The Mystery of Marie Rogêt,* was rejected both by his friend Snodgrass, who was editing a Baltimore paper, and by a Boston weekly. Poe had had the ingenious idea of transferring a real New York murder mystery to Paris, and of suggesting a new solution to it. Although he felt convinced that it would attract attention, and offered it to the Boston paper for $50 and to Snodgrass for $40, instead

of the $100 that he said would have been *Graham's* rate, neither
editor was interested. Whether he submitted it to Griswold for consideration is not known. In the end the story ran through three
issues of *Snowden's Ladies' Companion,* a rival to *Graham's,* and
he can hardly have received less than $40 for it. Two other stories
were published in 1842: *The Mask* [later *Masque*] *of the Red Death*
and *The Pit and the Pendulum;* and in June 1843 *The Gold-Bug*
won a prize of $100 offered by the *Dollar Newspaper. The Tell-
Tale Heart* was printed by James Russell Lowell in his magazine
The Pioneer, but Lowell was able to pay only $10 for it. It may be
that Maria helped the family finances by doing some teaching, and
it is certain that Poe borrowed money. There is more than one
letter in which he apologizes for his inability to repay a loan, and
probably there were other loans of which we know nothing.

The association with Lowell began in November 1842, when Poe
suggested that he might write "a short article each month" for
Lowell's new periodical. Lowell in reply said that he was pleased
to have "the friendship and approbation of almost the only *fearless*
American critic," and gave him *"carte blanche* for prose or verse."
The Pioneer lasted for only three issues, and Poe contributed to
each of them. When the magazine had to be given up, partly because
Lowell was suffering from a serious eye disease, Poe generously
waived payment for the last two contributions, saying that the periodical's death would be "a most severe blow to the good cause—
the cause of a Pure Taste." He enclosed a prospectus of his own
new magazine, *The Stylus,* explained that he was going to give a
series of portraits of American literati with critical sketches, and
that he would be glad "if I could so arrange matters as to have
you *first.*"

In some ways this friendliness is surprising. Lowell was a New
Englander from Cambridge, home of the Brahmin literati. Like his
clerical father and his future wife he was a convinced abolitionist,
and there were very few subjects on which he would have agreed
with Poe. On the other hand he was young and poor, and these
were recommendations in Poe's eyes. Lowell was in his early twenties at the time he launched *The Pioneer,* and had so little prospect
of supporting himself that his marriage was delayed for four years.
The strongest recommendation, however, was his deep and lasting
admiration for Poe, who was prepared to admire him in return.

In the meantime plans for *The Stylus* went on, together with the negotiations in relation to that government job. Since Poe had no money, it would seem that the first depended on the second, but that was not quite the case. In February 1843, he told his old Washington friend Thomas that he had found a backer:

> I have managed, *at last*, to secure, I think, the great object—a partner possessing ample capital, and, at the same time, so little self-esteem, as to allow me entire control of the editorial conduct. He gives me, also, a half interest, and is to furnish funds for all the business operations.

For once Poe's optimism was not outrunning the facts. This ideal figure actually existed, in the person of Thomas Cottrell Clarke, who had signed an agreement relating to the production of illustrations for the new magazine. *The Penn* was perhaps thought to be too local a name, or one that had been tarnished by its failure to appear, and the magazine was now to be called *The Stylus*. No agreement between Clarke and Poe has survived, but there is no reason to doubt Poe's statement in February 1843 that articles of co-partnership had been signed and sealed for some weeks.

Clarke published in Philadelphia a weekly paper called the *Saturday Museum*, and that February a biographical piece on Poe, written by a young friend of his named Henry B. Hirst, took up the whole large first page. "Put together" would perhaps be a better description, for the page included thirty-two laudatory views of Poe's stories which had been provided by him, as well as similar praise of his poems. This was accompanied by a portrait, or, as the subject called it, a caricature. "I am ugly enough God knows, but not quite so bad as that." In the following week the prospectus appeared in the paper, headed:

Prospectus of the Stylus:
A Monthly Journal of General Literature
To Be Edited by
EDGAR A. POE
And Published, in the City of Philadelphia, by
CLARKE & POE

The prospectus naturally resembles that for *The Penn*, with similar emphasis on the fact that in physical appearance the periodical "will far surpass all American journals of its kind." Edgar A. Poe is named firmly as the editor, and his previous editorial success is described. The sketches of American writers are named as a particular attraction. There is stress on a rigorous approach, absolute independence, aloofness from personal bias, and on "a criticism self-sustained: guiding itself only by the purest rules of Art."

In spite of these good prospects, Poe was not altogether easy. Before Clarke came on the scene he had suggested partnership to an eccentric and well-to-do poet from Georgia, Thomas Holley Chivers. The difficulty, he explained, was only in providing money for the first two or three numbers. "After this all is sure, and a great triumph may, and indeed *will* be achieved." He went into details showing that with fine thousand subscribers he and Chivers would each get an income of $10,000 a year. A mere $1000 was needed to get started. But Chivers—although he was a nomad who wandered from one region and hotel to another, and although he expressed the utmost admiration for Poe's genius—was extremely evasive when it came to the question of money. Then there was the matter of the governmental sinecure, a dream that often seemed about to materialize. There was a chance it seemed of a Custom House appointment in Philadelphia, a really perfect position because it meant that Poe would not have to move. A man named Thomas S. Smith was given the collectorship, and Poe waited to be called and sworn in by Smith. When he saw in the paper that somebody named Pogue had been appointed, he called on Smith, confident that Pogue was a misprint for Poe. Smith, however, was brusquely rejective, speaking scornfully of Robert Tyler and saying that he had orders from *President* Tyler to make no more appointments.

Poe was not the man to take such a rejection meekly, and he no doubt made it clear that Smith would be obliged to appoint him, whether he liked the idea or not. He suggested to Thomas that Robert Tyler should procure a few lines from his father, positively ordering Smith to give Poe the place. He complained also of "the low ruffians and boobies—men . . . without a shadow of political influence or *caste*—who have received office over my head." It is easy to imagine the hauteur with which Poe treated the bureaucratic Smith.

He was a hard man to help, but Thomas did his best. He saw that Robert Tyler was made aware of the *Saturday Museum* piece, expressed excitement about *The Stylus,* and suggested that a visit to Washington might clinch the government position and also secure several subscriptions. Poe could give a lecture, and be presented to the President. With these hopes and possibilities in mind Poe borrowed money from Clarke, and in March 1843 went off to Washington.

The visit was a disaster. Thomas was ill, and Poe was left in the care of his convivial friend Jesse Dow. There was a party on the evening of his arrival and he was, according to Dow, "over-persuaded" to drink some port. He ended the evening in a poor state, was ill on the following day, and subsequently was what Dow called "unreliable." He visited the government departments and got some subscriptions, but when he and Dow called at the White House and saw Robert Tyler, Poe's condition was such that it was thought inadvisable for him to have an interview with the President. Later he insisted on wearing his cloak inside out, and at another party became embroiled in an argument with a heavily whiskered Spaniard whose mustaches he found comic. After four days of this, on the day before the lecture was to be given, Dow decided that Poe had better go home, and put him on the train. Dow sent on a letter to Clarke suggesting that Poe should be met when he arrived, and adding some friendly but sad reflections:

> He exposes himself here to those who may injure him very much with the President. . . . He does not understand the ways of politicians nor the manner of dealing with them to advantage. How should he? . . . Mr. Poe has the highest order of intellect, and I cannot bear that he should be the sport of senseless creatures, who, like oysters, keep sober, and gape and swallow everything.

Poe got home safely, went to see Clarke who as he said made light of the matter, and wrote a jaunty letter apologizing to Dow and his wife, and to the Spaniard with the mustaches. But although he brushed off the affair, the damage done was deep and permanent. Robert Tyler had been shocked by Poe's condition, and there was no further question of intervention by the President. Poe recognized soon after his return from Washington that his chance of a government job had gone, and within a short time support for *The Stylus* had gone too. Perhaps Clarke had been more shaken than he showed at the time by news of that drinking bout; perhaps he ran into trouble with his other publications. At all events, by June 1843 he had withdrawn from their contract, and Poe was writing to Lowell to say that his magazine scheme had exploded. "I have been deprived, through the imbecility, or rather through the idiocy of my partner, of all means of prosecuting it for the present. Under better auspices I may resume it next year."

In the spring or summer of 1841 Poe was visited at home in Philadelphia by a handsome young man in his mid-twenties, open-faced, energetic and enthusiastic. This was Rufus Wilmot Griswold, who was to become his literary executor, tell lies about him, add to or excise passages from his letters, and in general blacken his name.

Griswold had been trained as a printer, but left his home in Vermont when he was fifteen to become a literary journalist. In 1837 he was licensed as a Baptist clergyman, and so was entitled to put Reverend or Doctor before his name. The two had met when Poe learned that Griswold was preparing a collection of American poets, and called at his hotel to see the young man. Griswold already had considerable journalistic experience, as assistant or part editor of half a dozen more or less sensational journals, including the *New World,* which sometimes had a page eleven columns wide and more than 4 feet long. He was just entering on the career as anthologist that was to make him celebrated. *The Poets and Poetry of America* was followed by *The Female Poets of America, The Prose Writers of America, The Poets and Poetry of England,* and many other collections.

Poe sent him some poems, along with the inaccurate biographical memoir quoted at the beginning of this book, and invited him home. Griswold remembered the house as cheaply but tastefully furnished, and Poe as a very quiet, gentlemanly figure dressed with simplicity and elegance. He paid one visit when Poe was watching by Virginia's sickbed, and observed "the singular neatness and the air of refinement in his home." The two men seem to have been on good terms at this time. In the "Autography" series written for *Graham's,* Griswold is described as a gentleman of fine taste and sound judgment, a poet of no ordinary power, and somebody whose "knowledge of American literature . . . is not exceeded by that of any man among us." Griswold in his turn praised Poe's poems, although he included only three in his anthology.

Although Griswold was later to do Poe great injury, it seems that the first difference between them came about because of Poe's jealousy that he should have been replaced at *Graham's* by a younger man who was being paid more money. From this time onward his references to Griswold in letters to friends are contemptuous or dismissive. "He is a pretty fellow to set himself up as an *honest* judge, or even as a capable one," and he tells a story of Griswold suggesting that he should write a review of the poetry anthology, which Griswold would pay for and then place in a magazine. "This, you see, was an ingenious insinuation of a *bribe* to puff his book. I accepted his offer forthwith, wrote the review, handed it to him and received from him the compensation—he never daring to look over the M.S. in my presence." This curious transaction actually took place. Poe praised the anthology, although with some qualifications, and the review was sent by Griswold to a Boston paper, with a note saying that he and Poe were not on the best terms. Poe's share in this transaction was not particularly creditable, although no doubt he needed the money. Again, however, it seems that he did not forgive Griswold for making the suggestion. A little later he told Snodgrass that Griswold's book was a most outrageous humbug, and wrote to another correspondent in terms which have already been quoted.

Griswold on his side was telling stories about Poe's unreliability and drunkenness and suggesting also, like others, that he often used opium. All the evidence about this comes at second or third hand. There were many people who drank with Poe and saw him under the influence of drink, but nobody who admitted to smoking opium with him or seeing him after he had taken the drug. All the stories about Poe's opium taking are like the account of his cousin Rebecca Herring, who is supposed to have said (the story comes as retailed to a third party many years after Poe's death) that she had often seen him in a sad condition from the use of opium at home in Philadelphia.

There is no proof that he used the drug seriously, as did Wilkie Collins, and no more than indications that he used it at all. Some of the stories, however, deal with the fusion of dream and reality in a way that suggests Poe knew the effects of opium. Much more firmly based are stories about the wildness of his behavior during the later years in Philadelphia, especially when Virginia was ill or funds were particularly short. He would disappear for days and then be brought home—either in the company of friends or after a search by Maria—pale, remorseful, and almost in a state of collapse. There is an elaborate but not fully authenticated tale of a disappearance that lasted for several days, at the end of which Poe was found wandering in woods near Jersey City. According to Griswold, "he walked the streets, in madness or melancholy, with lips moving in indistinct curses, or with eyes upturned in passionate prayers . . . and at night, with drenched garments and arms wildly beating the wind and rain, he would speak as if to spirits." If allowance is made for the romantic language there can be no doubt that many of these stories were true, in particular those dealing with outings in the company of his brandy-drinking young friend Henry Hirst, and the engraver John Sartain who customarily drank absinthe.

If Poe knew that Griswold was spreading such stories, that would have deepened the enmity between them. It is true also that Griswold was the sort of evangelical New Englander for whom Poe had little respect, yet the force of detestation seems extraordinary, on Griswold's side as well as his own. Griswold was a genial personality, handsome, theatrical and irresponsible, but he showed in no other aspect of his life the sustained malice that he displayed toward Poe. Whatever is said about their relationship must be conjectural, but it does seem likely that Griswold both attracted and repelled Poe. He did not adore women ethereally, like Poe, but was physically attracted to them, as his three marriages show. And he swam happily and easily in the journalistic waters that often almost drowned Poe. Pride and considerable vanity played their parts on Griswold's side. By the summer of 1843 the two men were no longer on speaking terms.

CHAPTER XI

NEW YORK AGAIN

*My life has been whim—impulse—passion—a longing for solitude—
a scorn of all things present, in an earnest desire for the future.*
—Edgar Allan Poe to James Russell Lowell, July 2, 1844

New-York, Sunday Morning
April 7 (1844) just after breakfast

My dear Muddy,

We have just this minute done breakfast, and I now sit down to write to you about everything. . . . We went in the cars to Amboy about forty miles from N. York, and then took the steamboat the rest of the way.—Sissy coughed none at all. When we got to the wharf it was raining hard. I left her on board the boat, after putting the trunks in the Ladies' Cabin, and set off to buy an umbrella and look for a boarding-house. I met a man selling umbrellas and bought one for 62 cents. Then I went up Greenwich St. and soon found a boarding house. It is just before you get to Cedar St. on the west side going up. . . . For breakfast we had excellent-flavored coffe, hot & strong— not very clear & no great deal of cream—veal cutlets, elegant ham & eggs & nice bread and butter. I wish you could have seen the eggs—and the great dishes of meat. I ate the first hearty breakfast I have eaten since I left our little home. Sis is delighted, and we are both in excellent spirits. She has coughed hardly any and had no night sweat. She is now busy mending my pants which I tore against a nail. I went out last night and bought a skein of silk, a skein of thread, & 2 buttons a pair of slippers & a tin pan for the stove. The fire kept in all night.—We have now got 4$ and a half left. Tomorrow I am going to try & borrow 3$—so that I may have a fortnight to go upon. I feel in excellent spirits & have'nt drank a drop—so that I hope so to get out of trouble. The very instant I scrape together enough money I will send it on.

This letter is almost unique in Poe's correspondence for its domestic concern and cheerfulness. He stresses his efficiency, his sobriety, his pleasure in food, Virginia's good health, like a child looking for approval. Maria had been left behind in Philadelphia, partly to sell books and forward letters, partly it seems because they lacked money for her journey. With typical clumsiness she sold or pawned a book that did not belong to Poe, sparking off some recriminatory correspondence when the sale became known. The permanently desperate condition of the family finances is very clear, and so is the extent to which Poe's mood depended on Virginia's health.

The move to New York was made because he was unable any longer to earn a living in Philadelphia. Nobody doubted his journalistic ability and flair, but his drinking and critical quarrelsomeness were too well known for anybody to employ him on terms that he would have been prepared to consider. He sold his stories, but not for large sums of money, and although he gave lectures on American poetry during his last months in the city, these were not especially profitable. When Poe was in trouble, his instinct was always to move away from it in the hope that things would be better elsewhere.

And sure enough, within a week of his arrival he pulled off one of the brilliant journalistic deceptions which he managed so skillfully, and which always gave him great pleasure. He sold to the *Sun*, one of the city's many newspapers, a hoax story about a balloon crossing the Atlantic, with Harrison Ainsworth among the passengers. The story gained something from the paper's adroit presentation, with an apparently hasty insertion in one edition and then the full story published as an "extra." The headlines read:

ASTOUNDING NEWS!
BY EXPRESS VIA NORFOLK!
THE ATLANTIC CROSSED IN THREE DAYS!

Signal Triumph of Mr. Monck Mason's FLYING MACHINE!!!!

The story caused excitement of a kind not known again until Orson Welles's *War of the Worlds* was broadcast nearly a century later. According to Poe, the square surrounding the *Sun* building was besieged, "ingress and egress being alike impossible," for several hours. The regular Saturday edition announced the news, and then the extra was delivered, containing full details of the flight. Again according to Poe, they were bought up regardless of price. "I saw a half-dollar given, in one instance, for a single paper, and a shilling was a frequent price."

The story was unsigned, but its author was soon known, and the cleverness with which the part-scientific, part-journalistic tone was maintained must have been recognized. A comparison of *The Balloon-Hoax* with a story of mechanical marvels written by Poe nine years earlier, *The Unparalleled Adventure of One Hans Pfaall,* makes his development in this kind of writing apparent. *Hans Pfaall,* which is about the balloon ascent to the moon of a bankrupt bellows-mender, is not meant to deceive, but the possibilities of deception inherent in such themes was evidently something that remained with Poe. It might be supposed that the perpetration of this success-ful joke would have put its author in demand; instead, it seems to have reinforced a feeling that he was not entirely trustworthy. The *Sun* had known exactly what it was doing, but it may have been in other editors' minds that Poe was capable of playing a joke on them, as well as on their readers.

His account of the story's success comes from one of seven letters he wrote for a little Pennsylvania magazine called the *Columbia Spy,* which had recently been acquired by two youths, both under twenty years old. The letters, published under the title *Doings of Gotham,* show Poe's informal everyday journalism at its best. He was easy and casual here, as he rarely was in life, getting in an occasional glancing blow at enemies like Griswold, but in general commenting on the New York scene with ironical good humor. Al-ways an economical man in a literary sense, he adapted for use here fragments of articles he had published before, and later used bits of these letters for his columns of "Marginalia." But it is keenness of observation that makes these articles brilliant journalism. He had, as he said, roamed "far and wide over this island of Manhattan," and over Brooklyn too. His ironical vein is shown in a description of a typical Irish squatter's shanty:

> It is, perhaps, nine feet by six, with a pigsty applied externally, by way both of portico and support. The whole fabric (which is of mud) has been erected in somewhat too obvious an imitation of the Tower of Pisa. A dozen rough planks, "pitched" together, form the roof. The door is a barrel on end.

He observed the decay of old mansions, and predicted accurately that in thirty years "the whole island will be densely desecrated by buildings of brick, with portentous *facades* of brown-stone, or brown-stonn, as the Gothamites have it. . . ." The insufferable dirtiness of the streets, the annoyance caused by street-criers, and the greater annoyance given to the sensitive by the clatter of vehicles over the round stones which paved the streets were noted, together with the unsuccessful attempt to close saloons on Sunday, and the pleasures of using a pair of sculls in going round Blackwell's Island. There was an account of a walking race in which the winner was supposed to have done 10 miles an hour (Poe commented typically that he had done that speed himself) and a wistful glance at the glories of Tiffany's. A passage on the architecture of Brooklyn is worth quoting because it shows the acute observing power he brought to any subject with which he was even briefly involved:

> Brooklyn . . . has, it is true, some tolerable residences; but the majority, throughout, are several steps beyond the preposterous. What can be more sillily and pitiably absurd than palaces of painted white pine, fifteen feet by twenty?—and of such is the boasted "city of villas." You see nowhere a cottage—everywhere a temple which "might have been Grecian had it not been Dutch"—which might have been tasteful had it not been Gothamite—a square box, with Doric or Corinthian pillars, supporting a frieze of unseasoned timber, roughly planed, and daubed with, at best, a couple of coats of whitey-brown paint. This "pavilion" has, usually, a flat roof, covered with red zinc, and surrounded by a balustrade; if not surmounted by something nondescript, intended for a cupola, but wavering in character, between a pigeon-house, a sentry-box, and a pig-sty. The steps, at the front door, are many, and bright yellow, and from their foot a straight alley of tan-bark, arranged between box-hedges, conducts the tenant, in glory, to the front-gate—which, with the wall of the whole, is of tall white pine boards, painted sky-blue. If we add to this a fountain, giving out a pint of real water per hour, through the mouth of a leaden cat-fish standing upon the tip-end of his tail, and surrounded by a circle of admiring "conches" (as they call the strombuses), we have a quite perfect specimen of a Brooklyn "villa."

Nothing is known about Poe's association with Eli Bowen and Jacob L. Gossler, the young men who ran the paper, nor how much he was paid, nor why his letters ceased after only a few weeks.

Perhaps the second and third of these questions are connected. In retrospect it is astonishing that a man who could write articles and notes with such ease and skill should have found it hard to make a living. This was the case, however. Within a few weeks the euphoria in that first letter had faded. Life was just as difficult in New York as it had been during the last months in Philadelphia. The sale of stories to *Godey's Lady's Magazine* was of some help (they included one of his most famous short detective stories, *The Purloined Letter*), but he was not well paid, although Sarah Hale, who accepted them, was commended by him in the *Spy* as "a lady of fine genius and masculine energy and ability." (She wrote "Mary Had a Little Lamb.") Poe was often offered less money than his contemporaries because his poverty was known. There must have been many occasions when he accepted terms that others would have rejected out of hand. It seems that what he needed was the Custom House sinecure, but such a solution is too simple for the problems of his self-destructive character. If he had secured the position, he would surely have put himself into a situation where he had to be dismissed from it. Throughout his adult life Poe struggled against self-induced privations, yet the struggle was real and the agonies it caused were genuine.

Maria, with the cat Caterina, joined Poe and Virginia after two or three weeks, and in the summer they moved to a farmhouse 4 or 5 miles out of town, at what would now be near 84th Street and Broadway. Here they boarded with the farmer's wife, Mrs. Brennan. The landscape was beautiful, and the surroundings rural. To get into New York you took a stage which passed near the house, or walked up a mile or so to a dock from which the boat left at seven each morning. There were a good many children and animals about the farm, but Poe seems not to have been disturbed by them, and for a time he was delighted by his surroundings and his cheerful hosts. He and Virginia had a room under the eaves, Maria one downstairs, and there was a study in which he worked. Virginia, however, was growing noticeably weaker, and by one account it was sometimes necessary for him to carry her from the room to the dinner table. He would go for long walks into the wooded country around, and then sit writing in the study. When stories and articles were completed, they would be taken into New York by the faithful Maria, who went the editorial rounds trying to sell them.

This temporary retreat from the literary world can be viewed in several ways, one of which is certainly that of a man trying to discover some deep reality about his own nature. There was a division in Poe's mind between the work he did to provide food and clothing for his family, work like *The Balloon-Hoax* and the *Columbia Spy* articles, and other pieces that expressed ideas already adumbrated, which were being slowly formulated into a philosophy of existence. Poe was looking for truths which went beyond the hopeless reality of his life, something outside and transcending the rational, and he played with the possibility that they might be found in some continuance of physical life after death. So in *Mesmeric Revelation,* which was written during the spring or early summer of 1844, he makes an imaginary experiment in mesmerism the basis for an assumption that death is only a metamorphosis, and that the life we endure is a preparation for a future which is "perfected, ultimate, immortal." This may sound like orthodox Christian doctrine, but in Poe's hands it is much more a basis for speculation, for instance, that "pleasure, in all cases, is but the contrast of pain," so that *"positive* pleasure is a mere idea" and does not truly exist. *The Facts in the Case of M. Valdemar,* published rather more than a year later, uses the same sort of speculation for the purposes of a sensational story. Can death be averted by mesmerism? When it is known that M. Valdemar must die within twenty-four hours, he is put into a mesmeric trance, and in it announces: "I am dead." He stays in a condition that might be called suspended death for seven months, without breath or blood pressure. When he is taken out of the trance, the words "Dead! dead!" come from his tongue, and then his body rots away in less than a minute into "a nearly liquid mass of loathsome—of detestable putridity."

The origin of these stories was Virginia's illness. The names of the protagonists, Vankirk and Valdemar, begin with V, and both are dying of tuberculosis like Virginia. *Mesmeric Revelation* is a serious attempt to express Poe's ideas, *M. Valdemar* a piece of almost pure sensationalism. Yet the serious work hardly exists as a story, while the sensational one has an undeniable power, and an air of authenticity. In England it was printed as a pamphlet about a remarkable scientific experiment. Poe's hackwork and the pieces he regarded seriously interpenetrated each other, and he was so avid for praise that he was prepared to applaud almost any friendly criticism, no matter how ill-judged or foolish.

The ideas passing through his mind were expressed at this time to Lowell more nearly than to anybody else. Lowell was to write for *Graham's* a biography of Poe to accompany a steel portrait, and asked him not for facts, which he already possessed, but for a spiritual autobiography giving *"your own estimate* of your life." The request stirred Poe profoundly, and the long letter he wrote in reply seems to be a genuine attempt at analyzing his own character. Lowell had blamed himself for indolence, and Poe admitted it as one of his own besetting sins. The reader of this book may carry away an impression of steady, unremitting work, but Poe was not referring to journalism, and he was writing truthfully when he said that "I have . . . rambled and dreamed away whole months, and awake, at last, to a sort of mania for composition. Then I scribble all day, and read all night, so long as the disease endures." That he should use the word "disease" of his writing "mania" is significant. He opened his heart in this letter also, as he had never done before, about his basic dislike of ideas proposing social or intellectual improvement:

> I live continually in a reverie of the future. I have no faith in human perfectibility. I think that human exertion will have no appreciable effect upon humanity. Man is now only more active—not more happy—nor more wise, than he was 6000 years ago. The result will never vary—and to suppose that it will, is to suppose that the foregone man has lived in vain—that the foregone time is but the rudiment of the future—that the myriads who have perished have not been upon equal footing with ourselves—nor are we with our posterity. I cannot agree to lose sight of man the individual, in man the mass.

Such ideas were glancingly critical of Lowell's own beliefs. Poe went on to discuss the relationship between matter and spirit in terms that a little echoed *Mesmeric Revelation* and a little prefigured *Eureka* ("the unparticled matter, permeating & impelling, all things, is God. Its activity is the thought of God"). Such remarks may have puzzled Lowell, but the passage that followed them is clear enough, and is perhaps the most accurate self-criticism Poe ever made:

> You speak of an "estimate of my life"—and, from what I have already said, you will see that I have none to give. I have been too deeply conscious of the mutability and evanescence of temporal things, to give any continuous effort to anything—to be consistent in anything.

Lowell's biography praised Poe as America's most discriminating, philosophical, and fearless critic, although he added that the critic sometimes seemed to mistake his phial of prussic acid for his ink-stand. He added that "Mr. Poe has that indescribable something which men have agreed to call genius." It would have been difficult not to be pleased by such words, and Poe expressed gratitude. Such mutual high opinions between such different personalities are best maintained by correspondence, however, and the only meeting between the two was a signal for the end of their friendly relationship. In 1845 Lowell called upon Poe in New York, and both men were disappointed. Poe was, Lowell said later, not tipsy but "a little soggy with drink"—a fact confirmed by Maria Clemm, who stayed in the room throughout, and later assured Lowell that "the day you saw him in New York *he was not himself.*" The Bostonian also felt that Poe did not quite live up to descriptions of him. His dapper neatness Lowell put down as being simply small, his interestingly pale (or olive) complexion as clammy-white. He noted the fine eyes and head, but observed also that the head receded sharply from the brows backward. What others had thought of as elaborate courtesy appeared to Lowell a manner formal, and even pompous. And Poe's view of Lowell? "I was very much disappointed in his appearance as an intellectual man. He was not half the noble looking person that I expected to see."

Poe's description of Lowell comes on the authority of Thomas Holley Chivers, the Georgian poet. The relationship between Poe and Chivers had an undertone of comedy. It is clear that Poe's interest in Chivers was as a potential backer for his magazine. Chivers on his side showed admiration for Poe's poetic genius by the imitation that is supposed to mark sincerity (although he claimed with occasional justice that Poe was the imitator), and for the exalted quality of his mind, but managed always adroitly to sidestep the question of putting up any considerable sum of money. So Chivers wrote to Poe in May 1844 about his projected magazine, saying that he should be paid $10,000 a year as editor, and adding paragraph upon paragraph of transcendental criticism about Poe's views on matter and spirit. But his interest in the magazine went no further than to suggest that *The Sibyl* would be a more poetical title than *The Stylus*. Why, he complained a month or two later, did Poe not answer, when his letters gave Chivers "such intellectual delight—the highest pleasure that a man can enjoy on earth—such as the Angels feel in heaven"? He went on to several more paragraphs of meditation about the nature of the soul and the quality of belief, but said nothing about backing *The Stylus.*

Poe had not given up the idea of the magazine. He wrote to Lowell (this was before their unhappy meeting) suggesting that a dozen men of letters might each subscribe $100. Their names should be kept secret, and a single blackball would be enough to exclude an undesired applicant. Poe and Lowell, as the original stockholders, would issue the first invitations, and an editor would be elected periodically from among the stockholders. Poe also wrote to the scholar Charles Anthon, outlining the prospects for *The Stylus* and asking that Anthon should use his "unbounded influence" with the brothers Harper. There was more than his usual wildness in these suggestions, for neither he nor Lowell had any money, and he had not been in touch with Anthon for some years. Lowell's reply is not known, but it cannot have been encouraging. Anthon approached the Harpers, but told Poe that they had "complaints" against him, and were not interested.

It may be that Poe's rejection of journalistic work was deliberate, but it must have been clear at least to Maria Clemm that it could not continue if they were to survive. In September 1844, on her rounds trying to beat up some work for Eddie, she called on Nathaniel Parker Willis, editor of the *New York Mirror.* Willis was a figure of more than merely local importance, a poet, playwright, and essayist as well as editor. Poe's sharpest reference to him has already been quoted on page 77. He had, more moderately, called Willis a graceful trifler in a letter to Lowell, and later was to pin him down with accuracy as a man who " 'pushed himself,' went much into the world, made friends with the gentler sex, 'delivered' poetical addresses, wrote 'scriptural' poems, travelled, sought the intimacy of noted women, and got into quarrels with notorious men." The barely concealed contempt of this reference was ingeniously fused with mild praise, just as in reviewing Willis's drama *Tortesa,* Poe had begun by saying that it was the best American play yet written, and then catalogued its faults at length. Willis had no reason to feel friendly toward Poe, but he was a generous man. Maria Clemm did not seem to him, as she had to Lowell, a rather ordinary uncultivated woman, but rather one "made beautiful and saintly with an

evidently complete giving up of her life to privation and sorrowful
tenderness." Her manners were unconsciously refined, her mournful
voice impressive. In a phrase, she seemed to Willis an angel on
earth.

So Willis agreed to employ Poe as what he called critic and subed-
itor, at what was no doubt a low salary. He must have known that
he was making a good bargain, providing Poe did not, as he had
been led to expect, arrive drunk at work or fail to arrive at all.
During the few months he spent on the paper, however, Poe's behavior was perfect. He was never late, never drunk, always industrious.
He was treated with a deference owed to his "pale, beautiful, and
intellectual face" and his evident genius; but when asked to modify
a criticism, he readily agreed, "far more yielding than most men,
we thought, on points so exceedingly sensitive." One might put it
differently by saying that Poe was complaisant because he was never
emotionally involved in the work he was doing. Within a few weeks
the family had moved back into the city, first to a cramped apartment
on 85 Amity Street, Greenwich Village, and then to a boarding
house on 195 East Broadway.

It was toward the end of his time at the *Mirror* that Poe published
the poem which made his name known beyond the comparatively
narrow circle of those interested in literature, and for a short time
seemed likely to change the whole course of his life. It is probable
that he had been working on "The Raven" for two or three years.
There are stories that he read an early version of the poem to the
farmer's wife, Mrs. Brennan, although an assertion that the "pallid
bust of Pallas" stood on a shelf in the Poes' part of the farmhouse
seems to be apocryphal. By January 1845, in any case, the poem
was finished to its author's satisfaction and had been sold to the
American Review. Or was he satisfied? He left himself a loophole
by publishing it under the pseudonym of Quarles, but at the same
time acknowledged authorship by allowing Willis to publish it in
the *Mirror* with his own name attached. A prefatory note presumably by Willis (although one can never be sure, with Poe, that he
did not write it himself) claimed that the poem was "unsurpassed
in English poetry for subtle conception, masterly ingenuity of versification, and consistent sustaining of imaginative life and 'pokerish-
ness.' . . . It will stick to the memory of everybody who reads it."
About the last assertion, at least, there has never been any argument.

CHAPTER XII

SOMETHING LIKE FAME

There is a small steam engine in his brain which not only sets the cerebral mass in motion, but keeps the owner in hot water.
New York Weekly Mirror, *July 5, 1845*

"THE RAVEN" is probably the most famous poem written by any American, and its success was immediate. Parodies appeared within a few weeks of publication. Lines and phrases were quoted from it in print, as they have been ever since. And its success renewed interest in Poe as a writer. In July 1845 the New York firm of Wiley & Putnam published twelve stories under the title *Tales* by Edgar A. Poe, and later in the year *The Raven and Other Poems* appeared. Poe was dissatisfied with the selection from his stories, in which he had no hand, but he must have been pleased by the terms, which were a royalty of 8 cents a copy on a book that sold for 50 cents. The book of stories, which included the four tales of ratiocination, was much better received than earlier collections. The book of poems had been chosen by Poe, and he omitted both "Tamerlane" and "Al Aaraaf," as well as some other early poems. It received mostly lukewarm or hostile reviews.

In a prefatory note Poe was characteristically defensive about his poems, saying that "I think nothing in this volume of much value to the public, or very creditable to myself. Events not to be controlled have prevented me from making, at any time, any serious effort in what, under happier circumstances, would have been the field of my choice." Elizabeth Barrett, to whom the book had been dedicated, wrote to tell him that she heard of people haunted by the "Nevermore" of "The Raven," and that an acquaintance who owned a bust of Pallas could no longer bear to look at it in the twilight. She added that "our great poet, Mr. Browning," had been much struck by the poem's rhythm. She expressed herself rather differently to Richard Hengist Horne, whose *Orion* Poe had called the greatest epic ever written, saying that the poem did not appear to her the expression of a sane intellect. "There is a fantasticalness about the 'sir or madam,' and things of the sort, which is ludicrous, unless there is a specified insanity to justify the strains."

Was "The Raven" a great poem, or even a good poem? It seems that Poe himself was never sure. Rather more than a year after its publication, he gave an account in the essay on *The Philosophy of Composition* of the process by which it had been written; this made it seem like a kind of exercise, a work conceived in the spirit of the tales of ratiocination. " 'The Raven' has had a great run, Thomas," he wrote exultantly to his friend in Washington, "but I wrote it for the express purpose of running—just as I did the 'Gold-Bug,' you know. The bird beat the bug, though, all hollow." The note struck here of deliberate contrivance is amplified in the essay. The picture of the poet sitting down to produce a work about the death of a beautiful woman because that was, "unquestionably, the most poetical topic in the world," and then carefully working out all the details—including the production of a kind of sample stanza— may have been meant as one more demonstration of analytic power. Poe wrote in a letter that it was his best specimen of analysis. It was deeply shocking, however, to those who viewed poetic composition as a matter of inspiration. Lines like:

> Tell this soul with sorrow laden, if within the distant Aidenn,
> It shall clasp a sainted maiden whom the angels name Lenore,
> Clasp a rare and radiant maiden whom the angels name Lenore

appeared in a different light if the soul with sorrow laden and the sainted maiden were, as one might say, deliberately devised stage properties. Nothing Poe said could damage the impression made by the poem, but he did his best.

Nevertheless, in the weeks after "The Raven" appeared, it must have seemed to him that he was at last being taken at his own estimation. He was invited to lecture, he was taken up by New York literary society, he became for a few heady weeks the editor of his own magazine, although it was not *The Stylus*. Another man,

many other men, could have turned this sudden celebrity to commercial use; in Poe's hands it melted away like butter before a fire.

Between three and four hundred people listened in the library
of the New York Historical Society to the author of "The Raven"
talking about the poets and poetry of America. It was a talk that
he had given before, and he repeated his praise of some writers
he had attacked in print, like Longfellow, Bryant, and Halleck. He
praised also some American women poets, in particular Mrs. Frances
Osgood. In giving this lecture Poe cut out all the caustic remarks
he had previously made about Griswold. The editor had sued for
peace in a letter which began: "Although I have some cause of
personal quarrel with you, which you will easily enough remember,
I do not under any circumstances permit, as you have repeatedly
charged, my private griefs to influence my judgment as a critic,
or its expression." Griswold went on to say that he wanted to include
Poe in his new anthology of American prose writers. Poe was not
unmoved or unforgiving. His reply, marked "Confidential," said that
"Your letter occasioned me first pain and then pleasure:—pain, because it gave me to see that I had lost, through my own folly, an
honorable friend:—pleasure, because I saw in it a hope of reconciliation." He went on to blame an unnamed mischief-maker, and said
that he hoped Griswold could forget the past.

The glimpse of editorship came about in the first instance through
Lowell, who gave Poe's name to a friend, Charles F. Briggs, who
was eager to start a new paper. Briggs was the author of a novel
called *The Adventures of Harry Franco* which had had sufficient
success for him to use the pseudonym of Harry Franco when writing
other fiction. Like others who fell out with Poe, he was a good-
natured, lively, extrovert.

> There comes Harry Franco, and, as he draws near,
> You find that's a smile which you took for a sneer;
> One half of him contradicts t'other; his wont
> Is to say very sharp things and do very blunt . . .

Lowell wrote a little later in his *Fable for Critics*.

In January 1845, Briggs had started the *Broadway Journal*, in
which literary reviews occupied most space, with articles about
painting and theatrical comment also prominent. There were poems,
but no stories. Within a few weeks of its appearance Poe had left

the *Mirror* and joined the new paper as one among a trio of editors, Briggs himself and a music critic named Watson being the others. Briggs was told "shocking bad stories" about Poe by Griswold, but ignored them. He was immensely enthusiastic about *The Gold-Bug,* which he thought among the most ingenious stories he had ever read, and the *Journal* printed "The Raven." Poe, Briggs assured Lowell, was a misunderstood man. The arrangement made was that he should have one-third of the profits, which at this time did not exist, although he told Thomas that the editorship would pay him well in the end.

Briggs's feeling that Poe was a misunderstood man did not last long. In his last weeks at the *Mirror* Poe had engaged in a campaign against Longfellow as a plagiarist. He had used the term of Longfellow before, but now he widened the accusation to include passages from Longfellow's play *The Spanish Student,* in which he found enough similarities to his own dramatic fragment *Politian* to "establish at least the *imitation* beyond all doubt." He suggested too that Longfellow had plagiarized Bryant. The similarities are very slight, and of a kind that one could easily find with a little industry in almost any two poets approaching similar themes. The whole controversy, in which a correspondent calling himself "Outis" defended Longfellow and ironically suggested that "The Raven" owed something to "The Ancient Mariner," was carried on by Poe at great length and with extraordinary fervor. (It is quite possible that he himself was "Outis," stoking the fires of argument.) Perhaps these accusations were a means of absolving himself from his own more serious plagiaristic sins. He continued the controversy in the *Broadway Journal.*

To find one's literary editor bringing over from another paper such a dangerous theme, and pursuing it with such unswerving determination, must have been unnerving for Briggs. He tried to make the best of it, however, assuring Lowell that Poe was only his assistant, and saying also that the best thing was to let him ride his hobby horse of plagiarism until he was tired of it. The controversy would call attention to the paper, and really Poe admired Longfellow and would say so before he had done. Poe might not be exactly a misunderstood man but he was a very good fellow, although his sharpness had made him enemies, and abominable lies had been told about him by "The Rev. Mr. Griswold of Philadelphia."

But the view of Poe as a very good fellow lasted no longer than the idea that he was a misunderstood man. By the end of June Poe was drinking hard and frequently, and Briggs decided to remove his name from the masthead. "I was taken at first with a certain appearance of independence and learning in his criticisms, but they are so verbal, and so purely selfish that I can no longer have any sympathy with him." Lowell said in reply that he had made Poe an enemy by doing him a service, and added that he was lacking in "that element of manhood which, for want of a better name, we call character."

Briggs did not in fact get rid of Poe. He seems to have been outmaneuvered in some negotiations to continue the paper with a new publisher, and in the end abandoned it to his partner John Bisco. In July Bisco and Poe signed a new agreement, under which Poe was to be the sole editor, "uninterfered with by any party whatever," and was to receive not a third but half of the profits. Briggs felt that he had been treated badly, and his allusions to Poe were bitter when he wrote to Lowell. He had not, he said, given the shadow of a cause for ill-feeling. "On the contrary he owes me now for money that I lent him to pay his board and keep him from being turned into the street."

It is very likely that this was true. Thomas had written in May asking if Poe could repay money lent to him by Jesse Dow on that ill-fated visit to Washington, and Poe said in reply that there had never been any chance of his repaying Dow "without putting myself to greater inconvenience than he himself would have wished . . . the Devil himself was never so poor." He added rather haughtily that he was sorry Dow had taken to dunning in his old age. In the same letter he made that tactless remark about the bird and the bug.

The emotional strain of Virginia's continuing illness, and of achieving success which was in a financial sense a mirage, was too much for Poe. He had been sober for a year or more, but now went on drinking bouts each of which left him "dreadfully unwell," as he told Evert A. Duyckink, who occasionally acted as a kind of agent for him. He added to Duyckink that he was going to retire to the country for six or twelve months, in the hope that he might recover health and spirits. One glimpse of him in drink is given by the librarian of the Astor Library, who met Poe on Broadway, and was told that he had arranged to read "The Raven" before Queen Victoria and the royal family. Another comes from the ineffable Chivers, who in the summer of 1845 met Poe for the first time, and one day saw him tottering from side to side down Nassau Street, "drunk as an Indian." While Chivers was steering him home they met Poe's old antagonist Lewis Gaylord Clark, of the *Knickerbocker Magazine.* Poe, restrained by Chivers from attacking Clark, rushed forward and shook hands with him instead, and according to Chivers the following conversation took place:

Clark: Why, Poe! Is this you?
  Poe: Yes, by God! This is Poe. Here is my friend Dr. Chivers from the South.
Clark: What! Dr. Chivers, the author of so many beautiful poems?
  Poe: Yes, by God. Not only the author of some of the beautifullest poems ever written any where, but my friend, too, by God!
Chivers: I was very much pleased with Willis Gaylord Clark's poems.
  Poe: What business had you to abuse me in the last number of your magazine?
Clark: Why, by God, Poe, how did I know the article referred to was yours? You had always attached your name to all your articles before, and how in Hell did I know it was yours?

Chivers was an embroiderer of reality rather than a creator of total fiction. One can believe in the basic truth of the encounter without accepting every word of what is put down. Poe's final comment after they had parted from Clark: "A damned coward, by God!" rings particularly true. So does the final scene in which Poe, after being brought home with difficulty, was put to bed by Mrs. Clemm, who then lamented the family's fate:

Oh! my poor Virginia! She cannot live long! She is wasting away day by day—for the doctors can do her no good. But if they could, seeing this continually in poor Eddy, would kill her—for she dotes upon him. . . . He has been here in bed for a whole week with nothing in the world the matter with him—only lying here pretending to be sick, in order to avoid delivering the Poem promised, before one of the literary societies of the city.

On the following day Chivers, finding him in bed, agreed with Mrs. Clemm that he was pretending to be sick to avoid the reading. It seems uncharacteristic of Poe to shun the limelight, but there is no doubt that reading in public imposed a strain on him, and according to Briggs another reading arranged at New York University could not be given because he was drunk. Soon after this, Chivers refused a request for the loan of $50. "I do not believe that it would have done for him to have had money," he piously remarked in his memoir, and Poe was in little danger of getting it from his rich friend. Three months later, after his return to Georgia, Chivers wrote: "You say you have not touched a drop of the ashes of Hell since I left New York. *That's* a *man."*

During this visit, Poe told Chivers that he was "in the damnedest amour you ever knew a fellow to be in in all your life," with a lady in Providence who had asked to see him that day. "Her husband is a painter—always from home—and a damned fool at that." The lady referred to was Frances Sargent Osgood, whose mild sentimental verses with such titles as "The Dying Rose-Bud's Lament" and "Your Heart Is a Music-Box, Dearest" ("With exquisite tunes at command,/Of melody sweetest and clearest,/If tried by a delicate hand") had already been praised by Poe for their tenderness, earnestness, passion, and "true imagination as distinguished from its subordinate, fancy." Her husband, Samuel Stillman Osgood, was a portrait painter, and she was in her middle thirties when Poe met her, a small, delicate, lively woman with two children, who was happy to conduct a literary flirtation with the author of "The Raven." She was consumptive, and survived her admirer by only a year. But after his death she remembered how deeply she had been moved at their first meeting by his proud and beautiful head, by the blend of sweetness and hauteur in his expression, and the almost cold gravity of his greeting, which had "so marked an earnestness that I could not help being deeply impressed by it."

Fanny Osgood had a childishness of appearance and a playfulness of manner ("I never can go the dignified," she told a friend) that greatly appealed to Poe, and the two wrote verses addressed to each other. One of Poe's, to be sure, had already been addressed to his cousin Rebecca Herring and then to Eliza, the daughter of Thomas W. White; now it served again, addressed to F——s S. O——d, as a reply to her "Echo Song," which had appeared in the *Broadway Journal:*

> I know a noble heart that beats
>   For one it loves how "wildly well"
> I only know for *whom* it beats;
>   But I must never tell!

It was Poe's Israfel who had not loved but sung "wildly well," and now he replied:

> Thou wouldst be loved?—then let thy heart
>   From its present pathway part not!
> Being everything which now thou art,
>   Be nothing which thou are not.

He added to this discreet compliment another poem, written ten years before but now addressed to F—— ("My soul at least a solace hath/In dreams of thee"), as well as several newly written pieces, including a punning quatrain, a Valentine, and a poem addressed to "——" and signed "M." This last was in reply to a reproachful poem of Frances Osgood's written under the pseudonym of Violet Vane:

> Perhaps you think it right and just,
>   Since you are bound by nearer ties,
> To greet me with that careless tone,
>   With those serene and silent eyes

The reference to Virginia was answered by an equally oblique reference to Samuel Osgood, from whom Fanny was temporarily separated:

> We both have found a life-long love;
>   Wherein our weary souls may rest,
> Yet may we not, my gentle friend,
>   Be each to each the *second best?*

Nothing could be much more decorous, or fit in less well with the story of being in "the damnedest amour you ever knew a fellow to be in." Chivers is an unreliable witness, and all the evidence we have suggests that this was on both sides an intensely conducted but unpassionate affair. It was not the only emotional involvement which Fanny Osgood permitted herself during the months of alienation from her husband. She was, one commentator said, "loved of all men who knew her," and one of them was Griswold, who wrote poems to her, and to whom she dedicated a book. But this came later. In 1845 it was Poe to whom she addressed poems.

It is said that he pursued her, and certainly they were much together. During the summer and autumn of this year he was in demand among New York's literary ladies. He found it easier to maintain relationships with women than with men. In the presence of what one of his later flames called "superior" (that is, literary) women, he was serious, respectful, adoring and arrogant, and he had the gift of making any woman in whom he was interested feel that she was the exclusive object of his attention. He did not so much talk to them as, according to one of them, "fall into a sort of eloquent monologue, half dream, half poetry." The role of worshipful lover was a part Poe played frequently in the drama of his life. To Virginia he was the anguished husband; to Mrs. Osgood the lover who knew that she was distant and unattainable; to other poetesses a man of sorrows who both invited and forbade intimacy by the melancholy dignity of his manner. The parts he played for men, the Southern gentleman, the savagely skeptical critic (Briggs was particularly disturbed by the violent egotism of his opinions), the man of letters stooping to journalism, were less appreciated. The admiration felt for him by other men was almost always intellectual; the feelings he inspired in women were emotional. To say that he played these parts is not to suggest that they were deliberately assumed. Poe's nature was histrionic, and it would be idle to ask what reality lay beneath the masks he assumed. The reality was the sum of all the parts he played.

Among the women writers whom Poe met at literary parties and gatherings this year were such forgotten poetasters as Anne Charlotte Lynch, Elizabeth Ellet, Sarah Anna Lewis, and Jane Ermina Locke. The men who came to Mrs. Lynch's or other salons included Willis, Bryant and Halleck. Poe was sometimes called on to read "The Raven," which he did very quietly and with a total absence of declamation. Opinions about his reading of poetry vary. Some liked the music of his voice and the deep seriousness of his manner, while others felt that he lacked power and "rather *cantilated* than read," as Chivers put it. But his conversation, and even more his presence, impressed almost everybody. There must have been something discouraging to the levity of party conversation in Poe's threadbare neatness, his elaborate courtesy, and the sad seriousness of his customary manner—a seriousness that made his smile even more captivating by its rarity. He talked, one American diplomat who heard him said, "with an abstracted earnestness, as if he were dictating to an amanuensis," and almost all of those who heard him were moved by his directness and sincerity. His pride and his poverty were equally evident.

Virginia was sometimes present at Mrs. Lynch's evenings in Waverly Place, but seldom took part in the conversation. At the home of Seba Smith, a poet who had been severely castigated by Poe, she is glimpsed in public for the last time, in a homemade gown, sitting pale and smiling beside the fire while her husband recited "The Raven." His liking for the company of women can hardly have escaped her attention, but she voiced no objection to it, or to his relationship with Mrs. Osgood.

All this was something like fame, but it was fame that paid no bills. Poe depended for money largely on the *Broadway Journal*, but gave to the weekly only a small part of the time and care that had been devoted a decade earlier to the *Southern Literary Messenger*. He reprinted many stories, poems and critical pieces, sometimes using one of his several pseudonyms, Littleton Barry. He became the paper's dramatic critic, and commented shrewdly and freshly on the plays he saw. The *Journal*, however, did not flourish like the other papers with which he had been editorially connected, and John Bisco decided to give it up. In October he agreed to sell his rights in it to Poe for $50 in cash plus a note at three months for the full amount of debts due. But where was even this small sum to come from? Poe wrote an ironic letter to Kennedy, telling him that "by a series of manoeuvres almost incomprehensible to myself, I have succeeded in getting rid, one by one, of all my associates in the *Broadway Journal*," and adding that if he could hold the paper for a month, he would be safe. Kennedy sent good wishes but no money. Chivers was asked for $45 which he promised to, and possibly did, send. Some who had little reason to like him were more generous. Fitz-Greene Halleck lent him $100, the editor and journalist Horace Greeley $50, and Griswold by his own account $25. This money enabled Poe to buy the paper, and to see his name on the front page as "Editor and Proprietor," but not to keep it afloat. Within a few weeks he had sold a half-interest, on the consideration that the buyer was responsible for the most recent debts, and in January 1846, the *Broadway Journal* ceased publication. Poe's valedictory note said that "Unexpected engagements demanding my whole attention . . . I now, as its editor, bid farewell—as cordially to foes as to friends." It was the last time he had a direct editorial relationship with any periodical. None of the loans was repaid.

To the failure of the paper was added a lecturing catastrophe. In October 1845 Poe visited Boston, where through the agency of Lowell he had been invited to lecture. The audience was large, but perhaps not particularly friendly. Poe's attack on the Bostonian idol, Longfellow, and his dislike for New England transcendentalism, were well enough known. It seems to have been taken for granted that he would recite a new poem, and another "Raven" would no doubt have been warmly greeted. But there was no new poem, and when Poe followed as speaker a local politician named Caleb Cushing, he first made some hostile remarks about didacticism in poetry, which might have been taken to refer to Longfellow or Lowell, and then read the obscure "Al Aaraaf." This was followed, at special request, by "The Raven," but by this time some of the audience had begun to leave.

Later in the evening, perhaps under the influence of drink, Poe told four Bostonians (including Cushing and a Shakespearean lecturer named Hudson) that he had hoaxed the audience by reading a poem written when he was twelve years old. Hudson, at least, was indignant. He told the tale to Cornelia Wells Walter, editor of the Boston *Evening Transcript,* and she began a campaign of savage personal raillery against Poe as poet. ("This capacity, it seems, had been deteriorating since Mr. Poe was ten years of age, his best poems having been written before that period.")

Poe replied in the *Broadway Journal* with scornful comments about the Bostonians ("Their hotels are bad. Their pumpkin pies are delicious. Their poetry is not so good"), and saying that nobody could have thought that he would compose an *original* poem for such people. "Al Aaraaf," which had been written "before we had fairly completed our tenth year," was quite good enough for a Boston audience. The insults were of a kind that had been commonplaces of his criticism for years, and he had been accustomed to assume that those insulted, like Willis and Longfellow, would forgive even if they did not forget. He was approaching a time, however, when there would be no more forgiving and forgetting.

CHAPTER XIII

FORDHAM, AND DISASTER

*Believe me, there exists no such dilemma as that in which a gentleman
is placed when he is forced to reply to a blackguard.*
        —*Edgar Allan Poe to George W. Eveleth, January 4, 1848*

ON February 14, 1846, Valentine's Day, Virginia sent Edgar a Valentine in the customary form by which the first letter of each line spelt his name. It is the only piece of verse she is known to have written:

> Ever with thee I wish to roam—
> Dearest my life is thine.
> Give me a cottage for my home
> And a rich old cypress vine,
> Removed from the world with its sin and care
> And the tattling of many tongues.
> Love alone shall guide us when we are there—
> Love shall heal my weakened lungs;
> And Oh the tranquil hours we'll spend,
> Never wishing that others may see!
> Perfect ease we'll enjoy, without thinking to lend
> Ourselves to the world and its glee—
> Ever peaceful and blissful we'll be.

Three or four months later her wish was realized when Poe rented for $100 a year a cottage at Fordham, 13 miles from the city. It was a shingled building of a single floor, with a porch extending along its front, and an attic above. The construction was the simplest form of American frame building, and the cottage itself was similar to hundreds of others built early in the nineteenth century. On the ground floor was a sitting room with stone fireplace and brick hearth, a small back room, and a kitchen. There were two more rooms in the attic. Fordham was a rural area, and the cottage was situated on top of a small hill, with a cherry tree and lilac bushes separating it from the road. There were pleasant walks in several directions, including one along the recently completed course of an aqueduct which Poe particularly favored. Yet it was not inconvenient; a station on the Harlem railroad a mile and a half away took you quickly into the city.

Poe worked sometimes in the sitting room, which had windows opening on two sides, sometimes in the coved attic. There is some doubt about the sleeping arrangements, one historian placing the Poes' bedroom downstairs and another saying that they slept in one of the attic rooms. There was by the standards of the time pitifully little furniture, but the place was scrupulously neat, and like their other homes bore the mark of a delicate and individual taste. Mary Gove—by Poe's account a mesmerist, phrenologist, Swedenborgian, and homeopathist—was charmed by everything when she came to see the family, the green grass outside as smooth as a carpet, the sitting room with its check matting and hanging bookshelf containing presentation copies, and most of all by the inhabitants. She found Maria Clemm tall, dignified, and most ladylike, a strong and stalwart figure who "appeared to be a sort of universal Providence for her strange children." Virginia, raven-haired, pale-faced, and brilliant-eyed, looked very young, but when she coughed appeared to be "rapidly passing away." And the master of the house held the same fascination for the Swedenborgian homeopathist that he had for other women. She gives a glimpse of the poet at play. A game of leaping, or long jumping, was proposed on a walk taken through the woods with other visitors. Poe outjumped the other men in the party, but burst his gaiter-shoes when landing. "O Eddie, how *did* you burst your gaiters?" Maria asked when they returned. If only an editor who had a poem in his hands would accept and pay for it, she said, Eddie could buy some new shoes.

Other visitors to Fordham give glimpses of the Poes' poverty, but also stress the charm of the place and the happiness of the household. One found the cottage half-buried in fruit trees, and the garden containing clumps of rare dahlias and beds of mignonette and heliotrope. There were by the same account rare tropical birds in cages, to which Poe gave keen and delighted attention. The other side to this idyllic picture is that for some weeks he was mysteriously ill. His illnesses were sometimes matters of convenience, but in the spring of 1846 it does seem that he was mentally and physically unable to work. He was wary, for the moment, of any more lecturing. When invited by the Literary Societies of the University of Vermont to lecture to them, he declined. That his desire for publicity remained unabated is shown by his request to Duyckink that he should get an editorial paragraph put in the press saying that "continued ill health, with a pressure of engagements," was the cause of the refusal.

Poe's propensity for literary flirtation now caused serious trouble. He had printed in the *Broadway Journal* not only Fanny Osgood's verses to him, but also a piece by another poetess, Elizabeth Ellet. This may be supposed to have referred to him, particularly because of its reference to that voice which thrilled the ladies:

> Ah! ne'er such a voice, I'll confess,
>   In its low, murmuring tones I have heard,
> So deep with emotion's excess—
>   Yet soft as the tones of a bird.

Whether or not he gave Mrs. Ellet encouragement and then rejected her—for in this case he seems to have been pursued, as in relation to Fanny Osgood he was undoubtedly the pursuer—she became sufficiently jealous to spread stories about the Osgood-Poe relationship. She too had visited Fordham, and there, she said, had been shown by the distressed Virginia some fearful paragraphs in one of Mrs. Osgood's letters. Mrs. Osgood indirectly retorted in print with several poems about slander and innocence, all of them printed in the *Broadway Journal,* which carried personal and particular meanings to those who knew the story. Mrs. Ellet, pressed for an apology by Mrs. Osgood, replied a little ambiguously that the letter sent her had "wrung my heart in convincing me how grossly you have been misrepresented and traduced." The letter shown her by Virginia Poe must have been a forgery. Why should Poe have forged it? She did not explain, beyond saying that he would not stop at such a crime. "Had you seen the fearful paragraphs which Mrs. Poe first repeated and then pointed out—which haunted me night and day like a terrifying spectre—you would not wonder that

I regarded you as I did." But she went no further in the way of apology than saying that she would never listen again to a tale of scandal, and that it was unfortunate for both of them "that we ever had any acquaintance with such people as the Poes."

The matter was not allowed to rest. With Fanny Osgood's agreement a committee of two—Anne Lynch and the formidable feminist Margaret Fuller—came to Fordham and asked Poe for the return of his letters from Mrs. Osgood. He apparently handed them over, but said angrily that Mrs. Ellet had better look after her own letters. By his own account he then felt ashamed of his words, made a package of Mrs. Ellet's letters to him, and left them at her door. Mrs. Ellet, however, was not prepared to stay under the imputation of having had love letters returned by Poe. Her brother, Colonel Lummis, went looking for him with a pistol, and when Poe learned this and tried to borrow a pistol himself from a young acquaintance named Thomas Dunn English, he was told by English that his surest defense would be to retract the charge that Mrs. Ellet had written him love letters. The affair ended not with shooting but with a fist fight, and not with Lummis but with English. According to English, Poe then took to his bed badly beaten, and sent a letter to Colonel Lummis saying that if he had mentioned letters from Mrs. Ellet it must have been in a fit of temporary insanity. According to Poe, the fight went quite the other way, and he had to be dragged from the "prostrate and rascally carcass" of English. He said nothing of the accusation that he had lied about Mrs. Ellet's letters, and of course if his tale was true he could not prove it, because the letters had been returned.

All this became known, and was interpreted in ways very unfavorable to Poe. The incident naturally marked the end of his relationship with Mrs. Ellet, whom he accused subsequently of sending anonymous letters to Virginia. That Virginia knew something of the scandal is shown by the line in her Valentine about "the tattling of many tongues," and she must have been upset by the visit of the two censorious ladies. Other stories told, about the extreme distress of Virginia and the anxiety of Maria Clemm, are conjectural. So, of course, is the nature of Poe's relationship with Fanny Osgood. His first biographers, in good Victorian style, assumed that it was platonic. Recent writers, in tune with modern feeling, have made different assumptions. To think that the two were physically lovers seems to me to ignore the essentially literary nature of the poems, and also radically to misread Poe's character as it is shown in his life and suggested in his work. Whatever unconscious motives may have moved him, his conscious view of love was wholly ethereal. Everything suggests that he would have shuddered away from sexual contact.

Relations between the Poes and Fanny Osgood seem to have survived the Ellet affair, at least for a while. Certainly there was a time when Virginia was pleased by the friendship. Mrs. Osgood tells a story of visiting the Poes just before they moved to Fordham, when he was completing a set of papers on "The Literati of New York City." He told her that the length of the paper on which they were written showed his estimation of the writers' importance. Virginia then helped him to unroll the papers, until at last "they came to one that seemed interminable," so that it stretched from one corner of the room to the other. " 'And whose lengthened sweetness long drawn out is that?' said I. 'Hear, hear,' he cried, 'just as if her little vain heart didn't tell her it's herself.' " She was not only given more space than better known writers, but the brief character sketch which succeeded an account of her as poet was written in a lyrical, although perfectly discreet, manner:

> She is ardent, sensitive, impulsive; the very soul of truth and honor; a worshipper of the beautiful, with a heart so radically artless as to seem abundant in art—universally respected, admired and beloved. In person she is about the medium height, slender even to fragility, graceful whether in action or repose; complexion usually pale; hair very black and glossy; eyes of a clear, luminous gray, large, and with a singular capacity of expression. In no respect can she be termed beautiful (as the world understands the epithet,) but the question "Is it really possible that she is not *so?*" is very frequently asked, and *most* frequently by those who most intimately know her.

The publication of these sketches about the New York literati in *Godey's Lady's Book* between May and October 1846 marked almost the end of Poe's career as journalist and critic. They compounded the damage done to his reputation by the Osgood-Ellet affair, which was common literary gossip, and his attitude in relation to the Boston lecture. He had been regarded as erratic and unreliable, but now it was agreed that he was malicious and treacherous as well, a man who could on no account be trusted.

Part of his reason for writing the sketches was given by him to the phrenological mesmerist Mary Gove, when he said that to praise an unworthy author was an unpardonable sin, but that "if one he loved better than his own life" were writhing on the rack, the venality might be excused. "Would you blame a man for not allowing his sick wife to starve?" But an uncommercial motive existed too. This kind of gossipy literary journalism was something that Poe, as the earlier "Autography" articles show, very much enjoyed writing. The sketches did not, in fact, give offense by their occasional logrolling but by what was felt to be their frequent malice. Godey, who published them, seems to have known that he was onto a good thing. He advertised the series widely, and the demand for the first installment was so great that it had to be reprinted. Poe's introduction sounded very threatening, with its contemptuous dismissal of the most successful writers as busybodies, toadies and quacks, who manufactured their reputations by assiduously courting editors and everybody else connected with newspapers. Hawthorne, "scarcely recognised by the press or by the public," was not acknowledged as a genius because "first [he] *is* a poor man, and, second, he is *not* an ubiquitous quack." Longfellow, on the other hand, who was "a man of property and a professor at Harvard," with "a whole legion of quacks under his control," was regarded as "a poetical phenomenon, as entirely without fault as the luxurious paper upon which his poems are invariably borne to the public eye." Poe's intention was, he said, to give "my own unbiased opinion of the *literati* (male and female) of New York," and also to give "very closely if not with absolute accuracy" the opinion of them expressed by "conversational society in literary circles."

That a reprint of the first article was called for is a tribute to Poe's acidulous critical reputation, rather than to the content of the papers. To read the accounts of these writers, most of whom never had more than a local reputation, is to wonder not at their savagery but at their gentleness. The first installment gave sketches of the Reverend George Bush, professor of Hebrew in the University of New York ("as an oriental linguist it is probable that he has no equal among us"), George H. Colton, editor of *The American Review* ("so marked and immediate a success has never been attained by any of our five dollar magazines, with the exception of the *Southern Literary Messenger*"), Willis ("Mr. Willis's career has naturally made

him enemies among the envious host of dunces whom he has out-
stripped in the race for fame"), and of four other figures of whom
only Briggs had even then any wide reputation. Only in dealing
with his former collaborator did Poe allow urbanity to desert him.
As a novelist, he said, Briggs was an obvious imitator of Smollett,
and his criticism was, as might be expected of a man who was "grossly
uneducated" and had "never composed in his life three consecutive
sentences of grammatical English," ludicrously bad. His personal
appearance was "not prepossessing," marked as it was by a low,
narrow forehead, a "pert-looking" nose, and small gray eyes which
were "not so good." Each sketch ended with a physical description
of the subject, and certainly these were sometimes sharp. Willis
was praised for the ease and grace of his carriage, his well-cut mouth
and fine teeth, but still the lower part of his face was too heavy,
and "neither his nose nor his forehead can be defended; the latter
would puzzle phrenology."

There were thirty-eight "Literati" sketches, and they ranged
in length from five hundred to five thousand words. The actual
criticism they contain is generally consistent with what Poe had
already written elsewhere, from his denigration of conceits in Donne
and Cowley to the view that even the best American poets were
overrated. There are some passages of unblushing flattery, and a
few in which, rather mildly, he paid off old scores. His view of
Laughton Osborn is representative of the first, the piece on Lewis
Gaylord Clark of the second. Osborn had written to Poe a few
months earlier, asking who had described his satirical poem "The
Vision of Rubeta" as a "gilded swill trough overflowing with Dunciad
and water" in the *Broadway Journal*. It had, naturally enough, been
written by Poe, but he denied this and said that he did not know
the reviewer's name. In the "Literati" Osborn was given generous
space, and although Poe provided an escape vent for his literary
conscience by saying that "The Vision of Rubeta" was very censur-
ably indecent, he said also that it was decidedly the best satire produced by an American. Clark was treated gently, although in part
ironically, nothing worse being said of him than that he had no
particular editorial character. Apart from that, "Mr. Clark once did
me the honor to review my poems, and—I forgive him."

In October the series came to an end. Poe said that the sketches
had been discontinued because people insisted on considering as

criticism what he had intended as lively gossip, and that he thought too little of them to guard sufficiently against haste, inaccuracy, and prejudice. This is a half-truth, like much else that he said and wrote, for he was prepared to denigrate them and at the same time was delighted to know that they were making a stir. One reason for discontinuing the series may have been that the stock of New York literati was running low; but another, certainly, was the nervousness increasingly felt by Godey, who put disclaimers into more than one issue of the magazine to the effect that the opinions expressed were Poe's, and that his own role was purely that of publisher.

In 1843 Poe had been paid $5 a page for his contributions to *Godey's*. One would like to think that three years later he was paid more highly, but whatever he received was insufficient recompense for the disrepute into which the series brought him, and the wounding personal attacks made on him because of it. The most bitter of these came from Clark and from Hiram Fuller, who had known Poe during his months on the *Mirror*, and must have disliked him intensely. Fuller, now the editor of the *New York Evening Mirror*, made attacks that were woundingly personal. Poe's poverty was known, and so was his occasional drunkenness. Fuller jeeringly said that "a man must be sadly in want of money who resorts to such methods of raising it," and doubted that Poe could express an honest opinion because of "his infirmities of mind and body . . . his unfortunate habits, his quarrels and jealousies." He ended with a physically descriptive portrait in Poe's own vein that made him only an inch or two over 5 feet in height, mentioned his quick, jerky, "almost waving" walk, and said that his tongue showed itself unpleasantly when he spoke most in earnest.

Clark's abuse was even coarser. After calling Poe "the jaded hack who runs a broken pace for common hire" and "the wretched inebriate whose personalities disgrace a certain Milliner's Magazine," he went on to an imaginary portrait of a "poor creature" who had called at his office, a figure so pitiful

> that every spark of harsh feeling toward him was extinguished, and we could not even entertain a feeling of contempt for one who was evidently committing a suicide upon his body, as he had already done upon his character. Unhappy man! He was accompanied by an aged female relative who was going a weary round in the hot streets, following his steps to prevent his indulging in a love of drink;

but he had eluded her watchful eye by some means, and was already
far gone in a state of inebriation.

Poe might and did reply, including in the next installment of
the "Literati" a paper on a former editor of the *Knickerbocker,*
Charles Fenno Hoffman, which enabled him to refer in passing to
"that dreary realm of outer darkness, of utter and inconceivable
dunderheadedness, over which has so long ruled King Log the Second, in the august person of one Lewis Gaylord Clark." But he
was fighting with inferior weapons, in a field where his chances of
using them were becoming restricted. He sent Fuller's attack to
the editor of a St. Louis paper, saying that Fuller had been forced
to leave Providence on account of several swindling transactions,
and asking for a rebuttal of his statements as well as the insertion
of a puff for his own poems and stories. But no puffs or rebuttals
could dam the tide rising against him.

There was one further quarrel in which Poe became involved
through the "Literati" sketches, with Thomas Dunn English, and
this was in some ways the most damaging of all. English was a genial,
rumbustious young man with a medical degree from the University
of Pennsylvania, who had published a thesis on phrenology that
had attracted Poe's attention. The two had been on friendly terms
in Poe's days on *Burton's.* The cause of Poe's animus against him
seems to have been English's attitude in the Ellet affair, although
English was of a physical type—large, genial, exuberant—that Poe
found antipathetic. English, who had attended two good preparatory
schools, was justifiably annoyed to find himself termed "a man without the commonest school education," to be told that he was incapable of writing grammatically, to be called not more than thirty-
five when he was in fact twenty-seven, and to read Poe's casual
remark that "I do not personally know Mr. English." His reply,
however, was of a brutality that made even Griswold wince. English
said that he had lent Poe money which had not been repaid, suggested that Poe had committed forgery, and gave contemptuous
accounts of his behavior when drunk. He referred to the "severe
treatment" he had given Poe for his "brutal and dastardly conduct,"
presumably toward Mrs. Ellet, mentioned his "frequent quotations
from languages of which he is entirely ignorant," and in an ultimate
paragraph summed him up as "not alone thoroughly unprincipled,

base and depraved, but silly, vain and ignorant—not alone an assassin in morals, but a quack in literature."

Poe wrote an equally vitriolic rebuttal which he expected Godey to print, but Godey had had enough. He sent Poe's answer to a paper of small circulation in Philadelphia, paid $10 to have it printed, and debited Poe with the cost. English replied in contemptuous terms, and Poe then filed suit for libel against Hiram Fuller and his partner, who owned the *Evening Mirror,* in which English's letters had appeared.

The libel suit stopped the correspondence, but not the gossip. Even friends now told stories of Poe's drunkenness, and said that he had brain fever or was being sent to a retreat for the insane. The tale of Mrs. Ellet and the letters was widely though not accurately known, and Poe's part in it was felt to have been discreditable. English, who had fled to Washington to avoid involvement in the libel action, published pseudonymously a novel entitled *1844, or The Power of the "S.F.,"* into which he inserted passages caricaturing Poe under the name of Marmaduke Hammerhead. Fanny Osgood was also caricatured in the book under the name of Mrs. Flighty— a poetess who wrote verses which "resemble a large quantity of water, with a homeopathical addition of milk." Hammerhead is characterized as a man who "never gets drunk more than five days out of the seven; tells the truth sometimes by mistake . . . and has never, that I know of, been convicted of petit larceny."

Much of this may seem trivial, but its effects were not. The storm caused by the publication of the "Literati" marked the end of Poe's career as a critic. Editors were no longer prepared to consider contributions from a writer whose opinions were so personal, and so likely to cause offense. In the three years of life left to him, he was to publish by way of criticism little more than a notable article on Hawthorne and some further encomia of Fanny Osgood.

CHAPTER XIV

THE DEATH OF VIRGINIA

You say—"Can you hint to me what was the terrible evil which caused the irregularities so profoundly lamented." Yes; I can do more than hint.
Edgar Allan Poe to George W. Eveleth, January 4, 1848

POE'S further illness during the latter part of 1846 may have been partly diplomatic, designed to keep away duns, to act as a salve for his conscience during periods of idleness, and to provide an excuse for his heavy drinking. The family's poverty and Virginia's steady decline were apparent to visitors. Mary Gove, when she visited the cottage in late autumn, found Virginia lying on a straw bed, wrapped in her husband's greatcoat, with the tortoiseshell Caterina lying close to her for warmth. Mary Gove approached Mrs. Marie Louise Shew, the daughter of a doctor, and an energetic and religious woman with a practical turn of mind, who did not know the Poes or care much about literature, but who soon became the organizer of a subscription which raised $60 in the first week, as well as a feather bed and clothing to cover it.

Bad news travels fast, especially in relation to somebody disliked by as many people as Poe. On December 15 a paragraph appeared in the *New York Express* saying that "Edgar A. Poe and his wife are both dangerously ill with the consumption," and that "they are so far reduced as to be able barely to obtain the necessaries of life." Willis saw the paragraph, and took the occasion to write a well-meant but unfortunately phrased editorial. In this he said that he had received some money for Poe sent by an anonymous admirer, and that he would be happy to forward "any other similar tribute of sympathy with genius." His attempt to rescue Poe's name from disrepute was phrased even more unhappily. He stressed how admirably Poe had conducted himself as a colleague, but emphasized the effect of drink on him by saying that one day "he came into our office with his usual gait and manner, and, with no symptoms of ordinary intoxication, he talked like a man insane." The poet Mary Hewitt had also been busy on the Poes' behalf, trying to raise a contribution for them from editors. She said in a letter to Fanny Osgood that the matter had got into print, and that she feared Poe's pride would be hurt.

No doubt it was, and perhaps it occurred to him that these appeals echoed those made for his mother before her death. He wrote an admirably dignified letter to Willis. Admitting his poverty, Virginia's illness, and the fact that he had himself "been long and dangerously ill," he said that he had still never suffered materially from privation, and that although pursued by enemies he still had many friends. "Even in the city of New York I could have no difficulty in naming a hundred persons, to each of whom—when the hour for speaking had arrived—I could and would have applied for aid, and with unbounded confidence, and with absolutely *no* sense of humiliation." But these brave words were denied by the facts. On January 29, 1847, he wrote to Mrs. Shew telling her that his wife was failing fast and suffering much pain. Mrs. Shew arrived only in time to make her farewells, for on the following day Virginia Eliza Poe died. She was a little more than twenty-four years old.

She was buried in the vault at Fordham belonging to the Valentines, who owned the cottage. Willis came to the funeral, with another New York editor named Morris, and half a dozen women mourners, including Mrs. Shew, who had now taken charge of the poet and his affairs. She made sure that Virginia was buried in fine linen, which greatly gratified Maria Clemm. "If it had not been for her, my darling Virginia would have been laid to her grave in cotton," she said. After the funeral Mrs. Shew sent medicines and flowers to Poe, who was in a state of collapse. "What we should do without you now is fearful to think of," Maria wrote to her. "Eddie says you promised Virginia to come every other day for a long time, or until he was able to go to work again. I hope and believe *you will not fail him.*"

Mrs. Shew had no intention of failing him. She raised another subscription, which paid off immediate debts, and took turns with Maria in nursing the feverish and sometimes delirious Poe. She also made her diagnosis of the illness, which she gave to Dr. Valentine Mott, a physician who knew Poe. She suggested that even when in good health Poe had a lesion of one side of the brain, and that as stimulants and tonics only made him insane, she had not much hope that he could be saved from brain fever "brought on by extreme suffering of mind and body." She thought, however, that there was hope for him if he lived quietly and stored up his physical resources. To this end she urged him to eat fish, in particular clams and oysters, "to supply brain power by the phosphates lost in his much thinking," as she later put it. Mrs. Shew noted in detail at Poe's request various tales of his early life, all of them fictional. They ranged from the account of a scar on his shoulder, which he said had been received through a quarrel about a girl in a foreign port, to stories that he had written a poem later credited to George Sand and a novel attributed to Eugène Sue.

Perhaps Poe was delirious. Or perhaps he was joking—a possibility that in his case can never be ruled out. His illness did not stop him from writing some verses which he gave to Mrs. Shew on Valentine's Day, a little more than a fortnight after Virginia's death. They began

Of all who hail thy presence as the morning—
Of all to whom thine absence is the night

Nor did illness stop him from writing letters, including one to a young admirer named George W. Eveleth, who wrote to tell him that the Philadelphia *Saturday Evening Post* was accusing him of plagiarism in relation to the book on conchology. A day or two later he wrote to Horace Greeley, asking him to deny a statement made in his *Tribune* which seemed to endorse English's accusation of forgery. Poe had just won his libel action. His attorney had offered to settle for $100, but he was awarded $225.06, the 6 cents being an indication that the defendants had to pay court costs. It seems that most of the money was swallowed up by Poe's own costs, but the victory was still sweet. He celebrated it by telling Eveleth, in his least engaging tone, that "the costs and all will make them a bill of $492," which was "pretty well—considering that there was *no* actual 'damage' done to me."

The ambivalence of Poe's nature was clearly shown in the months after Virginia's death. He was firmly enough fixed in life, sufficiently aware of what he was doing, to sound that triumphant note about winning the libel action, and to write a letter of thanks to Judge Robert T. Conrad for befriending him on a trip to Philadelphia which seems to have begun as an attempt to obtain commissions and which certainly ended in heavy drinking. He regarded himself as an expert on all aesthetic matters, and by May was able to carry out Mrs. Shew's suggestion that he should furnish the music room and library of her new house. No doubt he did so in accordance with the views he had expressed years earlier, in the article on *The Philosophy of Furniture,* that straight lines and right angles should be avoided, and that the soul of an apartment was always the carpet, which must show "distinct grounds, and vivid circular or cycloid figures." He praised some of the other furnishings in the house with characteristic fulsomeness, and "wondered that a little country maiden like you [has] developed so classic a taste & atmosphere."

Later in the year Mrs. Shew induced him to go to a midnight service with her, but he rushed out when the passage, "He was a man of sorrows and acquainted with grief," was spoken and repeated. Yet he was far from entirely rational, and there is no doubt of his grief. Tales of his wandering from bed at night to sit beside Virginia's tomb, and of Maria Clemm sitting for hours beside him may not be literally true, but they suggest the depth of his distress. His agony was expressed in "Ulalume," and in *Eureka,* a long prose poem about the nature of the universe and the place of man in it. Apart from these, he produced nothing during the year except *The Domain of Arnheim,* the revised version of a story he had written five years earlier.

It is said that "Ulalume" was written after a clergyman who visited Fordham saw and was shocked by the household's poverty, and by Maria's complaint that Eddie could get no regular employment worthy of his abilities. He assured Poe that verses written specifically for recitation could not fail to be financially profitable. It is said also that the setting came from a visit paid by Poe to a tomb at Mamaroneck which is approached by an avenue of pine trees, the "alley Titanic/Of cypress" in the poem. The stories may be true, although one would have thought that he hardly needed reminding that verse recitations were popular after the impact of "The Raven." But in any case the emotional impact of the poem, as of the later "Annabel Lee," is clearly linked with Virginia's death and burial. "Ulalume" was written in June, but was rejected by one magazine, and then accepted by another in lieu of an essay on *The Rationale of Verse* for which he had already been paid. In an attempt to achieve a success similar to that of "The Raven," Poe had the poem published anonymously, and then asked Willis to reprint it in his *Home Journal,* questioning its authorship. The obliging Willis did as he was asked, ending a paragraph of praise with the question: "Who is the author?" No furore similar to that created by "The Raven" followed. In the end, almost a year later, Poe was driven to answering the question himself by saying that the poem was not by Willis, but "is known to be the composition of EDGAR A. POE."

Toward the end of the year he recovered his spirits. In a letter to his young disciple George Eveleth, he said that he had been driven to drink by Virginia's illness. Each time her life was in danger he had become "insane, with long intervals of horrible sanity," and during these times he had drunk "God only knows how often or how much." A cure, however, had come through his wife's death. "This I can & do endure as becomes a man—it was the horrible never-ending oscillation between hope & despair which I could *not* longer have endured without the total loss of reason."

Now it was time to rebuild his life. He proposed to do so through the publication of *Eureka,* and—of course—through *The Stylus.*

CHAPTER XV

AT A DISTANCE FROM LIFE

*Touching "The Stylus":—this is the one great purpose of my literary
life. Undoubtedly (unless I die) I will accomplish it.*
        Edgar Allan Poe to Philip Pendleton Cooke, August 9, 1846

POE was able always to adopt a double view of everything he undertook and of everything that happened to him. He prided himself
on his ability as a logical thinker, but was perpetually fascinated
by the powers he attributed to things inexplicable by reason. Poetry
seemed to him a form of magic: phrenology offered answers to the
problems of the personality by suggesting that its nature was predetermined; the idea that life and death might co-exist within one
body was the basis of some of his most powerful stories. This inter-
penetration is evident in *Eureka,* which was subtitled "A Prose
Poem." The work was, he said in a prefatory note, dedicated to
those who feel rather than to those who think, and it was intended
for "those who put faith in dreams as in the only realities." It was
as a poem that he wanted the work judged after he was dead, yet
at the same time it was a Book of Truths. "The Beauty that abounds
in its Truth" was in reality the truth itself. To Eveleth he described
the book's subject succinctly, although perhaps no more intelligibly:
"The General Proposition is this:—Because Nothing was, *therefore*
All Things are."

Eureka will be discussed in detail later. Here it is perhaps enough
to say that it is a discourse dealing among other things with the
nature of mortality and the origin of the world. It was introduced
to the public through a New York lecture. As Poe wrote to Willis,
he would avoid all possibility of squabbling by choosing a nonliterary
subject. "I have chosen a broad text—'The Universe.'" In February

1848 he delivered the lecture in the library of the New York Historical Society. He had hoped for an audience of three or four hundred,
but only sixty came. The press reports were appreciative, although
he said that they had absurdly misrepresented his ideas. George
Putnam, who had accepted the book for publication, later described
his interview with Poe in relentlessly facetious terms. Poe had suggested that "Newton's discovery of gravitation was a mere incident
compared with the discoveries revealed in this book," and had gone
on to say that the smallest first printing should be fifty thousand
copies. Putnam published an edition of five hundred and gave the
author an advance of $14. The money was a loan, and the canny
publisher made Poe sign a document promising to repay it if the
sales had not been sufficient to earn the sum by the end of the
year. It is possible that Putnam's memory played him false and that
he printed 750 copies, but in any case the small edition had not
sold out a year later. The book had few reviews, and most of them
were uncomprehending or unfriendly.

Whatever may be thought of the arguments in *Eureka,* Poe was
right in considering it his most complete achievement, in the sense
that it was an attempt to comprehend philosophically the themes
treated most often in his stories and poems. Yet it is true also that
the book reflects the growing separation in his mind between the
world existing all around him, that painful visible world in which
Virginia had died and in which he was compelled to consort with
people he despised in order to earn a living, and the world of speculation and of dreams in which he would have preferred to live, and
which he tried to reach through the medium of drink. And the
complications or subtleties do not end there, for Poe enjoyed the
world of literary journalism at the same time that he despised it.
He took pleasure in drubbing nonentities, and was quite at home
bandying insults with English. Even while writing *Eureka,* he was
planning a book of which little more than the title page remains:

LITERARY AMERICA
Some Honest Opinions about our Autorial
Merits and Demerits
with
Occasional Words of Personality
by
Edgar A. Poe

The design was for something like a longer and larger "Literati," but it was barely begun.

The Stylus also was a link with the real world, a project of which the purpose was eminently rational, even though the idea that it would ever appear demanded faith. The death of Virginia, the removal of this loved but greatly demanding image of the ideal woman, meant in practical terms that a shadow upon Poe's actions had been lifted, and he may unconsciously have felt this. He could now devote himself wholly to *The Stylus,* and to the renaissance it would bring in American literature. It was to be completely his own, with no question of others participating in the editorship or of a publisher exercising control. To Willis and others he rehearsed the possibilities, as he had often done before, in terms of the numbers of subscribers needed, the certainty of finding them if he made a trip South and West "among my personal and literary friends—old college and West Point acquaintances," the difficulty of making the trip because he lacked money. With an audience of only sixty the lecture had failed to provide the necessary funds, and he was a little embarrassed by the ever-ready Willis's announcement of the new magazine, although he consoled himself with the thought that this premature announcement would push him into action a little more quickly. "I mean to start for Richmond on the 10th March," he told Eveleth, but lack of money and very likely some heavy drinking prevented him from doing so until July 1848. There was one occasion at this time when a clergyman friend of Mrs. Shew's found him "crazy-drunk in the hands of police" after a three-day spree, and took him home 11 miles to Fordham.

In the end the delivery of his lecture on the Poets and Poetry of America at Lowell in the heart of New England produced some of the funds, and it is possible that Charles Astor Bristed, a grandson of John Jacob Astor III, supplied most of the rest. Bristed had helped Poe before, and it seems unlikely that he was able to resist a letter saying that "my last hope of extricating myself from the difficulties which are pressing me to death, is in going personally to a distant connexion near Richmond, Va, and endeavoring to interest him in my behalf."

Poe stayed in Richmond for three weeks. The return to the South, the scene of his childhood and of his first great success as editor, overwhelmed him. John R. Thompson, then editor of the *Messenger,* wrote in October to Philip Pendleton Cooke that Poe had been "horribly drunk and discoursing *Eureka* every night to the audiences of Bar Rooms." Thompson had tried unsuccessfully to get him to write something specially for the *Messenger,* and in the end had accepted his essay on *The Rationale of Verse.* His friends, Thompson said, had tried to get him sober, but "were compelled at last to reship him to New York." A year later Thompson expanded what he had written into a narrative with many unlikely and inexact details, but there seems no doubt of the essential truth of the story he told at the time. Poe saw the Mackenzies and his sister Rosalie, he challenged the editor of the Richmond *Examiner* to a duel that did not take place, and by one account he called daily upon a widow named Jane Clark, who reminded him of Virginia. He recited "The Raven" to a small party, which included Rosalie, and very likely he also read aloud parts of *Eureka.* He made no attempt to get subscribers for *The Stylus.*

In truth he was incapable now of concentrating for long upon anything but his own emotional condition. Women were indispensable to him as objects of worship, images to be both idolized and platonically loved. With Virginia gone, his susceptibility to women was variously expressed. It is said, on rather slight evidence, that he asked Fanny Osgood to elope with him. There was also Mrs. Shew, whose spirit he called an angel's; there was the New England poetess Jane Ermina Locke, who was distantly related to Fanny Osgood; there was Estelle Anna Blanche Robinson Lewis, the daughter of a prosperous Cuban, who was married to an attorney from whom Poe is said to have borrowed money. Mrs. Lewis signed the name Stella to many of her verses, for she too was a poet. With all of them he flirted, by most of them he was flirtatiously pursued. The female poets regarded him as a decayed lion, into whose mouth their heads must be placed in order to prove that he had no teeth. And then there were also Sarah Helen Whitman and Annie Richmond, two women whom he pursued much more seriously.

The minor figures may be dealt with first. Mrs. Shew stands apart from the others, in the sense that she had no interest in literature and was concerned with Poe, as with Virginia, chiefly as a medical case. She was plain, and deeply religious. This did not stop him from idolizing her, and she was responsible for his writing of "The Bells." Poe came to her house one day in a disturbed state, and said that he had to write a poem, but that the neighboring church bells were distracting him. She then wrote out: "The Bells, by

E. A. Poe," and the line: "The Bells, the little silver Bells." Poe completed the verse, and another after she had suggested "The heavy iron Bells." He was then totally exhausted and went to bed, where he slept for twelve hours. On the next day she took him back to Fordham in her carriage.

Mrs. Shew, unlike many witnesses in the Poe case, has an air of truthfulness. This first version of the poem, to which he put her name as author, contained only two verses, and so did a version sold later by Poe for $15. He expanded it more than once, and received for it in all a total of $45. The end of their relationship was abrupt, and came because a young theological student read *Eureka*, discovered pantheistic views in it, and communicated his disquiet to Mrs. Shew. Perhaps this reinforced her uneasiness about Poe's general strangeness, an uneasiness which extended to being slightly afraid of Caterina. The letter that she wrote breaking off communications brought a reply that was both agonized and incoherent, which must be quoted although it is too long to be given in full. It begins:

> Can it be true Louise that you have the idea in your mind to desert your unhappy and unfortunate friend and patient? You did not say so, I know, but for months I have known you was deserting me, not willingly but none the less surely—my destiny—
> Disaster following fast, following faster, &c
> I have had premonitions of this for months I my good spirit, my loyal heart! . . . I have read over your letter again, and again, and can not make it possible with any degree of certainty, that you wrote it in your right mind.

Her last visit to Fordham had been made in the company of a clergyman:

> How can I believe in Providence when *you* look coldly upon me, was it not you who renewed my hopes and faith in God? . . . & in humanity Louise I heard your voice as you passed out of my sight leaving me with the Parson, "The man of God, The servant of the most High." He stood smiling and bowing at the madman Poe!

The letter ends:

> I am a coward, to wound your loyal unselfish and womanly heart, but you must know *and be assured*, of my *regret*, my *sorrow*, if aught

> I have ever written has hurt you. My *heart* never *wronged you* . . .
> I will try to overcome my grief for the sake of your unselfish care
> of me in the past, and in life or death, I am ever yours gratefully
> & devotedly

After Poe's death Mrs. Shew regretted her severity, but they never
met again.

Mrs. Locke and Mrs. Lewis belonged to that category of lady
poets from the tedium of whose conversation Poe is said to have
fled out into the fields when they visited Fordham, leaving them
in the kitchen to talk to Maria Clemm. Or at least that is true of
Mrs. Lewis, whose *Records of the Heart* and *Child of the Sea* he
reviewed in terms that were no less ecstatic because he was in
debt to her husband Sylvanus. Stella was in her early twenties, and
did not discourage the literary amorousness to which Poe was inclined. He sent her a sonnet embodying "a riddle which I wish to
put you to the trouble of expounding," which when discovered revealed her name; he wrote letters of introduction for her; revised
her long romantic poem "The Prisoner of Perote," and then said
in print that it was her most impressive work; puffed her poems
in more than one notice, and went so far as to suggest to Griswold
that in *The Female Poets of America,* "you have not *quite* done
justice to our common friend Mrs. Lewis; and if you could oblige
me so far as to substitute, for your no doubt hurried notice, a somewhat longer one prepared by myself (subject, of course, to your
emendations) I would reciprocate the favor when, where, and *as*
you please." It is not clear how this could have been done, since
Griswold's book had been in print for some months, but the logrolling intention is plain enough. Poe—and also particularly Maria
Clemm—remained on terms of warm friendship with the Lewises
for the rest of his life.

Mrs. Locke had been responsible for arranging the lecture at
Lowell. She had also given some help in Virginia's illness, and later
without having met they engaged in correspondence which was
on his side characteristically romantic and obscure. There was, it
seemed, a question that he dared not ask her, and she naturally
wanted to know what it was:

> You will not suspect me of affectation, dear friend, or of any
> unworthy passion for being mysterious, merely because I find it im-
> possible to tell you *now*—in a letter—what that one question was

which I "dare not ever ask" of you. . . . Tell me nothing—I ask nothing—which has any reference to "worldliness" or the "fear of the world." Tell me only of the ties—if any exist—that bind you to the world.

Was he asking whether she was a widow? If so he must have been disillusioned when they met, for Mrs. Locke was in her forties and had a husband and a large family. On this visit he met a neighbor of the Lockes, Nancy Locke Heywood Richmond, and was immediately attracted to her. Within a few months he was writing her love letters saying "I love you, as no man ever loved woman" at almost the same time that he was writing to another woman, Sarah Helen Whitman, imploring that she would "write me *one word* to say that you *do* love me and that, *under all circumstances,* you will be mine." The tragicomedy of his romantic involvements was about to begin.

CHAPTER XVI

THE DESPERATE HEART

We confess to a half-faith in the ordinary superstition of the signifi-cance of anagrams when we find, in the transposed letters of Edgar Poe's name, the words a God-peer.
—*Sarah Helen Whitman,* Edgar Poe and His Critics, *1860*

POE'S entanglements with Helen Whitman, Annie Richmond, and then with his first love Elmira Shelton, are the stuff of French farce. He proposed to marry Helen Whitman, he would certainly have wished to marry Annie Richmond had she been free, he also wanted to marry the widowed Mrs. Shelton. How can one take any of this seriously? Yet although Poe's conduct was ridiculous, there was nothing comic about his misery. His letters at this time were written by a man at the end of his tether, no longer able to think clearly or act reasonably.

His words are appeals from a desperate heart, crying out for help. What sort of help, what was it that he wanted from women? Not sexual pleasure, certainly, which was as remote from him now as it had been throughout his life. Physical beauty? Fanny Osgood had a kittenish prettiness and Annie Richmond seems to have been attractive, but Helen Whitman was in her middle forties and noted for the individuality rather than the beauty of her appearance. A spiritual quality? Yes, it would seem that he looked for this, and Helen Whitman's reputation as "the Seeress of Providence" was one of her attractions for him; but there was little that could have been called spiritual about Elmira Shelton. It seems that, as nearly as one can phrase it, he hoped for the re-creation of the past, the duplication of a time in which he had been part of a family. He was looking also for a sensibility complementary to his own, aware of the truths he had uttered in *Eureka*. Yet to say all this is to put the matter too explicitly, for in a conscious sense he longed only to love and be loved.

Helen Whitman, as she preferred to be called, had been a widow for fifteen years when she met Poe. She lived in Providence, Rhode Island, with her masterful mother and her eccentric sister. She was intelligent, well read in two or three languages, wrote verses, and was deeply interested in spiritualism. Like other women who interested Poe, she was unconventional only in the most respectable way. She felt drawn to him because they had been born on the same day of the year, and the other-worldly and romantic tone of his poems and stories greatly appealed to her. She sent a poem to a Valentine party at which many of the New York literati were present, Mrs. Osgood and Mrs. Ellet among them, which might certainly be taken as a declaration of interest. The poem was on the theme of "The Raven," and the tone of its ten verses fluttered the company when it was read:

> Then, Oh! Grim and Ghastly Raven!
> Wilt thou "to my heart and ear
> Be a Raven true as ever
> Flapped his wings and cried 'Despair'?"
> Not a bird that roams the forest
> Shall our lofty eyrie share.

Poe was clearly the Raven, the lofty eyrie was Fordham, and if it was to be shared, was she not declaring a desire to live emotionally in that lofty eyrie too? The poem was anonymous, but since it was sent from Providence its authorship was not in doubt. Poe had caught a glimpse of this Helen nearly three years earlier, when he had visited Providence with Fanny Osgood. Now he first sent her the poem "To Helen," torn out of his 1845 volume, and then wrote a poem in blank verse which he posted to her. The unsigned poem began:

> I saw thee once—once only—years ago;
> I must not say *how* many—but *not* many

went on to describe her visionary beauty, "clad all in white, upon a violet bank" among "the upturned faces of a thousand / Roses that grew in an enchanted garden," and ended with a recollection of eyes which had lighted his lonely pathway home that night:

> I see them still—two sweetly scintillant
> Venuses, unextinguished by the sun!

That first view, she said later, had been of her standing on the front step and not lying on a violet bank as she did in the poem; but she was still pleased. She responded, although not immediately. She learned that Poe had been making enquiries ("her poetry is, beyond question, *poetry*—instinct with genius," he told one correspondent), and sent a coy poem, anonymous like his own, which reached him on the unhappy visit to Richmond. His next move was to write her a letter in a disguised hand, signed by one of his several pseudonyms, Edward S. T. Grey, asking for her autograph. This she left unanswered, but he now took a decisive step by calling at her house, bringing with him a letter of introduction. He called and he conquered, or perhaps was conquered, a consummation desired both by Edgar and his Helen. Ten days after his visit, on October 1, he wrote a romantic, incoherent, extremely literary love letter. It was in reply to one sent him by her of a much more down to earth kind. He might try to convince her, she said, that "my person is agreeable to you—that my countenance interests you," but her appearance was in fact disappointingly variable. Although admiration of his genius made her feel "like a child" in his presence, in reality it was the other way round in terms of age. (In fact, she was six years the older.) Poe replied that she was mistaken about their ages, and in any case, "if illness and sorrow have made you seem older than you are—is not all this the best of reason for my loving you the more? Cannot my patient cares—my watchful, earnest attention—cannot the magic which lies in such devotion as I feel for you, win back for you much—oh, very much of the freshness of your youth?"

He said much else in a letter that covered, in his neat hand, page after page, and made his linking to this Helen seem an irresistible fate that he had tried hard to deny. On that first sight of her he had positively refused to pay a visit in company with Mrs. Osgood. "I *dared* not speak of you—much less see you. For years your name never passed my lips, while my soul drank in, with a delirious thirst, all that was uttered in my presence respecting you." Then had come

the Valentine—and he recited the sequence of events afterwards,
up to the moment of their first meeting:

> As you entered the room, pale, timid, hesitating, and evidently
> oppressed at heart; as your eyes rested appealingly, for one brief
> moment, upon mine, I felt, for the first time in my life, and trem-
> blingly acknowledged, the existence of spiritual influences altogether
> out of the reach of the reason. I saw that you were *Helen—my*
> Helen—the Helen of a thousand dreams.

Later, when they sat together in a cemetery, he had put his
arm round her waist and positively declared himself. "I said to you,
while the bitter, bitter tears sprang into my eyes—'Helen, I love
now—now—for the first and only time.'"

It has been said that both the parties engaged in this correspondence were playacting, and that this was no more than the sentimental adventure of two self-conscious poets. There is certainly an element of make-believe in her confession of a fatal illness (she was
to live another thirty years) so that, "were I to allow myself to love
you, I could only enjoy a bright, brief hour of rapture and die,"
and his dramatic comment: "Alas Helen! my soul!—what is it that
I have been saying to you?—to what madness have I been urging
you?" Yet for Poe playacting came naturally, and as Scandal says
in *Love for Love* there may be little difference between continued
affectation and reality. The idea that neither Poe nor his Helen
was serious is denied by their actions.

Their relationship followed a predictable course, bearing in mind
that Helen's spiritual feelings covered a highly practical and conventional nature. She must already have known the erratic reputation
of her lover, but now she consulted friends, heard nothing good
from them, and asked him what he had to say of suggestions about
his drinking and his quarrelsomeness. Her letter prompted a hysterical cry of self-justification which seems both artificially confected
and sincerely felt. He was most deeply wounded by the words that
she said she had often heard used about him, that he had great
intellectual power but *"no* principle—*no* moral sense." The extraordinary rhodomontade of the reply suggests that Poe really was unaware of the way in which many people regarded him:

> Is it possible that such expressions as those could have been
> *repeated* to me—to me—by one whom I loved—ah, whom I *love—*

by one at whose feet I knelt—I *still* kneel—in deeper worship than man ever offered to God?—And you proceed to ask me *why* such opinions exist. You will feel remorse for the question, Helen, when I say to you that, until the moment when those horrible words first met my eye, I would not have believed it *possible* that any such opinions could have existed at all:—but that they *do* exist *breaks my heart* in separating us forever.

How, he wondered, had these stories come about when, with the exception of occasional excesses to which he had been driven by intolerable sorrow, he had erred only "on the side of what the world would call a Quixotic sense of the honorable—of the chivalrous"? For this in youth he had thrown away a large fortune "rather than endure a trivial wrong," out of chivalry he had married "for another's happiness, where I knew that no possibility of my own existed." The explanation was that he had been the victim of private enemies, including "a woman whose loathsome love I could do nothing but repel with scorn" (this was Mrs. Ellet), and of public ones like Fuller and English. He also told Helen that she lived among his enemies. "Had you read my criticisms generally . . . you would see why all whom *you* know best, know *me* least, and are my enemies." Her letter, together with his recent discovery that she was comparatively rich while he was poor, had destroyed forever his dream of a life passed with her on "the banks of some quiet river, in some lovely valley of our land":

> Here, not *too* far secluded from the world, we exercised a taste controlled by no conventionalities, but the sworn slave of a Natural Art, in the building for ourselves a cottage which no human being could ever pass without an ejaculation of wonder at its strange, wierd [*sic*] and incomprehensible yet most simple beauty. Oh, the sweet and gorgeous, but not often rare flowers in which we half buried it!—the grandeur of the little-distant magnolias and tulip-trees which stood guarding it—the luxurious velvet of its lawn—the lustre of the rivulet that ran by the very door—the tasteful yet quiet comfort of the interior—the music—the books—the unostentatious pictures—and, above all, the love—the *love* that threw an unfading *glory* over the whole!—Ah Helen! my heart is, *indeed, breaking.*

The cottage is reminiscent of Fordham, and also of those cottages in which virtuous characters lived in Dickens; the full-blown language might have been spoken by David Poe when he trod the boards; the whole thing is intensely literary—but after all, Poe was an intensely literary man writing to a literary lady. Mrs. Whitman, at any rate, wavered a little. When she wrote it was indecisively, or so it seemed to Poe. Her letter reached him in Westford, Massachusetts, where he was staying with the Richmond family, and he told her that he would come to Providence.

He came to Providence. By his own account, he spent an agonized, sleepless night, in the morning bought two ounces of laudanum, and returned to Boston. There he took half the laudanum with the intention of ending his life, but was saved by an unnamed friend and by the fact that his stomach rejected the drug. Within a day or two he was back in Providence. Helen had expected to see him on November 4, but on the 7th she received a letter saying that he was very ill and should go home. "If you cannot see me— write me *one word* to say that you *do* love me and that, *under all circumstances,* you will be mine." An interview followed, several interviews.

She showed Poe letters warning her against him, some prompted perhaps by Griswold, who had asked his friend Horace Greeley: "Has Mrs. Whitman no friend within your knowledge that can faithfully *explain* Poe to her? Mrs. Osgood must know her." Whether or not Mrs. Osgood wrote, several people told her what might be expected in a life with Poe. Her formidable mother, Mrs. Power, was opposed to the marriage. On the other side there was a genius who was clearly suffering agonies—his anguish is revealed in the daguerrotype taken of him during these days—and said that he could be saved by her love. In the end Poe was so frantic with excitement and misery during one visit to the house that even Mrs. Power said that Helen should promise him anything he wanted. His passionate appeals, "awful even to sublimity," as she said, rang through the house. She agreed that she would marry him, making the condition only that he should abstain from drink. A triumphant Poe returned to Fordham, and on November 18 wrote to her from the steamboat:

> My own dearest Helen, *so* kind so true, so generous—so unmoved by all that would have moved one who had been less than angel:— beloved of my heart of my imagination of my intellect—life of my life—soul of my soul—dear, dearest Helen, how shall I ever thank you as I ought.

So it was settled. They were to be married.

Poe had met Annie Richmond in July 1848, when he went to lecture in Lowell. At some time in October he sent her a note introducing Stella Lewis, "of whose poetic genius you will remember I spoke so much at length in my late lecture." The note is addressed *"To my very dear friend,"* but gives no hint of particular intimacy. The next letter, however, written from Fordham just after his return from Providence, is a love letter written in very similar terms to those he had been using when writing to Helen:

> So long as I think that you *know* I love you, as no man ever loved woman—so long as I think you comprehend in some measure, the fervor with which I adore you, *so* long, no worldly trouble can ever render me absolutely wretched. But oh, *my darling, my* Annie, my own sweet *sister* Annie, my *pure* beautiful angel—*wife* of my soul—to be mine hereafter & *forever in the Heavens*—how shall I explain to you the *bitter, bitter* anguish which has tortured me since I left you?

He tells her about taking the laudanum, and the letter makes it plain that although Helen knew nothing of Annie, Annie knew all about Helen, and had advised marriage to her. She is made responsible for the proposal. His soul had "revolted from saying the words which were to be said" to Helen Whitman; but still, in Providence, "I saw *her,* & spoke, for *your* sake, the words which you urged me to speak." Were those words irrevocable, would Annie not relent? And he invokes the prospect of another cottage, one with a different ambience:

> It is not *much* that I ask, *sweet sister Annie*—my mother & myself would take a small cottage at Westford—oh *so* small—so *very* humble—I should be far away from the tumult of the world—from the ambition which I loathe—I would labor day & night, and with industry I could accomplish *so* much—Annie! it would be a Paradise beyond my wildest hopes—I could see some of your beloved family *every* day, & you often—oh VERY often—I would hear from you continually—regularly & *our* dear mother would be with us & love us both—oh *darling*—do not these pictures touch your inmost heart?

Mrs. Clemm had written to Annie begging her to come to Fordham, and he reinforced this with one of those desperate appeals that we have read before:

> Ah beloved Annie, IS IT NOT POSSIBLE? I am so *ill*—so terribly, hopelessly ill in body and mind, that I feel I CANNOT live, unless

I can feel your sweet, gentle, loving hand pressed upon my forehead—oh my *pure, virtuous, generous, beautiful, beautiful sister
Annie!*—is it not POSSIBLE for you to come—if only for a little week?

When eight days had passed without word from Annie in reply
to this letter, Poe wrote in distraught terms to her young sister
Sarah Heywood, stressing "how *purely* I love her," and imploring
her to answer and tell him if anything was wrong. On the previous
day he had written to Helen Whitman saying: "I dread the Future—
and you alone can reassure me."

What should we make of all this? Most of Poe's biographers have
drawn a distinction between the courtship of Helen and his feeling
for Annie, which as one writer has said "was not a literary adventure;
it was a heartfelt love." This does not seem to be right. The language
used to both women is equally hyperbolic and ethereal. It is true
that there is a discernible lowering of the temperature in Helen's
case when Annie is occupying his attention, but it would be easy
to find similar passages in letters to both women. Nor will it do to
say that Poe was a self-conscious actor. Of course he was, but that
is not a fully satisfactory explanation of this simultaneous approach.
The truth is surely that he was at this time on the borders of sanity.
Mrs. Shew's diagnosis of a brain lesion may not have been far off
the mark.

With this said, the whole affair must seem to us more extraordinary—even more extraordinary—than it appeared at the time. The
American literary ladies of the period give the lie to Donne's lines:

> Love's not so pure and abstract as they used
> To say, that have no mistress but their Muse.

For them love was essentially an aesthetic and unworldly emotion, and sexual intercourse (a phrase which of course they would
not have used) was decidedly something else. Helen Whitman's attitude has already been suggested. She dressed almost always in white,
was a strong believer in the occult, and is said to have carried a
handkerchief soaked in ether which she occasionally sniffed. Her
ideas about literature were marked by that thin, high, transcendental
thinking that Poe most disliked—she was almost one of the artistic
Bostonians he had labeled Frogpondians in her yearning for the
ineffable sublime. Annie Richmond, married to a prosperous manu-
facturer of wrapping paper, and a contented wife and mother, was
another matter. Her husband appears to have known of her platonic

love affair with Poe, and at this time to have accepted it. In a sketch
by Poe called *Landor's Cottage,* she was described as "a young
woman about twenty-eight years of age—slender, or rather slight,
and somewhat above the medium height," with "spiritual gray"
eyes and light chestnut hair. She destroyed the letters Poe sent to
her, and we know them only from the perhaps incomplete copies
she made. Like most of the women closely connected with him,
she was sentimental in a commonplace way, and like others felt
that she was succoring a man of genius. The exotic quality of this
Southern songbird never failed to impress women.

Poe passed the weeks that followed his engagement in an emotional turmoil. He warned Helen that Mrs. Ellet would use every
conceivable chicanery to stop the marriage, including "anonymous
letters so skillfully contrived as to deceive the most sagacious." Even
Mrs. Osgood had been "for a long time completely blinded by the
arts of the fiend." Such warnings were interspersed with literary
comments on a new poem Helen had sent him, with reproachful
references to the enmity of Mrs. Power, and with a hint that he
saw in his future wife a possible backer for *The Stylus.* Was she
ambitious, did she have faith in him?

> Would it *not* be "glorious," *darling,* to establish, in America, the
> sole unquestionable aristocracy—that of intellect—to secure its su-
> premacy—to lead & to control it? All this I *can* do, Helen, & will—
> if you bid me—and aid me.

A document drawn up, no doubt at the request of Mrs. Power,
by which Helen's estate was transferred to her mother "for her
own use," must have disabused him of such hopes, although he
signed the document without objection. If, as he had said earlier,
her possession of money was an obstacle to their marriage, that
obstacle was now removed. But doubts were stirring in his mind.
He was going to Providence to lecture, and on the day before he
left New York met Mary Hewitt, who asked whether he was going
there to be married.

"No, Madam, I am not going to Providence to be married, I
am going to deliver a lecture on poetry." After a pause he added,
"That marriage may never take place."

The lecture was delivered on December 20, and was a great
success. The subject was "The Poetic Principle," and nearly two

thousand people attended. Afterwards he had a drink with some young men, but was not intoxicated. On Saturday, December 23, he wrote a note to the local clergyman, asking him to "have the kindness to publish the banns of matrimony between Mrs. Sarah Helen Whitman and myself," and also one to Maria which said simply: "My own dear Mother—We shall be married on Monday, and will be at Fordham on Tuesday on the first train."

Could they have been married on Monday, Christmas Day? At any rate they were not. We have only Helen Whitman's word for what happened, but although her stories varied over the years they amounted essentially to a feeling that she could not go through with the marriage. On the 23rd, she said, in what is perhaps the most probable of her accounts, they went out riding and visited a circulating library. There, "a communication was handed me cautioning me against this imprudent marriage & informing me of many things in Mr. Poe's recent career with which I was previously unacquainted"—perhaps of his interest in Mrs. Richmond. She was also told that he had been drinking that very morning, and although this was "in no degree perceptible," she felt it to be decisive. Should one come to the conclusion that she was never serious? That seems an overstatement. The pressures being exerted against the marriage were strong. They ranged from her mother, through her considerable circle of literary acquaintances, to such Providence friends as William J. Pabodie, who liked Poe but thought that she would be foolish to marry him. She endured the final scene with a feeling of "intense sorrow," and he pleaded with her to say that she would grant him another interview. Her mother broke in upon these farewells, by one account telling Poe the time of the next train for New York. He left the house speaking of the intolerable insults he had suffered from her family, and she never saw him again.

So it was over. For both of them it was in a way a relief, yet both also felt afterwards that it had been a chance missed. Thinking, brooding, and in the end writing about Poe became one of Helen's chief occupations after his death, and for him the blow both to his hopes and his pride was severe. The thought that marriage to her would somehow have helped to launch the magazine was certainly in his mind, and any kind of rejection was something that he now found it harder than ever to bear. He tried to replace the uncomfortable facts by a more congenial version in a letter to her—sent first of all to Annie, who then sealed it and mailed it from Boston—in which he complained about rumors insulting to himself, and said that so far, "I have assigned no reason for my declining to fulfil our engagement—I had none but the suspicious & grossly insulting parsimony of the arrangements into which you suffered yourself to be forced by your Mother." He asked her to disavow a rumor that after the banns had been published once, she had gone to the clergyman and asked him to stop further proceedings. It is not certain whether she replied. Poe had sent the letter to Annie so that she should see that he had not behaved badly, and she was convinced, or perhaps needed no convincing. Mr. Richmond seems to have liked Poe, but his family, who lived in Providence, thought Poe "a very *unprincipled* man to say the least."

Throughout all this time Poe was much in need of money. The Eastern papers and magazines were no longer interested in him as a contributor, and he was reduced to looking for new and inferior markets, like the *American Whig Review,* to whom he sent an article in the hope that they would give him $10 for it, or the Boston *Flag of Our Union,* which as he said himself was "not very respectable." He sent to the *Messenger* material some of which, like his "Marginalia," had been published before, and was happy to accept a beggarly $2 a page from them.

These difficulties did not appear in his letters to Annie, which gave a wholly different picture. Engagements to write, he said, were pouring in on him every day, including two proposals in the last week from Boston. Even in the heart of Frogpondia he was acknowledged. Fifty pages of "Marginalia" had gone to the *Messenger,* enough for ten months. He had made permanent engagements with every magazine in America. The lowest payment he got was $5 a page, and since he could easily average a page and a half a day, he would soon be out of financial trouble. But his troubles—and this also of course he did not say—were not only financial. As the New Year of 1849 arrived, the year that was to be the last of his life, he was losing both the ability and the desire to write. Concentration for a long period of time had become increasingly difficult. To Annie, after the brave words about magazine sales, he said: "I have had a most disturbing headache for the last two weeks . . ."

CHAPTER XVII

A SOUTHERN GENTLEMAN
GOES HOME

Mr. Poe was a man of great riches and fame,
And I loved him, I'm sure, though I liked not his name.
He asked me to wed. In a rage I said, No,
I'll never marry you and be called Mrs. Poe.

Old Song

THERE were times when Poe felt that there was no hope for him, that *Eureka* expressed all he had to say, and that since nothing could succeed *Eureka,* it was time for him to die. Sometimes, especially after drinking bouts, he knew himself to be very ill. Yet hope was not extinguished, for at other times he saw the chance of salvation in living with a woman who loved him and could relieve him of financial burdens, as Helen might have done. And always a more material and tangible salvation than the love of a woman, the ghost of *The Stylus,* haunted him. If the magazine could be founded, he felt, its success might even now change the course of his life. The record of his last months is one of slackening concentration and increasing confusion, through which occasional shafts of intelligence burst like lightning through thunder clouds, and during which emotionally he was totally absorbed in Annie Richmond.

His passion for Annie fed upon absence. If Helen's knowledge of him was based only upon occasional visits through three months of courtship, Annie knew him hardly at all. He had met her in July 1848, when he went to lecture in Lowell, and then again when he stayed once or twice at the Richmond family home. Was it perhaps partly for this reason that she remained an ideal woman—an ideal rather than a woman? We know little of her reactions to him, but probably if he had been able to carry out his often-expressed wish to live near to her, the resultant strain on her family relationships would have been intolerable. The kind of emotional demands he made could be more nearly fulfilled in absence than in presence.

Even love by correspondence imposed strains. Mrs. Locke, whose own correspondence with Poe has been mentioned, was beside herself with moral indignation about his projected marriage to Helen Whitman, and also about his friendship with Annie. It may well have been a letter from her that was handed to Helen at the circulating library, and there is no doubt that the Lockes did their best to break up Poe's relationship with Annie by gossiping, and eventually by writing to Mr. Richmond. Poe himself had already quarreled with them. He had done so, he told Annie, because they had maintained that it was through their patronage that the Richmonds were accepted in society, and "that your husband was everything despicable." He had immediately left the house, and so "incurred the unrelenting vengeance of that worst of all fiends, 'a woman scorned.'" No doubt there was some embroidering of truth in this account, but he made the Lockes' accusations a reason for not paying a visit:

> Not only must I *not* visit you at Lowell, but I must discontinue my letters & you yours—I cannot & *will* not have it on my conscience that I have interfered with the domestic happiness of the only being in the whole world, whom I have loved, at the same time with truth & with *purity*.

Poe went astray when he suggested that Charles Richmond had been influenced against him by the "malignant misrepresentations" of these "unmentionable nobodies & blackguards." On the contrary Mr. Richmond, the model of a trusting husband, had written angrily to the Lockes and had terminated their relationship. But still, Poe and Maria did not pay their visit. Correspondence, however, continued, and he sent to Mrs. Richmond a copy of the poem "For Annie" which was printed in the *Flag of Our Union*. The poem obviously reflects his feelings about his own illness:

> The sickness—the nausea—
> The pitiless pain—
> Have ceased, with the fever

> That maddened my brain—
> With the fever called "Living"
> That burned in my brain.

His spirit is now at peace, thanks to Annie:

> And so it lies happily,
>   Bathing in many
> A dream of the truth
>   And the beauty of Annie—
> Drowned in a bath
>   Of the tresses of Annie.

Poe thought this, he told her, the finest poem he had written. Whatever its poetic merit, it is certainly emotionally of a different order from the pieces laboriously concocted for Helen Whitman and Mrs. Shew. He was to write three more poems of which only one, "Annabel Lee," can be considered on anything like the level of his best work.

In these last months he wrote also the little sketch *Landor's Cottage,* a wistful, sentimental view of an imaginary cottage in which Annie is living (although not with the narrator, who views the scene with detachment as an outsider); a strongly anti-democratic tale of the future called *Mellonta Tauta;* a very slight squib called *X-ing a Paragrab;* the last of his hoax stories, *Von Kempelen and His Discovery,* which describes the turning of lead into gold; and *Hop-Frog,* a tale on quite a different plane from the rest of his work during this last year. The sadistic story of the revenge taken by Hop-Frog the dwarf and court jester when forced to drink wine by the King reflects Poe's own impotent fury against those he thought of as his slanderers. Hop-Frog persuades the King and his councillors to dress up as orang-outangs (the King loves crude practical jokes), dresses them in garments soaked with tar and covered in flax, sets fire to them, and escapes with his girlfriend Trippetta.

The story's agonized brutality contrasts remarkably with Poe's coy comments about it to Annie. "Only think of your Eddy writing a story with *such* a name as 'Hop-Frog.' You would never guess the subject (which is a terrible one) from the title, I am sure." It was published in the despised *Flag of Our Union,* and so was the Von Kempelen story, which he hoped would repeat the success of *M. Valdemar.* The California gold rush made the subject topical, and as he wrote to Evert Duyckinck, "such a style, applied to the gold-excitement, could not fail of effect." If, as he expected, nine people out of ten believed it, then the story would serve a useful purpose by putting a check to the gold fever. Duyckinck had been helpful to Poe in the past, but he rejected the story for his *Literary World,* even though it was offered to him for $10.

Poe was now prepared to write almost anywhere, for almost any sum of money. His only reliable market was the *Messenger.* There he gave a great puff to Stella Lewis and another to Fanny Osgood, and made a bitter attack on Lowell's *Fable for Critics.* This long comic poem about American literary figures is by turn adroit, amusing, awkward and amateurish. Poe viewed it very harshly. It had been published anonymously, and,

> But for some slight foreknowledge of the literary opinions, likes, dislikes, whims, prejudices and crotchets of Mr. James Russell Lowell we should have had much difficulty in attributing so very *loose* a brochure to him. The "Fable" is essentially "loose"—ill-conceived and feebly executed as well in detail as in general.

He quoted disapprovingly some of the lines about himself, which are in fact among the liveliest in the poem:

> Here comes Poe with his Raven, like Barnaby Rudge—
> Three-fifths of him genius, and two-fifths sheer fudge;
> Who talks like a book of iambs and pentameters,
> In a way to make all men of common sense d——n metres

Perhaps Poe's disapproval had something to do with the fact that he was dealt with much more briefly than some very minor writers, but he based it on other grounds. Lowell, he said, praised only Bostonians. "Other writers are barbarians, and satirized accordingly—if mentioned at all." And what could one expect of such a bigot? "Mr. Lowell is one of the most rabid of the Abolition fanatics; and no Southerner who does not wish to be insulted, and at the same time revolted by a bigotry the most obstinately blind and deaf, should ever touch a volume by this author." He was, of course, writing for Southerners. The review appeared anonymously, but its authorship was evident, and it says something for Lowell's generosity of mind that it did not affect his feelings about Poe's genius.

There was no solace anywhere but in the prospect of *The Stylus,* although he told his old friend Thomas that he was in better health than he ever knew himself to be, and his young admirer George Eveleth that *Eureka* was accomplishing all that he had prophesied and more. All this was whistling in the dark, but in April 1849 he received a letter which looked as if it might make his dream come true.

The letter was from Edward Howard Norton Patterson, a young man of twenty-one who lived in Oquawka, Illinois. Patterson had been given the local paper by his father on coming of age, but he had larger ambitions. He wanted to publish a magazine, and he wanted the literary contents to be exclusively under Poe's control, "not doubting that even a cheap Magazine, under *your* editorial control, could be made to pay well, and at the same time exert a beneficial influence upon American Literature." Poe must have rubbed his eyes as he read the words. Detailed figures, estimates of profits? Nothing was easier than for him to produce them, as he had done so often before. He demurred only at the idea of cheapness, and put the case for a magazine that was better produced and more expensive, costing $5 a year. To obtain the necessary thousand subscribers he proposed to make a tour in the West and South, lecturing as he went to pay expenses. Publication from Oquawka, however, presented a problem. Who had heard of Oquawka? Poe proposed to put on the title page: "Published simultaneously at New York and St. Louis," said he would soon be starting for Richmond, and asked Patterson to send him $50 to await him on his arrival.

Patterson, as his reply made plain, was perfectly serious. He went into some detail of his own, agreeing to the idea of putting New York and St. Louis as points of publication, but insisting that the actual place of printing should be Oquawka because he had an office and a printing plant there. He sent the $50 to John R. Thompson, editor of the *Messenger*. The prospective editor, however, stayed in the East, probably because he lacked money to make the journey. He went to Boston and Lowell, spent a week with the Richmonds, and told Annie that he would start for Virginia on June 11. He did not leave, however, until the 29th. Stella Lewis helped the household at Fordham with money, and it does not seem that Poe was drinking, but barely enough came in to buy food for Maria Clemm and her Eddy.

His actual departure is marked by one of those conversations that one feels to have been invented, even though it may in fact be true. The night before he left, he and Maria Clemm stayed with Mrs. Lewis, whose work he had praised so highly, and whom in person he found to be generous, sensitive and impulsive, marked by a romantic sensibility that bordered upon melancholy. On this evening she found him also to be melancholy. On leaving, Poe expressed a presentiment that he would never see her again, and asked her to write his life. Maria also said that he left in wretched spirits, after arranging his papers and telling her what to do with them if he should die. Once on the steamboat he became more cheerful. "God bless you, my own darling mother. Do not fear for Eddy! See how good I will be while I am away from you, and will come back to love and comfort you." These were the last words he spoke to Maria, according to her later recollection. At any rate, he left for Richmond.

He left for Richmond and she returned to Fordham. She waited for news which did not come, and in hope of money to enable her to live. After ten days she wrote a frantic letter to Annie, but Annie too had heard nothing. A little later Maria went to see Stella Lewis, and found there a letter written from Philadelphia. Its contents could not have cheered her. Poe wrote that he had been very ill with the cholera, "or spasms quite as bad," and asked for her to come to him so that they could die together:

> It is no use to reason with me *now;* I must die. I have no desire to live since I have done "Eureka." I could accomplish nothing more. For your sake it would be sweet to live, but we must die together. You have been all in all to me, darling, ever beloved mother, and dearest, truest friend.

He added that he had been taken to prison once since he came to Philadelphia, for getting drunk, "but *then* I was not," adding that it had been "about Virginia."

What had happened? The lost mental control of which he must sometimes have been aware was now acute. In Philadelphia he had gone to see John Sartain, who edited a magazine and was also the most celebrated American engraver on copper. Sartain had printed "The Bells" and was to print "Annabel Lee." The story he told in his reminiscences probably gained something from the fact that it was written nearly half a century after the events took place, but it fits too well into the pattern of Poe's behavior to be disregarded.

According to Sartain, Poe came into his engraving room asking for protection, saying that in the train he had heard two men who sat behind him planning to kill him and throw him off the platform of the car. It was for revenge, he said, "a woman trouble." He asked Sartain to remove his mustache so that he should not be easily recognized, and the engraver snipped away at it with his scissors. When it was dark they went for a long walk, and Poe told stories of having been put into a cell in Moyamensing Prison, and of attempts by the attendants there to kill or frighten him, including one in which "they brought out my mother, Mrs. Clemm, to blast my sight by seeing them first saw off her feet at the ankles, then her legs up to the knees, her thighs at the hips, and so on." Sartain took him home, put him to bed on a sofa, and sat up beside him. After staying a day or two Poe appeared to have recovered, and agreed that the men were a delusion. Sartain lent him money and he went off, as he said, to New York.

Sartain's is not the only story of Poe's Philadelphia adventures, for he was helped by other friends there who gave him money and did their best to keep him away from drink. There is no record of his having been put in prison. He did not go to New York (something which he may have suggested in momentary suspicion of Sartain), but continued his erratic journey South, and at last on July 14 reached Richmond. In a second letter to Maria Clemm, he said that his valise had been lost for ten days and that when it was found the two lectures it contained had been stolen, and in a third he told her that he had been "totally deranged" for ten days as the result of an attack of delirium tremens. He had reached Richmond with $2, of which he sent her one. The end of the letter suggests his almost childish reliance on her at times of trouble: "Oh God, my Mother, shall we ever again meet? If possible, oh COME! My clothes are *so horrible,* and I am *so ill.*" But she lacked money even to buy food, and had no prospect at all of getting to Richmond.

This, then, was catastrophe. Yet, as he had done so often before, Poe bounced back from these troubles into unfounded optimism. He had been saved in Philadelphia by the generosity of friends; he would put forth all his energies and try to write something; all was far from lost. He put up at the old Swan Tavern (he had by now collected Patterson's $50), saw old friends and made new ones,

was welcomed and cosseted. He visited the Mackenzies and saw
Rosalie. She took him on a visit at which he met Susan Archer Talley,
a young poet of whom he had said that "she ranks already with
the best of American poetesses, and in time will surpass them all."
It is not surprising that Susan Talley, then in her very early twenties,
was inclined to think well of him. She was impressed by his ease,
his grace, his dignity, and by the reserve that changed into warmth
when he realized her identity and took her hand. He seemed to
Susan Talley a refined, high-bred and chivalrous gentleman. And
no doubt this is how Poe momentarily saw himself, as a Southern
gentleman who had returned to take his proper place in Richmond
society.

But although he was accepted, as he had not been in the past,
the lecture that he gave was not well attended. No more than a
hundred people came to hear him talk about "The Poetic Principle,"
and since the tickets were priced at 25 cents, the return from the
talk was small. On the other hand, as he told Maria Clemm, those
present were enthusiastic, and "every body says that if I lecture
again & put the tickets at 50 cts, I will clear $100." Susan Talley,
who was there with her mother and sister and Rosalie, noted that
he used no manuscript (it was one of the two in the valise) and
that he stood quite motionless as he delivered the lecture. Afterwards Rosalie, radiantly happy, said: "Edgar, only see how the people
are staring at the poet and his sister."

Meanwhile, what of *The Stylus?* Poe had written a note to Patterson as soon as he recovered, saying that in Philadelphia he had
been arrested by the cholera, from which he barely escaped with
his life. Nearly three weeks passed before he wrote again, in rather
lukewarm terms. One has the impression that, subconsciously aware
of his own incapacity any longer to organize and run a magazine,
he was looking for a way of escape from the responsibility that
was being pressed on him. A cheap magazine, one with a $3 annual
subscription, would, he said, suggest namby-pambyism and frivolity.
"I could not undertake it *con amore*. My heart would not be in
the work." If Patterson changed his mind, of course—but it is obvious
that Poe did not think that likely. When Poe said that he awaited
a reply in Richmond, he must have thought that was the end of
the affair. He did not know his man. Patterson promptly agreed
to the $5 magazine, providing he was certain that a thousand people

would buy the first number. Was there an argument about the title?
"Adopt your own title. I leave this matter to you." And he continued:
"If the proposition meets your approval, you may immediately com-
mence your journey to St. Louis," which, taking things easily, he
should reach by the middle of October. There they would meet,
and make final arrangements.

Patterson received no reply to this letter. A few years earlier
Poe would have been delighted by the promise to lay out $1100
for the first issues. Now he did nothing, but lingered in Richmond.
He enjoyed the company of old friends like the Cabells and the
Stanards, and basked in the admiration of the young. John Allan's
widow was out of the city almost throughout the summer, so that
he was saved the possible embarrassment of any contact with her.
And he was again contemplating marriage.

This time the lady was Elmira Shelton, to whom he had considered himself engaged more than twenty years earlier when she
had been Elmira Royster. She had been a widow now for five years,
and had been left a sizable estate by her husband. The courtship
was brief. Elmira was told one day that a gentleman had called
and was waiting in the parlor. She recognized him at once, and
within a few days he was asking her to marry him. "I found out
that he was very serious and I became serious," she said years later.
"I told him if he would not take a positive denial he must give
me time to consider of it." One of Poe's biographers has brutally
said that Elmira had no attraction except wealth, and a daguerrotype
certainly makes her look both plain and formidable. Her teen-age
son and daughter were strongly opposed to the marriage. On the
other hand, she was no less susceptible than others to Poe's romantic
air, and there must have been something compelling also about
the idea of reviving an old love.

Did she say yes? It seems that in a hesitant way she did. At
the end of August or the beginning of September, Poe wrote enthusiastically to Maria about a number of things. The papers had been
full of his praise since the lecture, and he contrasted his success
with the failure of a lecturer on Shakespeare, who had "8 persons,
including myself & the doorkeeper." The husband of a Philadelphia
poet, Mrs. St. Leon Loud, had called on him and offered $100 for
help in editing her poems—an offer which he had immediately accepted. The work, he said, would not occupy him more than three

days. And among the accounts of visits paid and people seen, and invitations refused because he lacked a dress coat, he wrote about his marriage. Elmira had talked of visiting Fordham, but he was not sure if that would do. Upon the whole it would be better for Muddie to tell people at Fordham that he was ill, and "break up" there "so that you may come on here." Would they be happier at Richmond or at Lowell? Fordham itself was beautiful, and they could easily pay off their debt, but as he said twice in the letter, "I *must* be somewhere where I can see Annie." In her reply she was not to mention the name of Annie. "I cannot bear to hear it now—unless you can tell me that Mr. R. is dead." She was also to play a part in a deception to be practiced on Elmira, who had been told by Poe that he had kept a pencil sketch of her made long ago. The sketch evidently no longer existed, and he told her to say that she had looked for it without success. His last words have the comic effect of a throwaway line: "I have got the wedding ring.—and shall have no difficulty, I think, in getting a dress-coat."

One would be inclined to think that Poe was exaggerating the progress of his courtship, if Elmira had not herself written to Maria some three weeks later. The letter, with its assurance that "I am fully prepared to *love* you, and I do sincerely hope that our spirits may be congenial," is clearly that of a prospective daughter-in-law. She gives assurance of Edgar's sobriety, and although two bouts of drunkenness are mentioned by some friends, his stay in Richmond was fairly sober. (He was received into the Sons of Temperance at some time during his stay.)

The visit to Richmond stretched on and on. Two months after his arrival he gave the "Poetic Principle" lecture in Norfolk, to a small but appreciative audience. A girl of sixteen named Susan Ingram met him a day or two before the lecture at a party in a hotel, and remembered the scene as idyllic. The hotel was near the ocean, the water shone in the moonlight, Poe read his poems, and later copied out "Ulalume" and sent it to her. He came to see the Ingram family, and she remembered him as one of the most courteous men she had ever met. Although his pictures looked like him, they did not do him justice, because there was something in his face that they did not reveal. "Perhaps it was in the eyes, perhaps in the mouth, I do not know, but any one who ever met him would understand what I mean."

From the Norfolk lecture he made only enough to settle his hotel bill, with $2 over. He could not send any money to Maria, and she asked for help from Griswold, saying that she had been "without the necessaries of life for many days" and lacked money even to get to New York. In another letter she sent him a package containing an article, probably about Stella Lewis's poems, which she asked that he should publish exactly as it was written. "If you will do so I will promise you a favorable review of your books as they appear. You know the influence I have with Mr. Poe. Not that I think he will need any urging to advance your interest." Griswold's reaction is not known, but very likely he sent her some money. If he did, it was not enough to pay for the journey to Richmond.

Poe, back in Richmond, at last decided to make a move. He would give one more lecture, go to Philadelphia and spend those three days in editing Mrs. Loud's poems, then start for New York. Patterson and *The Stylus* may have been in his mind, but he did not write to Patterson, and showed no intention of being in St. Louis in October. And what about the marriage? *"If possible* I will get married before I start—but there is no telling," he wrote to Maria. He told her to write to him in Philadelphia, addressing the letter to E. S. T. Grey. She was to leave the letter unsigned, in case he did not receive it. Why was there no telling about the marriage? Perhaps he was deterred by Elmira's determination to retain control of her income or by the family's opposition. Whatever the reason, it is clear that neither of the parties felt any great urgency. Elmira said afterwards that there had been a partial understanding, although she did not think she would ever have married Poe. This seems to be contradicted by her letter to Maria Clemm.

Poe did not get married, but he did leave Richmond. The second lecture was better attended than the first, and must have put money in his pocket. A couple of days were spent in saying goodbye to friends. He stayed a night with the Talleys, and Susan remembered a meteor briefly appearing in the sky as he said goodbye. She remembered also that he showed her a letter from Griswold, agreeing to act as his literary executor, a letter not seen by anybody else. She was an imaginative young lady. Another night was spent at the Mackenzies', where he said goodbye to Rosalie. He paid a farewell visit to Elmira, who found him sad and suffering from fever, so that she thought he would not be well enough to leave. On the

same evening, however, Thompson of the *Messenger* thought him
in excellent spirits. Poe took the cane of a friend named Dr. Carter,
mistaking it for his own, ate supper at a restaurant on Main Street,
met some acquaintances there who found him both cheerful and
sober, and went aboard the boat for Baltimore. He told a number
of people that he expected to be back in two weeks, presumably
with Maria Clemm, after clearing up his affairs in New York. His
trunk, and some other baggage, was left at the Swan Tavern.

The Baltimore boat left on September 27, and reached the city
twenty-four hours later. It must be called remarkable, in view of
the thoroughness of American scholarship, that Poe's movements
during the next five days remain uncertain. It is said that he called
on one friend and dined with others, that he attended a birthday
party and felt bound to pledge his hostess in wine, that he went
by train to Philadelphia and was taken ill there, that he got on to
another train returning to Baltimore in mistake for going to New
York. There is no strong evidence to back any of these suppositions,
and if he went to Philadelphia he did not approach the Louds. In
truth we know nothing of these days except for the practical certainty that some of them were spent in drinking. There is something
very appropriate to the tragicomedy of his life and the ambiguity
of his work in the mystery surrounding these last days.

On October 3 his old acquaintance and correspondent Dr. Snodgrass received a note:

> Dear Sir,
>   There is a gentleman, rather the worse for wear, at Ryan's 4th
> ward polls, who goes under the cognomen of Edgar A. Poe, and
> who appears in great distress, & he says he is acquainted with you,
> and I assure you, he is in need of immediate assistance.
>
> Yours, in haste,
> Jos. W. Walker

Walker was a compositor on the Baltimore *Sun*. An election was
being held in the city, and the fact that Poe was found near a polling
station gave rise to suggestions that he had been given drink or
drugs and taken from one polling place to another to cast a multiplicity of votes. Again, there is no evidence to support this theory. When
Snodgrass reached him he was not merely the worse for wear, but
unconscious. He was wearing a poor thin shirt, not his own, but

still had Dr. Carter's malacca cane. Snodgrass, in company with Poe's uncle by marriage Henry Herring, took him in a carriage to Washington College Hospital. He was put in the care of the resident physician, Dr. John J. Moran.

Four days later, on October 7, he died. He was forty years and a few months old. Even about the circumstances surrounding his death a mystery remains. One account is given by Snodgrass and another by Moran. Or rather, there are accounts given by both men, which they elaborated over the years. Snodgrass, a temperance lecturer, said that Poe was in a condition of "beastly intoxication," something which again lacks other support. Of Moran's versions the first, given to Mrs. Clemm a few weeks later, is to be preferred. Poe was, he said, unconscious until the following day, when he moved into delirium, talking to "spectral and imaginary objects on the walls." On the next day he became more tranquil, but was not able to give coherent answers to questions. He said that he had a wife in Richmond, but did not know when he had left the city, or what had become of his trunk. Then delirium returned, and it took the efforts of two nurses to keep him in bed. He had been admitted on Wednesday, and on Saturday night "he commenced calling for one 'Reynolds,' which he did through the night until *three* on Sunday morning." He then became quiet, said, "Lord help my poor soul," and died.

The doubts that have been cast on Moran's story spring chiefly from the elaboration he made of it many years later, but there seems no reason to question its general truth. It is unlikely that he would have invented the story of calling for Reynolds. Who was Reynolds? Poe had no friend of that name, and the most likely candidate is Jeremiah Reynolds, whose projected American South Polar Expedition had influenced him in writing *Arthur Gordon Pym*. But this last cry, like much else in his life, offers a riddle unsolved.

Very few people attended the funeral. Neilson Poe had visited the hospital without being allowed to see his cousin. Now he and Henry Herring made the funeral arrangements. The service was conducted by a distant relative, the Reverend William T. D. Clemm, and the handful of people present included Snodgrass and Poe's cousin Elizabeth Morton Smith, to whom he had once written verses, as well of course as Henry Herring and Neilson Poe. In a letter to Maria Clemm, written two days after the funeral, Neilson Poe said that "Edgar had seen so much of sorrow—had so little reason to be satisfied with life—that to him, the change can scarcely be said to be a misfortune."

He was buried in the Poe family lot in the Presbyterian Cemetery in Baltimore. A few years later Neilson Poe ordered a tombstone for his cousin, but it was broken by a freight train that jumped the track into the marble yard where it was being prepared. The grave remained unmarked by any name, indicated only by the number "80," placed there by the sexton. This was the mortal end of Edgar Allan Poe.

EPILOGUE

THE HISTORY OF A REPUTATION

TWO of the Baltimore papers noticed Edgar Allan Poe's death, one in a paragraph, the other in no more than three lines. In New York a sympathetic half column appeared in the *Journal of Commerce*. In Richmond, naturally enough, the obituaries were longer. But the longest by far appeared in a New York paper, was in a personal sense almost totally hostile, and made accusations that were to be stamped on Poe's reputation for decades.

The obituary appeared on the day of the funeral in Greeley's *New York Daily Tribune,* and was written by Griswold under the pseudonym of "Ludwig." The first paragraph gives the tone in relation to Poe as a human being:

> Edgar Allan Poe is dead. He died in Baltimore the day before yesterday. This announcement will startle many, but few will be grieved by it. The poet was well known personally or by reputation, in all this country; he had readers in England, and in several of the states of Continental Europe; but he had few or no friends; and the regrets for his death will be suggested principally by the consideration that in him literary art lost one of its most brilliant, but erratic, stars.

The account repeated the errors of detail given to Griswold in Poe's own account, and similar errors appeared elsewhere. His talents were acknowledged, but every chance of personal denigration was taken. When he first appeared before Kennedy, "a tattered frock-coat concealed the absence of a shirt, and the ruins of boots disclosed more than the want of stockings." Not only did he walk the streets in madness or melancholy, and speak as if to spirits that "at such times only could be evoked by him from that Aidenn close by whose portals his disturbed soul sought to forget the ills to which his constitution subjected him . . . the Aidenn which he might never see but in fitful glimpses, as its gates opened to receive the less fiery and more happy natures whose listing to sin did not involve the doom of death"; but his experiences had "deprived him of all faith in man or woman." He had looked at the social world and regarded it as a fraud, a discovery which "gave a direction to his shrewd and naturally unamiable character." Yet this shrewd and unamiable man was unable to cope with other people. "Though he regarded society as composed of villains, the sharpness of his intellect was not of the kind which enabled him to cope with villainy, while it continually caused him overshots, to fail of the success of honesty."

Griswold was too clever a man to leave the piece so unbalanced. He wrote in praise of the conversation, "almost supramortal in its eloquence," which contained "imagery . . . from the worlds which no mortal can see but with the vision of genius," although he added that the conversational magician "himself dissolved the spell, and brought his hearers back to common and base existence, by vulgar fancies or by exhibitions of the ignoble passions." He praised the stories as "scarcely surpassed in ingenuity of construction," and said that the poems would "retain a most honorable rank," although he observed too that as a critic Poe was "little better than a carping grammarian." Few things in this subtle piece of dispraise could be labeled positively untrue, yet its total effect was to show Poe as an eccentric minor writer and a most disagreeable man. One of the finest touches was a passage quoted from a novel by Bulwer in description of a character named Francis Vivian. Poe, Griswold said, was in many respects like Francis Vivian:

> Irascible, envious—bad enough, but not the worst, for these salient angles were all varnished over with a cold repellent cynicism while his passions vented themselves in sneers. . . . He had, to a morbid excess, that desire to rise which is vulgarly called ambition, but no wish for the esteem or the love of his species.

And so on. The passage was set between quotation marks in the *Daily Tribune* to show that it was taken from Bulmer, but when it was reprinted in the memoir that served as Griswold's preface

to his edition of Poe's works in the following year the quotation
marks had disappeared, so that it stood as the writer's own opinion.

The Griswold obituary—for its authorship was generally known—
did not go uncontroverted. Willis, evidently shocked by it, wrote
a piece for his *Home Journal* in which he spoke of Poe's punctuality,
industry, courtesy, and patience, and attributed any unpleasant traits
to the disastrous effect upon him of "a *single glass* of wine." Other
old friends moved to his defense. The most outspoken of them was
Lambert Wilmer, who called the obituary a hypocritical canting
document written by a slanderous and malicious miscreant. "Some
circumstances mentioned by the slanderous hypocrite we *know* to
be false, and we have no doubt in the world that nearly all of his
statements intended to throw odium and discredit on the character
of the deceased are scandalous inventions." But Wilmer's word carried little weight against Griswold's, and even defenders like the
amiable Willis conceded the case against Poe in part by suggesting
that he was a Jekyll and Hyde character, and that Hyde appeared
as soon as he had started to drink. Willis's picture in his memoir
of Mrs. Clemm going round from one magazine to another, "thinly
and insufficiently clad," trying to sell a poem or an article, was bound
to stir more sympathy for this angel in adversity—to use his phrase—
than for the errant genius she was trying to support. Indeed, much
of his article was a plea for her rather than for Poe. The last sentences
read: "She is destitute and alone. If any, far or near, will send to
us what may aid and cheer her through the remainder of her life,
we will joyfully place it in her hands."

In fact Maria Clemm was neither alone nor destitute after Poe's
death. Annie and Elmira wrote to her in terms which, even allowing
for the language of the time, were extravagant in addressing a
woman they had never met. Annie's letter begins:

> Oh my mother, my darling, darling mother oh, what shall I say to
> you—how can I comfort you—oh mother it seems more than I can
> bear—and when I think of you, his mother, who has lost her all, I
> feel that it must not, no, it cannot be—oh, if I could but see you,
> do, I implore you, come to Annie as soon as possible.

And so on through some pages. Elmira wrote, with an ardor heated
rather than cooled by death:

Oh! how shall I address you, my dear, and deeply afflicted friend
under such heart-rending circumstances? I have no doubt, ere this,
you have heard of the death of our *dear Edgar!* yes, he was the
dearest object on earth to me; and, well assured am I, that he was
the pride of your heart.

Helen Whitman wrote more soberly, "to assure you of my sympathy
in your deep sorrow and of my unalterable affection for one whose
memory is still most dear to me."

Maria Clemm went off to stay with Annie; but before this, eleven
days after Poe's death, she gave Griswold a power of attorney to
collect and edit the works. The power of attorney mentions that
"it was the express wish and injunction of the Author before his
death that Dr. Rufus W. Griswold should compile and edit the same
in case of their publication." Whether or not Susan Talley was right
in saying that she saw a letter from Griswold, there can be no doubt
of Poe's desire that he should edit the works, even though Maria
Clemm later told a different tale. In January 1850 a selection of
poems and stories was published in two volumes, with Willis's memoir and the article Lowell had written some years earlier.

The production of the works with such speed does not reflect
any friendly feeling on Griswold's part. In a letter to Helen Whitman,
he said that *"I was not his friend nor he mine,* as I remember to
have told you." He had undertaken the work simply to oblige Mrs.
Clemm, but he gave Mrs. Whitman a word of warning about Poe's
"Muddie":

> I cannot refrain from begging you to be very careful what you say
> or write to Mrs. Clemm, who is not your friend, or anybody's friend,
> and who has no element of goodness or kindness in her nature, but
> whose heart and understanding are full of malice and wickedness.
> I confide in you these sentences for your own sake only, for Mrs.
> C. appears to be a very warm friend to me.

Griswold reiterated often that he had undertaken his editorial work
for nothing, and Mrs. Clemm received no payment, although she
was given several sets of the edition to sell for her own benefit.
Rosalie Poe also got no payment from the publication. She was left
homeless after the Civil War, and was reduced to selling pictures
of her brother in the streets of Richmond and Baltimore. She ended
her life in 1874, at a church home in Washington. The question of

who profited from the publication of the works remains a mystery. It may be that the sales did not cover the publisher's expenses, but this does not seem at all likely, for later in the year a third volume was published.

Maria Clemm's later life may be briefly summarized. She paid lengthy visits to several ladies in turn. They included Annie, who confided in her and later much regretted it; Mrs. Shew, who also found her untrustworthy; and Mrs. Lewis, with whom she fell out. She threatened at one time to descend on Mrs. Whitman, who managed to avert the visit. She paid a brief visit to Longfellow, who gave her $20. Dickens sent her a much larger sum of money, out of sympathy for her and admiration for Poe, and at various times other people contributed to her support in response to the begging letters which she wrote with some expertness. She talked endlessly, and with increasing inaccuracy, of the years spent with her beloved Eddie and Virginia. In the end the literary ladies all seem to have tired of her, and her last years were spent in a home in Baltimore, where she died in 1871.

In the third volume of the works Griswold republished his obituary in a form much enlarged, and much more unfavorable to its subject. His original article had been, he said, "unconsidered and imperfect, but, as every one who knew its subject readily perceived, very kind." He now added to it a number of grace notes. Some were untrue, like the statement that Poe had been expelled from the university, and that the prize for *MS. Found in a Bottle* had been awarded to him because his was the first legible manuscript found by the judges. Others were based on gossip, like the reference to a story, "scarcely suitable for repetition here," that Poe had done something discreditable in relation to the second Mrs. Allan which had caused his expulsion from home. Others still were purely malicious, like the tale of his saying to Burton: "Burton, I am—*the editor—of the Penn Magazine*—and you are—hiccup—*a fool.*" The English controversy and Willis's fund-raising enterprise were discussed in detail. Poe's audacity as a plagiarist was said to be "scarcely paralleled . . . in all literary history."

In a preface to the memoir, Griswold gave an account of his own relations with Poe, largely through their correspondence. In printing these letters he went in for wholesale forgery. The effect of the forgeries is twofold: first to show Poe's admiration for Griswold, and second to reveal him as a fawning figure, eager to please. One instance of Griswold's activities will be enough. In February 1848, Poe had written sending material for consideration in an anthology. To this letter Griswold added a preface, a middle section, and an appropriate coda. The preface established Griswold's generosity and Poe's poverty: "A thousand thanks for your kindness in the matter of those books, which I could not afford to buy, and had so much need of." The middle section, too long to quote, contained thanks for Griswold's praise and ended: "I can truly say that no man's approbation gives me so much pleasure." And the last phrase read: "Why not let me anticipate the book publication of your splendid essay on Milton?" Griswold did not hesitate to improve his own letters also, to stress his kindness and Poe's appreciation of it.

The effect showed not only to the credit of Griswold but even more emphatically to the discredit of Poe. Had he expressed contempt for Griswold in public, calling him a dexterous quack able to force even the most rubbishy work into notoriety by innumerable petty arts? He should now be made to grovel before the man he had attacked. As a subsidiary note, Griswold added material to letters other people had written to Poe, all of it included to show him in a bad light. He put in unfavorable remarks apparently made by Poe about other literary figures, one or two of them writers who might have been prepared to defend him. Some of Griswold's tampering is trivial, and by the lax textual standards of the time almost permissible, but all of it worked to Poe's detriment. As an editor Griswold made some minor changes, which were not outrageous by the prevailing ideas of editorial responsibility.

The memoir was transferred to the first volume when the works were reprinted and a fourth volume added, and for twenty years this remained the only edition of Poe's works. Its effect on his personal reputation was profound. Griswold was the authorized biographer, and what he said was naturally taken as authentic. Protesting voices were raised, particularly in the South, but they had comparatively little effect. When Griswold died in 1857, his triumph was complete.

His forgeries were not publicly known until the twentieth century, and their full extent was not realized until in 1941 Professor A. H. Quinn printed facsimiles of genuine letters beside the letters with additions made by Griswold for the printer. The revelation of what he did has raised curiosity about his character. As. W. H. Auden has said:

> That one man should dislike another and speak maliciously of him after his death would be natural enough, but to take so much trouble, to blacken a reputation so subtly, presupposes a sustained hatred which is always fascinating, because the capacity for sustained emotion of any kind is rare.

Poe's choice of his literary executor seems remarkable when one considers the enmity that had existed between the two men, but in fact it was simply an acknowledgment of Griswold's supremacy in his chosen literary field. He was the champion editor and compiler of his time. *Poets and Poetry of America* was a landmark, extraordinary as that may seem now when three-quarters of the writers included are forgotten. The book established a reputation which several later collections consolidated, and its popularity is shown by the fact that in little more than a decade the book was in its sixteenth edition. Poe's representation had been increased from three and a half to nine pages, which gave him a little more space than Lowell and a little less than Willis. For purposes of comparison it should be said that such poetasters as J. G. Brainard and Willis Gaylord Clark were given eight and six pages respectively.

Griswold was capable of behaving with much generosity to those who sought his help. C. G. Leland and Bayard Taylor are two writers of the period who found Rufe or Gris, as he was familiarly called, invariably kind and helpful. Handsome, theatrical in manner, and emotional in his approach to almost any subject, Griswold's mercurial personality impressed many men and charmed many women. But he wanted to have his own importance acknowledged. If his hatred for Poe had to be given any single cause, it would lie in Poe's openly expressed contempt for this diligent anthologist of the insignificant. But it is likely also that Griswold was in a curious way jealous of Poe. Certainly their lives ran almost parallel in some respects. In 1839 Griswold applied for an editorial post on the *Southern Literary Messenger,* and he succeeded Poe on *Graham's.* When he died he was only a year older than Poe. He succeeded Poe in the favors of Mrs. Osgood, who dedicated her last volume to him, and sent him a Valentine beginning "For one, whose being is to mine a star," which contained not only her name but also his own woven into the lines. His second marriage in 1845 was never consummated, and ended some years later in divorce. His last years, like those of Poe, were marked by the rapid advance of illness, in his case tuberculosis, and by domestic troubles and sorrows.

He followed Poe also in quarreling with Mrs. Ellet, in circumstances which throw light on both their characters. She was in the habit of visiting his rooms at New York University without his permission, and there opened drawers and read confidential papers. When he discovered this, they corresponded in the third person. "Mr. Griswold declines to furnish Mrs. Ellet with proof sheets or any early copy of his book entitled *The Female Poets of America*," he wrote, adding that "It strikes him that the relations heretofore existing between himself and Mrs. Ellet should have prevented any application from her on the subject."

After the book had appeared early in 1849, he accused her of writing anonymous articles about it: "Mr. Griswold is advised of all the attempts Mrs. Ellet has made for the injury of his book, and has read in MS some of the rejected articles she has written upon it." Mrs. Ellet replied that she would not object to the destruction of her review in proof, provided she was paid for it. Griswold, like Poe, accused her of writing anonymous letters. She may have done so, but she signed a letter to his wife, complaining that he had used "the most vituperative, foul and obscene language" about her in a public place, and that she was keeping various letters written by him "to protect myself against annoyance from an unscrupulous and deadly enemy." Maria Clemm, in a letter written a decade after Poe's death, said that Griswold had offered her $500 for "a certain lady's letters," and that fearing temptation she had burned them. If they were Mrs. Osgood's, as has been suggested, it is hard to see what use he could have had for them; but if they were Mrs. Ellet's, his eagerness would be intelligible.

It certainly seems in retrospect that Griswold was an unscrupulous and deadly enemy to Poe, yet it is unlikely that he saw himself in such a light. He often said that his memoir and his editorship were acts of pure altruism, and the publisher of the works confirmed that Griswold "never received a cent for his labors." Some of Poe's acquaintances regarded his view of Poe as an outrageous travesty, and wrote to say so. The most outspoken of these was George Graham, who said that the portrait was "a fancy sketch of a perverted, jaundiced vision," and attributed the tone of the memoir to Poe's summary critical disposal of some of Griswold's friends, so that "the present hacking at the cold remains of him who struck them down, is a sort of compensation."

But for every friend of Poe's who was made indignant by the memoir, there was another who felt that it was upon the whole just. Stella Lewis remained on friendly terms with Griswold, and so did Thomas, who had tried to get Poe the customs appointment. When Griswold died, his view of Poe was generally accepted. Poe was regarded as a poet of a genius most conspicuously shown in "The Raven"; a skillful writer of short stories and hoaxes, sometimes horrific but often rather mechanical; and an intelligent but absurdly prejudiced critic. The villainy of his character became more firmly established with almost every new criticism, as Griswold's edition of the works crossed the Atlantic. The Scottish literary clergyman George Gilfillan, an indefatigable and in his day famous anthologist and critic, enlarged on Griswold. Poe was, Gilfillan said, a combination of fiend, brute, and genius. "He was no more a gentleman than he was a saint. His heart was as rotten as his conduct was infamous. He knew not what the terms honour and honourable meant. . . . He showed himself, in many instances, a cool, calculating, deliberate blackguard." Gilfillan, however, did not deny his genius, thought that moral lessons could be derived from his life, and was prepared finally to say "Peace to the well-nigh putrid dust of Edgar Poe." He was no more emphatic than the editor of the *Edinburgh Review*, who said that the lowest abyss of moral imbecility and disrepute had not been reached until Poe was born.

It would be wrong to speak of Poe's reputation as reviving, for after his death interest in his work never flagged. The general view of him did, however, change a great deal in the third quarter of the nineteenth century, and quite radically in the fourth. The change was both biographical and critical. Helen Whitman's *Edgar Poe and His Critics,* published in 1860, tried to counter Griswoldian criticism by presenting a view of Poe as loving husband and brilliant talker, but since she rarely descended to detail the book had little effect. Her study played some part, nevertheless, in attracting the interest of the biographer who, more than any other single figure, was responsible for rescuing Poe from Griswold.

This was John Henry Ingram, an eccentric Englishman, who was greatly preoccupied with Poe for more than half a century. It is extraordinary that an Englishman, and one without a private income, should have been able to gather source materials that made him the greatest living authority on Poe; but Ingram was not an ordinary man. He maintained his mother and two sisters through what must have been an undemanding job in the Post Office, plus the money he received from books like his biography of Mrs. Browning, his very successful *Flora Symbolica: or the Language and Sentiment of Flowers,* and articles on various subjects. His principal occupation, however, was the life of Poe. From the late 1860s he corresponded with anybody in America who could tell him anything at all in the way of biographical detail. Four of the women most closely associated with Poe were still alive, and although Ingram did not obtain any information from Mrs. Clemm, Mrs. Whitman and Mrs. Richmond were both tremendously helpful. Mrs. Whitman sent manuscripts, news cuttings, magazine articles, and copies of letters, as well as writing an account of her own relationship with Poe. Annie Richmond, who as the years passed came more and more to think that knowing Poe had been the most important event in her life, made copies of the letters the poet had sent her, and gave him some of Poe's books. Mrs. Shew, Mrs. Lewis, the Poe family in Baltimore, and dozens of other friends and acquaintances sent reminiscences and materials. In 1874 Ingram began publication of a four-volume edition of the works, which he introduced by a controversial memoir, and six years later he published a full-length biography.

His work had considerable effect. The picture he painted of Poe as almost a model citizen, gentle, generous and industrious, was not much more accurate than Griswold's, but it attracted interest as the first full and coherent defense of the writer. He denied any suggestion of Poe's plagiarism, and admitted the drinking only so far as to say that toward the end of the writer's life, "sorrow and chronic pecuniary embarrassment drove him to the use of stimulants." He attacked Griswold's memoir, often very effectively, and said forthrightly that he would not discuss Poe's letters to Griswold because "there is pretty positive proof that some, if not the whole of them, are *fabrications.*" He had no proof of this, but had been told it by Mrs. Whitman.

The most indignant remarks about Griswold are contained in the memoir; the full-scale biography says less about him, although there is no lessening of acerbity. By this time Ingram had been fairly flooded with information from literary ladies. Some of it was personal and possibly accurate reminiscence, much was third- or fourth-hand evidence of an erratic kind, some was purely comic. With the passing years Mrs. Whitman became more convinced of her own family relationship with Poe. She told Ingram of an occasion when she had dressed as an Albanian chieftain for a tableau, and had appalled her mother by the physical resemblance she showed to Poe. She found that Ingram too had an affiliation with Poe, since Ing-ram meant "Son of the Raven." Mrs. Shew also sent him a great deal of material. Ingram seems to have been overwhelmed. Both ladies were given a chapter to themselves in the biography, and so was Annie, who was a later but almost equally frequent correspondent. Ingram was lured into mistakes, and into a lack of balance. For all his good intentions, he produced a biography that was misleading both about Poe's work and his personality.

The 1874 memoir gave impetus to an attempt that had been for some years brewing in Baltimore, to put up a memorial stone to Poe. It took a decade to raise enough money, but in 1875 the memorial stone, designed by the architect of the City Hall, was at last completed. Poe's body was removed to a new resting place in the churchyard, and Mrs. Clemm was placed beside him. The monument took the form of a block 8 feet high of veined Italian marble with a granite base. There was a medallion portrait on one panel with the writer's full name beneath it, and the frieze was ornamented by acanthus leaves and a lyre crossed with laurel. The memorial had been sponsored largely by local educationalists and teachers, and the actual ceremony was unhappily parochial. It took place in the Western Female High School, ladies composing the larger part of the audience, and many teachers were on the platform, where they were joined by Snodgrass, Neilson Poe, and Joseph Clarke, who had been Poe's headmaster long ago in Richmond. It says something of the disrepute still clinging to Poe's name, and the enmity he had roused, that of the poets invited only Walt Whitman attended. There was not much greater response to the suggestion that they might write an epitaph for inscription on the stone. Longfellow ignored the invitation and suggested a couple of Poe's own lines as an epitaph, Oliver Wendell Holmes regretted that he could not hope to be present, Whittier said that he did not care for monuments,

Helen Whitman's brief note merely wished the Poe Memorial Committee well.

English reactions were warmer, although Tennyson suggested that it would "be best to say of Poe in a reverential spirit simply Requiescat in Pace." Swinburne assured the Committee of Poe's imperishable fame, but must have disconcerted them by saying how much his reputation owed to "the laborious devotion of a genius equal & akin to his own"—that of Baudelaire. It was the respectable figure of Ingram's memoir that the Committee wished to commemmorate, not somebody akin to the maleficent author of *Les Fleurs du Mal*. In the end no epitaph was put upon the stone, and the proceedings had a slight flavor of absurdity about them.

The work—that is, the poems and short stories, for the criticism was little read after Poe's death—had grown constantly in popularity. Seven editions of the poetical works appeared in London during the 1850s, and the tales too were frequently reprinted. In France he had critical fame as well as public applause. "Edgar Poe, who isn't much in America, *must* become a great man in France," Baudelaire wrote in 1856 to Sainte-Beuve. The first serious criticism in France had come a decade earlier, in the form of a long article about the *Tales* in the *Revue des Deux Mondes*. But although this aroused interest, it was Baudelaire's passion for Poe that made him famous in France. Baudelaire spent much time in making translations of the stories, and wrote three essays about Poe which appeared in 1852, 1856, and 1857. The first of these relied heavily on a long article by John M. Daniel in the *Southern Literary Messenger*. Daniel, the hotheaded young man with whom Poe nearly fought a duel, was a passionate supporter of States' rights. His article excoriated the three Easterners—Griswold, Lowell, and Willis—whom he held responsible for the traduction of Poe. He painted a picture of a Poe who was already at university a great scholar, but also "the most dissipated youth" in that very dissolute place. He elaborated on Poe's own fictions about visiting Greece and Russia, saying that he had nearly experienced the knout in Siberia, and stressed his beauty, his genius, his poverty, his drinking, and his singularity.

It was Daniel's fictitious Poe, a genius and an outcast, who enchanted Baudelaire. Poe seemed to him a genius stifled by the American atmosphere in which his life had been passed. Like his French admirer, he felt a deep disgust for "democracy, progress and *civilization,"* and in his joking stories mocked the ignorant fools who surrounded him. He was an "aristocrat by nature even more than by birth," a "Byron gone astray in a bad world," who "imperturbably affirmed the natural wickedness of man," and understood that certain actions attract "only *because* they are bad or dangerous; they possess the fascination of the abyss."

Baudelaire was ready to regard this largely invented figure as one of the great storytellers and one of the profoundest and most subtle critics of all time. The effect of Baudelaire's writings, and even more of his translations from the stories, was immediate, intense and permanent. Mallarmé, a few years later, said that he had learned English the better to read Poe, and thought that the American had one of the most marvelous minds the world had ever known. Other French writers in the second half of the nineteenth century, Verlaine, Rimbaud, Huysmans and Gide among them, expressed themselves less emphatically but still saw Poe as a visionary genius with deep insight into the nature of humanity. The blend in him of the rational and the fantastic seemed to them extraordinarily profound. In France he was regarded as a writer and thinker upon the very highest level within a few years of his death. Near the end of the century Valéry wrote to Gide: "Poe is the only impeccable writer. He was never mistaken."

It was in reaction against all this, against Ingram, the French view, and a popularity that was thought to be of a largely vulgar kind, that Poe's most influential biographers worked. Richard Henry Stoddard and George Edward Woodberry, whose biographies appeared in the 1880s (in Stoddard's case as introduction to a six-volume selection from the works), were both temperamentally unsympathetic to their subject. Stoddard, who had emerged from a hard early life as shop boy and iron molder to become one of the most learned and influential critics of his time (his friends called him the Nestor of American literature), disliked Poe's theatricality and his aristocratic airs. He had also a personal reason for dislike, in the fact that he had sent Poe a poem called "Ode on a Grecian Flute" which he understood had been accepted for publication in the *Broadway Journal,* only to be told by Poe that the poem was a forgery. Stoddard's "life" replaced Griswold's memoir in a biographical section that retained the Willis and Lowell accounts of Poe; in it he condescended comfortably toward Ingram, and in effect supported Griswold:

If he was misunderstood while alive (of which there is no evidence), he is not misunderstood today, for what with Dr. Rufus W. Griswold on the one hand, and Mr. John H. Ingram on the other, a consensus of conclusions has been reached which is not likely to be disturbed. He belonged to the bright, but blasted brotherhood whose faults the world agrees to condone, partly because of the gifts which accompany them, and partly because of the misfortunes which they entail.

Stoddard's own conclusion, that "the character of Poe was as unlovely as the conduct to which it impelled him was willful," does not show much sign of condonation. He praised some of the poems, although he thought "Ulalume" represented the insanity of versification, and found it hard to believe that Poe was in earnest when he wrote such a "jingling melody" as "Annabel Lee." The best of the stories seemed to him masterpieces much limited by their constant theme of madness. Poe's madmen, he remarked acutely, were all criminals first, and the supremacy he granted the writer in this region is made to seem almost undesirable in itself. And the criticism? "It was the fashion while Poe lived to call him a critic, a delusion which could never have obtained in any country where the principles of criticism had been studied, and the practice of criticism cultivated." So spoke Nestor, and the fact that he had made an outstanding howler in denying that Poe wrote "Tamerlane" diminished very little the effect of his biography.

George Edward Woodberry, who wrote a biography published in 1885, and then in a much enlarged form in 1909, was a figure even more influential than Stoddard. Woodberry, who also collaborated in producing a ten-volume edition of the works, was a vigorous and intelligent critic, whose general views were of the New England transcendentalist kind that Poe so much disliked. He was a true descendant of Emerson and Lowell, and his subject would certainly have labeled him a Frogpondian. A democrat, and a very conscious rebel, Woodberry can have been drawn to write about Poe only because he was so alien, such a fascinatingly idiosyncratic symptom of a romantic disease. At the time of his first biography, Woodberry thought that "all the documents published by Griswold are genuine and ungarbled," and although he modified this view, he never publicly recanted it. Yet Woodberry was a critic of great perceptiveness, and he tried always to be just. His view was that Poe brought his own fate upon himself, and that no particular attention need be paid to the "idealized legend" built around him. He regarded him as "the son of Coleridge by the weird touch in his imagination, by the principles of his analytic criticism, and the speculative bent of his mind." He was sufficiently a New England moralist to add that "in imagination, as in action, his was an evil genius." Neither Stoddard nor Woodberry mentioned the French view of Poe as a transcendent genius, although Woodberry certainly must have known it.

All this drove Ingram frantic. His involvement with Poe had from the first been emotional as well as scholarly. Two aunts, his father, and one of his sisters had been insane, and although he often asserted his own reasonableness, the attraction held for him by Poe was clearly the fact that the writer moved so often on the edge of reason. He also had something of Poe's touchiness. He had once accused Mrs. Whitman of betraying him by giving material to a rival biographer, he had distressed Annie Richmond by printing some of her letters word for word where she had supposed that he would simply convey the ideas that they contained, he had gathered together the most important Poe collection in the world, he had written the definitive biography, and now here were these Americans borrowing his material but controverting his ideas, and saying (this was Woodberry) that the letters to Annie should not have been printed even while he made extensive use of them.

Passionately and bitterly Ingram attacked the Americans' views and accused them of stealing his materials. The biography published in 1902 by James A. Harrison, professor of history at the University of Virginia, as the first volume in his monumental seventeen-volume edition of the works, was marked, Ingram felt, by Griswoldism. So was Woodberry's two-volume biography of 1909, which was in any case so largely pirated from his own work, Ingram angrily and inaccurately said, that it could not be imported into Britain. Harrison had dared to question Ingram's scholarship, Woodberry to suggest that he had accepted too readily some of the literary ladies' reminiscences. It is true that Woodberry was still in 1909 implicitly a Griswoldian, ignoring the question of forgery which must have been revealed by his own researches, and saying that Griswold's characterization of Poe, "in substance though not in feeling, was the same as that which uniformly prevailed in tradition in the best-

informed literary circles in this country." He added that "the rebirth
of Poe's reputation took place in writers of the next generation."
Ingram believed, to the day of his unnoticed death in 1916, that
Poe had not been given his due.

By the time of the centenary, that rebirth had undoubtedly taken
place. Two hundred and fifty people attended a celebratory dinner
given by the Authors' Club in London. Sir Arthur Conan Doyle
presided, the American ambassador was the guest of honor, and
an Irish member of the family, Captain Poe, had been persuaded
to attend. Conan Doyle was in his bluffest form. Poe had not, he
assured the guests, been of a moping, brooding nature. To the contrary, he had been virile and athletic, a noted runner, swimmer,
and boxer. "He was no milksop or dreamer, but a proper lad of
his hands, full of healthy open-air instincts." He praised particularly
the originality of the tales, and asked: "Where was the detective
story until Poe breathed the breath of life into it?" The American
ambassador, Whitelaw Reid, was not so sure that Poe was free from
morbidity, nor that he was a great writer. Americans would be star-
tled by his European fame, he thought, and might be inclined to
rate Hawthorne, Emerson, or Benjamin Franklin more highly. Like
Conan Doyle, he mentioned Poe's bad luck in his choice of a literary
executor and biographer, and picked out for especial praise Woodberry's biography. Ingram, who was present, must have felt the
knife turn in the wound.

Similar celebrations took place in France and Germany, and in
five American cities—Baltimore, Boston, Philadelphia, Richmond,
and New York. In New York Woodberry addressed the Bronx Society
of Arts and Sciences, and said now much about genius and nothing
about an evil genius. He stressed Poe's poverty, mentioned only
in passing that the tales and poems bore "the legend and superscrip-
tion of pain and death," and praised him for having many friends,
and those friends the best.

The same views were echoed in speeches elsewhere. The Baltimore *Sun* summed up the situation when it printed a large cartoon
showing Uncle Sam carrying a bust of Poe into the Hall of Fame,
with the headline: "Poe *Is* Famous At Last."

PART TWO

THE WORK

THE CRITICISM

Visionary Poe and Logical Poe

POE'S life was one thing, his art another, or so it would seem at first glance. The life was spent in journalism, in producing stories that were written quickly through the need for money, in concocting tricks and hoaxes that would fool the public. Less and less did this life give time for the practice of poetry, yet it was as a poet that he had begun, and as a poet that he always regarded himself.

The pressures of life, then, seem to have crushed the artist. Yet this was not really so. One interest Poe holds for us is that he embodies several contradictions. He was alien to the American literary world, yet at the same time wholeheartedly part of it. The view of him as an orchid growing among cow parsley, a European born in the wrong continent, is not so much wrong as incomplete. He was an orchid, yet he was also very consciously a nineteenth-century American, who approached the problems of art as only an American of his time and place could have done. He is, as Edmund Wilson says, in his ideas a typical early nineteenth-century romantic, "closely akin to his European contemporaries," yet at the same time he adheres to a belief that artistic techniques can be logically and rationally explained, a belief that would have seemed to other romantic artists of the time uninteresting or untrue. He was, as James and Eliot suggested, often sensational, vulgar, provincial with "the provinciality of the person who is not at home where he belongs, but cannot get to anywhere else," yet this very provincial quality (if that is the right name for it) makes his best work uncomfortably memorable. A Poe who had spent his life in Europe would probably have been a mere teller of weird stories. The personal stresses he suffered would have been less extreme, he would have found it easier to make a literary living. It was the American scene Poe viewed with such contempt that helped to make his work unique.

His theory of art is in general that of nineteenth-century romanticism as it was stated by Coleridge. His particular distinction is that he pushed the theory further than Coleridge or any of his contemporaries, British or German. He is the first art for art's saker, a forerunner of Gautier and Walter Pater. From Coleridge Poe adopted the idea of a primary and a secondary imagination, the primary being that of everyday perception, the secondary that which breaks through the crust of the known, visible world into a further range of ideal vision, including poetic vision. He adopted this essential division but put it differently, adding glosses of his own, and drawing from it conclusions that would have astonished Coleridge. His ideas are naturally implicit in much of his criticism, but are made specific in three lectures, *The Philosophy of Composition, The Rationale of Verse* and *The Poetic Principle.* The last of these, which he delivered several times, constitutes his final statement about the nature of poetry.

Poe's version of Coleridge separated what he called the world of mind into three compartments: Pure Intellect, Taste, and Moral Sense.

> I place Taste in the middle because it is just this position which it occupies in the mind. . . . Just as the intellect concerns itself with Truth, so Taste informs us of the Beautiful, while the Moral Sense is regardful of Duty. Of this latter, while Conscience teaches the obligation, and Reason the expediency, Taste contents herself with displaying the charms, waging war upon Vice solely on the ground of her deformity, her disproportion, her animosity to the fitting, to the harmonious, in a word, to Beauty.

Poetry is concerned with our sense of the Beautiful, a sense achieved through Taste, which is the sole arbiter of Poetry. "With the Intellect or with the Conscience, it has only collateral relations. Unless incidentally, it has no concern whatever either with Duty or with Truth."

No other romantic theorist spelled out quite so specifically the conception that poetry existed in a region outside all ordinary human concerns. And Poe offered his own version of Coleridge's view of the secondary imagination by saying that poetry was an attempt to reach beyond this world into the unknown. "Inspired by an ecstatic prescience of the glories beyond the grave, we struggle by multiform combinations among the things and thoughts of Time to attain a portion of that Loveliness whose very elements perhaps appertain to eternity alone." The union of poetry with music was essential, and it was not so much in as *"through* the poem, or *through* the music"* that eternity could be glimpsed.

To this elaboration and enlargement of romantic theory, Poe added the idea that poetry's appeal must be immediate, and that it cannot last long. Poetry had less to do with the mind than with sensation. As early as the introductory letter to the volume of 1831 he had said that poetry was distinguished from science by having pleasure and not truth as its aim, and what he meant by pleasure was something approaching ecstasy. The ecstasy was necessarily transient; it followed that a long poem was a contradiction in terms. "That degree of excitement which would entitle a poem to be so called at all, cannot be sustained throughout a composition of any great length. After the lapse of half an hour, at the very utmost, it flags—fails—a revulsion ensues—and then the poem is, in effect, and in fact, no longer such." *Paradise Lost* was a series of short poems, joined by many tedious passages. *The Iliad* had probably been conceived as a series of lyrics. Poe would no doubt have denied the name of poem to *Don Juan, The Rape of the Lock* and *Hudibras.*

His belief was, then, that through or in poetry one glimpsed a beauty beyond ordinary human conception. The poet experienced, and his reader briefly felt, divine ecstasy—an experience which had little or nothing to do with duty, truth, intellect, conscience. But when such a position has been stated in these extreme terms (such claims were not made by Coleridge), problems arise which Poe was too intelligent to ignore. What was such poetry to have as subject, and in what terms could it be said? A poem uses the resources of language, and language involves meanings which at least imply the existence of qualities he had already dismissed as unpoetic. He opposed eloquently "the heresy of *The Didactic,*" and wrote scornfully about the particularly American and even particularly Bostonian belief that the expression of truth was the ultimate purpose of poetry. Truth, he said, in a brilliant phrase, has no sympathy with the myr-

tles. "In enforcing a truth, we need severity rather than efferves-
cence of language. We must be simple, precise, terse. We must
be cool, calm, unimpassioned. In a word, we must be in that mood
which, as nearly as possible, is the exact converse of the poetical."
If you replaced the idea of a poem that was true, or that inculcated
a moral, or that in some other way was related to ordinary living,
by the "poem *per se,* [the] poem which is a poem and nothing more,
[the] poem written solely for the poem's sake," what in the end
had you got? What would such a poem be about? If you were strictly
logical—and Poe prided himself upon the strictness of his logic—it
would be about nothing at all. From this self-evident absurdity he
sought to escape partly by admitting that what could be called trace
elements of duty, truth, and other aspects of the mind entered into
many fine poems, and also by insisting that originality was one of
a poem's chief virtues. The insistence upon originality, together with
the idea that a poem should be a kind of electric shock, are his
hallmarks as a theorist.

He uses the word "originality" in two different senses. Sometimes
it is in the sense of condemning a writer who is *not* original, who
has copied another. So he said that Mrs. Sigourney had acquired
the title of the American Hemans* "solely by imitation," and observed of his friend Hirst that although he had written some com-
mendable poems, others were marked by "a far more than occasional
imitativeness," which was "a sin in poetry, never to be forgiven."
From the beginning of his critical career, Poe bore down strongly
on this vice. In his first year of reviewing for the *Southern Literary
Messenger* he discovered the spirit of imitation in Kennedy, said
that Bulwer's novels were all echoes of each other, and attacked
a novel on the ground that it had no pretension to originality of
manner or style. Sometimes, as in the Longfellow controversy, he
accused other writers of actual plagiarism, occasionally from his own
work. Often these accusations were made on the slightest ground
or on no ground at all, like his suggestion that Elizabeth Barrett's
"Lady Geraldine's Courtship" was "a very palpable imitation" of
"Locksley Hall." This concern with plagiarism no doubt sprang
partly from his own inclination to pick up poetic rhythms and fictional themes from other writers, as well as from the actual plagiar-

* Mrs. Hemans, who wrote "The Boy Stood on the Burning Deck," was
highly regarded as a poet.

ism (that is, the large chunks lifted almost verbatim from other writers) in which he often indulged. But he called for originality in another, positive, sense. He believed that there were new themes to be discovered, new rhythms and metrical combinations to be used, and in this belief he was forever crying "Make it new!" with an enthusiasm like that of the young Ezra Pound. The object of poetry might be the expression of supernal loveliness, but Poe sharply distinguished here between ends and means. The means by which poetic effects were obtained should be defined and organized as closely as possible.

It would be an exaggeration to say that his attitude toward the purpose of poetry was European-romantic and his approach to the way of writing it American-materialist, but an exaggeration that held a basic truth. He had a concern with the means of doing things— extending from cryptography, criminal puzzles, and mechanical chess players to the forms of art—which is clearly linked with the development of American technology. Part of Poe wished to preserve poetry as a sacred mystery; another part wanted to demonstrate that the whole thing was a technical problem, which could be solved as one solves a cryptogram. These two parts might be termed Visionary Poe and Logical Poe.

It was Visionary Poe who conceived the poems, but Logical Poe who wrote them. Most of the horrific stories are the work of Visionary Poe, but the detective stories and the hoaxes belong to Logical Poe. For Visionary Poe, any art worth the name was in search of something different from, and finer than, ordinary reality. Logical Poe, however, believed that all literary effects were explicable, and that by the exercise of logic you could take a work of literature apart like a clock, and see how it functioned. In the struggle between Visionary and Logical Poe, and the fusion between them, rests the fascination of his personality and his art.

The most extreme theoretical approach of Logical Poe to art was made in the analysis of "The Raven" in *The Philosophy of Composition,* and of versification and prosody in *The Rationale of Verse.* This latter essay was probably completed in 1847, and was an enlargement of a piece written some years earlier. Logical Poe made a bluff, no-nonsense approach, saying that the subject of versification had been dealt with formerly in terms of "inaccuracy, confusion, misconception, misrepresentation, mystification, and downright ig-

norance, whereas in fact it was all very simple," and "included within
the limits of the commonest common sense." His knockabout attack
on previous analysts of versification is always enjoyable but at no
point convincing. His conclusions are often, and unusually, crude,
as in his brisk disposal of argument about long and short syllables.
"In general, a syllable is long or short, just as it is difficult or easy
of enunciation. The *natural* long syllables are those encumbered—
the *natural* short syllables are those *un*encumbered, with conso-
nants." Accented syllables, he observes casually, "are of course always long." The essay has been attacked by many, most effectively
by Yvor Winters, and has found almost no defenders. Logic of this
kind was not a scalpel suitable for cutting away to reveal the heart
of a poem, as is made even more evident in *The Philosophy of
Composition,* which appeared in 1846.

In a letter Poe called this essay his best specimen of analysis,
and there seems no justification for suggesting as some critics have
done that the piece was a hoax, any more than one can reasonably
call "The Raven" a hoax. Poe's statement of his intention is unequivo-
cal, and is made with the rawness that prompted both James and
Eliot to call him provincial:

> It is my design to render it manifest that no point in its compo-
> sition is referable either to accident or intuition—that the work pro-
> ceeded step by step, to its completion with the precision and rigid
> consequences of a mathematical problem.

The problem? To compose a poem that should "suit at once
the popular and the critical taste." Length? We know that a long
poem is not a poem at all, and around a hundred lines is settled
on. Next, the tone. To be universally appreciated, it must aim at
Beauty. What is the *tone* of Beauty's highest manifestation? One
of sadness, so the poem must be sad. It needs a keynote, which
will be in the form of a refrain. This will be repeated in each stanza,
and so should be short and forceful. It should also be sonorous. What
vowel is more sonorous than "o," what consonant can be better
linked to it than "r"? We are led quickly to "Nevermore," and since
repetition of this by a human being would be unreasonable, a non-
reasoning creature is indicated. A parrot perhaps? No, a raven,
"equally capable of speech, and infinitely more in keeping with
the intended *tone."* We have now a length, a tone and a refrain,

but still lack a subject. What is the most melancholy topic? Death. And when is death most poetical? When it is linked to Beauty. The demonstration is complete: "The death then of a beautiful woman is unquestionably the most poetical topic in the world." With all this settled, we move to the versification. "My first object (as usual) was originality . . ."

One may mercifully abstain from following Poe into his attempt to show that "nothing ever remotely approaching" his combination of meters and rhythms in "The Raven" had been attempted before. It has been said that the poem was not actually written in the way described, but although this may be true it is beside the point. The worst thing about the essay is that it should have been written at all, that Poe could have thought that readers would be impressed by such an account of a poem's purely mechanical creation and construction. But he saw no contradiction between the conception of poetry as divine ecstasy, and the idea that rules for producing the ecstasy could be laid down. Like much of his theory, *The Philosophy of Composition* reasons back from effect to cause. It tells us nothing about the process of artistic creation, but does say something about Poe's view of art. He often started poems and stories from the desire to say something inexpressible, and had then to look for a logical justification and form for its expression. Although he detested what one critic has called the parvenu industrialism and the doctrine of progress that were emerging as major aspects of American life, they still influenced him.

As an artist he was often damaged by this dichotomy between Visionary and Logical Poe. As a critic, however, he positively gained depth and subtlety in viewing other writers by tempering a constant view of the ideal with an equally constant view of his society's materialism. His critical achievement was based on finding a balance between the two, so that romantic perceptiveness and idealism were streaked always with a vein of severe commonsense. The combination of these qualities made him the first great American literary critic.

Cutting a Dash

Any reader of Poe's criticism, coming to it after the stories and poems, is likely to be surprised by its exuberance and unbuttoned freedom. This is true particularly of the work he did for the *Southern Literary Messenger* when he came to it as a young man of twenty-six. Logical Poe was in command, taking poems to pieces to show that they did not work, analyzing dismal books in deadly detail, speaking sometimes with impressive passion and at others with a tolerant playfulness only evident in his criticism and journalism.

The review of *Norman Leslie* has already been mentioned on page 56. Another example of this vein is one of the first reviews he wrote. The book is the anonymous *Confessions of a Poet,* and Poe begins by saying that "the most remarkable feature in this production is the bad paper on which it is printed, and the typographical ingenuity with which matter barely enough for one volume has been spread over the pages of two." The conclusion is:

> The author avers upon his word of honor that in commencing this work he loads a pistol, and places it upon the table. He farther states that, upon coming to a conclusion, it is his intention to blow out what he supposes to be his brains. Now this is excellent. But, even with so rapid a writer as the poet must undoubtedly be, there would be some little difficulty in completing the book under thirty days or thereabouts. The best of powder is apt to sustain injury by lying so long "in the load." We sincerely hope the gentleman took the precaution to examine his priming before attempting the rash act. A flash in the pan—and in such a case—were a thing to be lamented.

This is Poe at his most brutally jocose. It is not surprising that such reviews should have set people asking the name of their writer. They were written, of course, with that intention. Such coat-trailing is less evident in later reviews, but he was capable at any time of excoriating most woundingly work he thought wretchedly bad, as in his remarks about a poem called *Wakondah* by a New York literary man Cornelius Mathews. After much detailed technical criticism of versification and images the poem is characterized as trash, a mere jumble of incongruous nonsense and twaddling verbiage.

This acerbity was the aspect of Poe's criticism that attracted most attention, but in fact such outright denunciation was rare. It was much more common for him to offer a close, and at the time very unusual, textual analysis of a poem or novel, and then to pronounce judgment in terms which made an attempt at balance, although they perhaps did not please the author. In a long review of the Southern writer William Gilmore Simms, the author is attacked for his bad grammar, wretched taste, and inaccurate use of language. Some of the criticisms are trivial, but the accumulation of them is extremely damaging, and the conclusion that "In spite, however, of its manifest and manifold blunders and impertinences, 'The Partisan' is no ordinary work" will hardly have given much comfort. But Simms did not take offense, and much later, in his "Marginalia," Poe said that if one forgot Brockden Brown and Hawthorne, Simms was "immeasurably the best writer of fiction in America."

The critical ideas already outlined can be found behind almost every long article, and because they apply to poetry more easily than to prose, Poe was happier in writing of poets than novelists. Poetry was more easily susceptible to line-by-line analysis, and the best of his early criticism is relentlessly analytical. Joseph Rodman Drake's reputation in particular could hardly survive Poe's detailed examination of phrases and stanzas in terms of their absurdity, his adroit parody of one stanza, and his remark that "a thousand such lines may be composed without exercising in the least degree the Poetic Sentiment, which is Ideality, Imagination, or the creative ability." A similar, although much more friendly, analysis of Bryant was one of the last pieces he wrote for the *Messenger*. These two articles helped to make his critical reputation, and they were outside the range of any other American critic of the time in their detailed analysis, their intense energy, and their frequent reference back to first principles. He was inflexibly romantic, dismissing the *Essay on Man* as an "Essay in Rhyme," and regarding Donne and Cowley as crude writers lacking in art. These early reviews cut a dash, but they did something more. They stated a critical position with a firmness and clarity unmatched by any other writer of the time.

Poe and American Literature

Poe was unique in the attention he paid to American literature as something different from that written in English on the other side of the Atlantic. He had been from youth an eager and admiring reader of British magazines, especially *Blackwood's, Fraser's,* and the *Edinburgh Review.* The tone of authority, the easy colloquialism and bantering dismissiveness of *Blackwood's* in particular was something that in his early days as a critic he tried to take for his own. His air was by intention that of a British critic sympathizing with his American cousins for their rustic ignorance—and yet he was aware of being an American cousin himself, so that seriousness kept breaking in. He often deplored the inferiority of American literature, and still more the complacency with which many of his fellow countrymen regarded their own ignorance. The beginning of the Drake-Halleck review already quoted is a typical example. His attitude to American fiction was similar. When, in 1837, he praised Judge Beverley Tucker's *George Balcombe* as upon the whole the best American novel, he added: "we still do not wish to be misunderstood as ranking it with the more brilliant fiction of some of the living novelists of Great Britain." As a literary people, he said on another occasion, Americans were "one vast perambulating humbug." Criticism was corrupt, the relations between critic and publisher consisting often of "a direct system of petty and contemptible bribery." Reputations were made by puffing, but nobody took them seriously. As for the quarterly reviews, "who but an ass will put faith in tirades which *may* be the result of personal hostility, or in panegyrics which nine times out of ten may be laid, directly or indirectly, to the charge of the author himself?" If one believed the puffers the whole American atmosphere was redolent of genius, filled with magnificent poets and novelists; but everybody knew that this was not so. "It cannot be gainsaid that the greater number of those who hold high places in our poetical literature are absolute nincompoops," and the best he could find to say about his contemporaries on this occasion was that "Mr. Bryant is not *all* a fool. Mr. Willis not *quite* an ass. Mr. Longfellow *will* steal, but perhaps he cannot help it."

What was the extent of American talent? Poe admitted that there were in the country poets of the loftiest order, although he insisted: "we do *not* believe that these poets are Drake and Halleck," and found it hard to name them. Bryant, he said, was preeminent only in minor merits and was not comparable with the best living British poets. Longfellow was granted a vivid imagination and some ability, but he lacked "combining or building force" and had "absolutely nothing of unity," even if one ignored his tendency to plagiarism. Lowell was entitled to second or third place (or even, he suggested at another time, to first) among American poets, but he had an imperfect ear for rhythm, and possessed less artistic ability than some others.

There were occasions when he took a different line, complaining that Americans had unjustly been called an unpoetical people because they had proved themselves so adept in the arts and sciences of promoting material comfort. As he wittily observed: "Our necessities have been mistaken for our propensities. Having been forced to make railroads, it has been deemed impossible that we should make verse." But this was an expression of optimism rather than a claim for the greatness of any actual American literature. He said often that his countrymen had been overpraised, and he wrote about none of them in the terms he kept for Tennyson, Elizabeth Barrett or Dickens. The driving force of his criticism was directed toward the creation of standards which should not be lower than those of the best English periodicals. It was for this that *The Penn* and *The Stylus* were to be founded, to look at books as works of art rather than as histories or moralities or works of philosophy. The division he saw between the journalist and the critic was that the journalist might turn aside to discuss the opinions expressed in a book or to gossip about the author. The critic was concerned only with *"the mode* in which these opinions are brought to bear," and the word "criticism" could only properly be used of works that were in the first place artistic products rather than vehicles for the expression of opinion. Not all, or most, of Poe's own reviewing passed this test; but then, few of the books he wrote about could be seriously considered as artistic products. His accounts of them were designed to sweep away bad books and poems, and by extension to show the nature of good ones. Such reviews provided the entertainment that he thought it necessary to offer readers, but these destructive analyses of forgotten writers were not by his own standard criticism. When his sympathy was fully engaged, he produced work that was extraordinary in its perceptiveness.

Critical Samples

Many of the destructive analyses were remarkable performances. The consistency of Poe's attitude, and the way in which he referred back always to general principles, make his writing illuminate always something more than the work under discussion. The Drake-Halleck article contains a brilliant early statement of his attitude, a piece on the "National Melodies of America" expresses a view about the necessary mystic indeterminateness of music which is upon the whole clearer than anything he said later on the subject. Such instances could be multiplied. But his writing had its greatest impact where the subject was worth the intense attention he gave it, in the articles about Hawthorne, Dickens and Elizabeth Barrett. It is significant that only one of these was an American writer.

Poe wrote twice at length about Hawthorne, in 1842 and in almost his last serious critical article five years later. He felt that there was an occasional lack of originality in Hawthorne's themes, and was unable to refrain from the suggestion that one Hawthorne story contained "something which resembles plagiarism" from his own *William Wilson*. But his appreciation of a writer at this time little regarded by other critics was otherwise unstinting. "He has the purest style, the finest taste, the most available scholarship, the most delicate humor, the most touching pathos, the most radiant imagination, the most consummate ingenuity": and he picked out for special attention Hawthorne's quietly melancholy tone. He sensed also the limitations of the writer whom he called "the truest genius, upon the whole, which our literature possesses"—in a certain lack of vital energy, and an insistence upon allegory. Poe viewed other writers very often in terms of his own artistic ambitions, but although there is an element of special pleading for his own work in his insistence on the importance for the story writer of the "single effect" that he thought so vital in poetry, what he says applies wonderfully well to Hawthorne.

"Mr. Bulwer, through art, has almost created a genius. Mr. Dickens, through genius, has perfected a standard from which Art itself will derive its essence, its rules," he wrote in 1841, in comparing *The Old Curiosity Shop* with such a book as *Night and Morning*. He recognized that Dickens's character was in some ways similar to his own. (It could be said that Dickens presented in his art the manic and Poe the depressive side of a personality.) In an early, short review of *The Pickwick Papers* Poe picked out "A Madman's MS" for special praise, and almost every aspect of Dickens appealed to him, the horrific, the sentimental and the detective. He was, with some justice, pleased with himself for having discovered the principal deception in *Barnaby Rudge* when the book was appearing in serial form, although he was critical of the way in which Dickens deceived the reader. His complaint that the author may give the reader false information through the mouth of a character, but must not do so in his own person, was a forerunner of the detective story reader's insistence on "fair play." It is interesting, in view of his own stories of crime and mystery, that Poe deprecated Dickens's deception. "That this fiction, or indeed that any fiction written by Mr. Dickens, should be based in the excitement and maintenance of curiosity we look upon as a misconception, on the part of the writer, of his own very great yet very peculiar powers." He thought *The Old Curiosity Shop* a masterpiece, to which he granted even originality, as well as a "chaste, vigorous, and glorious imagination." He regarded *Barnaby Rudge* as a much inferior work, and put his objections in forceful detail. But with Poe as with Dr. Johnson, the value of the criticism is bound up with the struggle to see another artist through his own beliefs, and it is not important whether he is "right" or "wrong." Poe's view of Dickens is unique in its insights because his interpretation was so wholly individual. It remains memorable when fifty conventionally well-ordered pieces have been forgotten.

The deadly literalness that he could bring to reviewing, in particular to the reviewing of poetry, is shown by his comment on four lines by Elizabeth Barrett which another American critic had been unwise enough to call faultless and sublime:

> Hear the steep generations how they fall
> Adown the visionary stairs of Time,
> Like supernatural thunders—far yet near,
> Sowing their fiery echoes through the hills!

The paragraph of comment is very effective:

> Now here, saying nothing of the affectation in "adown"; not alluding to the insoluble paradox of "far yet near"; not mentioning the inconsistent metaphor involved in the sowing of fiery echoes; adverting but slightly as to the misuse of "like" in place of "as"; and to the impropriety of making anything fall like *thunder*, which has never been known to fall at all; merely hinting, too, at the misapplication of "steep" to the "generations" instead of to the "stairs"—(a perversion in no degree justified by the fact that so preposterous a figure

as *synechdoche* exists in the school-books:)—letting these things pass, we shall still find it difficult to understand how Miss Barrett should have been led to think the principle [sic] idea itself—the abstract idea—the idea of *tumbling down stairs,* in any shape, or under any circumstance—either a poetical or a decorous conception.

Did Logical Poe, the genial butcher, disapprove of Mrs. Browning? It would be reasonable to think so. In an essay of nearly ten thousand words on her *Drama of Exile and Other Poems* the butcher is at work for much of the time, discovering "a very palpable *bull"* in the opening of the title poem, making a glancing contemptuous comparative reference to Milton, complaining of the "unquestionably many, and generally inexcusable" affectations like 'ware, 'bide, and 'gins (aware, abide, begins) and of a far-fetchedness of imagery "reprehensible in the extreme," and her fondness for pet words like "down" and "leaning."

It comes as a surprise near the end of the essay to read: "That Miss Barrett has done more, in poetry, than any other woman, living or dead, will scarcely be questioned." There follow three pages of panegyric, rather praising what Elizabeth Barrett might have written than what she had actually produced. After the early part of the essay, this is at first bewildering. What has happened? Visionary Poe has emerged, to offer a view of the perfect poem embodying "the Shelleyan *abandon,* the Tennysonian poetic sense, the most profound instinct of Art, and the sternest Will properly to blend and vigorously to control all," and to say that Elizabeth Barrett might have written this poem, if only she had not been "contaminated by pedantic study of false models" and "seduced into the art of imitation." Visionary Poe was always ready to praise noble intentions. Logical Poe was never prepared to let slovenly execution go unremarked.

One must look at the other reviewing face of Poe. His readiness to do some of the puffing that he condemned has already been suggested. He was capable of wretched things, like telling Cornelius Mathews that his own savagely executed destruction of Mathews's poem was an "impudent and flippant critique" done by somebody else. One of the worst instances of this double dealing occurred in relation to Griswold. Poe's change of mind above the merits of *The Poets and Poetry of America* has been noted; but in 1843, after being replaced by Griswold at *Graham's,* he wrote in the Philadelphia

Saturday Museum the most vitriolic review that ever came from his pen. Its authorship was anonymous, but internal evidence shows that it was certainly inspired by Poe, even though his friend Henry Hirst may have done some of the writing. At the beginning the reviewer asks the purely formal question whether Griswold is "the man of varied talents, of genius, of known skill, of overweening intellect, he was somewhere pictured, or is he the arrant literary quack he is now entitled by the American press?" The answer is that Griswold is as ignorant of poetry as a Kickapoo Indian, and that his book must be subject to "unqualified condemnation" for its toadying tone and the utter incompetence in selection. Those omitted "should be gratified at their non-appearance in the volume before us, for if ever such a thing as literary ruin existed, or exists, nine-tenths of the *Poets* (!) of America are ruined forever by the praise of Mr. Griswold!" Nothing can excuse what was done by Griswold to Poe, but he certainly had cause to be offended. And Poe repeated part of the attack in one of his lectures.

That is the darkest face of Poe as critic; but he was liable also to overpraise wildly, especially when writing about those poetesses to whose charms he was susceptible. He seems at times to have been overwhelmed by the masses of material passing for poetry that came into his hands, and to have adopted the attitude of the regular novel reviewer who abandons the standards with which he started and greets ecstatically the best book that has come his way in the past month. Poe knew very well the worth, or worthlessness, of the ladies who sat at his feet while he talked, and conveyed that they understood perfectly his poetic susceptibilities because they were poets too. Perhaps it is asking too much of humanity to expect that he should have stated his views outright. He twisted about in dealing with their work, making a cunning qualification here and putting in a note of deprecation there, so that praise was never total. Fanny Osgood was wonderfully tasteful, and had "a happy refinement—an exquisite instinct of the pure—the delicate—the graceful," but "we should not venture to speak of her as the equal of Mrs. Maria Brooks in imagination and vigor, nor of Mrs. Amelia Welby in passionate tenderness and rhythmical skill." Mrs. Welby, although she lacked originality—a quality despised only by "the chlorine critics (the grass-green)"—had all the passion of Mrs. Norton, with a nicer ear. Mrs. Norton now, who was she? None other than, since the death of Mrs. Hemans, the Queen of English song. But by some ingenious sidestepping, Mrs. Norton is compared with Mrs. Hemans so that pros are made to balance cons. ("There are passages in some of her poems of greater power than any passages of like length in Mrs. Hemans' writings, though at the same time there are a far greater number of inferior lines.") He never wrote about Mrs. Whitman, but one may be sure that he would have been similarly dexterous in dealing with her.

Poe's Quality as Critic

Such waywardness says little more than that Poe was a flawed human being. The quality of his best criticism is unaffected by it. If one were asked why a selection from his six volumes of criticism would be valuable today, the answer would lie in the power generated by that conflict between Visionary Poe and Logical Poe. Many of the serious reviews are prefaced by a general statement of attitude. The statements are sometimes repetitive—for instance, the passage about truth's lack of sympathy with the myrtles used in *The Poetic Principle* appeared first some years earlier in a review of Longfellow's *Ballads*—but the total effect is to offer a view of art that is valuable through its very limitations. Poe never falters in his opposition to didacticism, and to morality as a suitable end for poetry. The conclusions he draws from his premises may sometimes seem to us absurd, as when he distinguishes "The Village Blacksmith" and "The Wreck of the Hesperus" as nearly excellent poems, yet his insistence on the Ideal and the Beautiful is permanently valuable. He pushes everything through further than other romantic critics, and his practice takes his theories to their relevant end. To ask as he does: "Might not this matter be as well or better handled in *prose?*" and to say that if it might, then it was no subject for poetry, may appear too simplistic, but its results provide many fine insights.

Visionary Poe would not be half so effective without the help of Logical Poe. What might, in the article on Longfellow, be no more than the statement of a position, is transformed by Logical Poe into a damaging technical attack done in terms of versification, with a remarkable distinction made between natural and artificial spondees. There is no close link between the theoretical condemnation of didacticism and the technical examination of Longfellow's verse, yet the two do complement each other. Poe did not speak the last word on Longfellow or on any other writer, but what he said was put always in wholly distinctive terms.

This means that as a critic he was often wayward, but never dull. In reading Johnson on Shakespeare one is not concerned with the abstract justice of his assessment so much as the impact made by the great plays upon a mind of wonderful weight and power. Poe is representative of a strain in nineteenth-century thinking, as Johnson was of the eighteenth. Like a true nineteenth-century American he is fascinated by anything new, from methods of printing to scientific theories, from travelers' discoveries to theories of grammar. He has an opinion about everything. About phrenology, for instance, which, again like a true nineteenth-century man, he thinks, "as a science, ranks among the most important which can engage the attention of thinking beings." Or about education, in relation to which he recommends the establishment in Virginia of district schools like those in New England. Or about slavery, where he puts his faith in "a degree of loyal devotion on the part of the slave to which the white man is a stranger, and of the master's reciprocal feeling of parental attachment to his humble dependant." As a critic he can be seen at his most characteristic, genial, ebullient, and unbuttoned—or if you dislike him, at his most maddeningly dogmatic and pretentious—in the "Marginalia" that he contributed to various magazines in the last six years of his life.

Two or three samples of these "Marginalia" will serve as a taste. One can hardly say that they give the flavor, for any selection of quotations would give different flavors, and I have chosen extracts of a very few lines, which hardly represent the frequent passages covering two or three pages:

> The drugging system, in medical practice, seems to me to be a modification of the idea of *penance,* which has haunted the world since its infancy—the idea that the voluntary endurance of pain is atonement for sin. . . . How else shall we account for the fact, that in ninety-nine cases out of a hundred, the articles of Materia Medica are distasteful?

> I have not the slightest faith in Carlyle. In ten years—possibly in five—he will be remembered only as a butt for sarcasm. His linguistic Euphuisms might very well have been taken as prima facie evidence of his philosophic ones; they were the froth which indicated, first, the shallowness, and secondly, the confusion of the waters.

I believe that Hannibal passed into Italy over the Pennine Alps;
and if Livy were living now, I could demonstrate this fact even to
him.

But really the "Marginalia" need to be read as they were printed,
as passages in a magazine, to produce their full effect. In the first
selection, for example, Poe rambles around the pleasures of marginal
jottings, with references to Bentham, Mill, Jeremy Taylor, Sir
Thomas Browne, melancholy Burton, and half a dozen others; offers
a note on Oriental Literature, a comment on Shelley, a jocular reference to Puseyism, a joke about authors, a sharp rebuke for theorists
who talk of man in his "natural state," a couple of paragraphs about
the "idiosyncras in the Divine system of adaptation"—and we are
as yet hardly a third of the way through. Some of the "Marginalia"
were lifted wholesale or adapted from other writers, some were
his own, some were fragments of old reviews reshaped.

It is good to be reminded that this is what Poe was like, or what
part of him was like. He was a wonderfully quick, intelligent and
perceptive man, with a butterfly mind that never rested for long
on a subject. He could write amusingly, provocatively and subtly
about anything, but the "Marginalia" suggest one reason for his
inability to earn a journalistic living. He intended to write down
to the level of his readers, yet rarely managed it. Profundity and
scholarship kept breaking in, and whether the scholarship was genuine or borrowed made little difference to readers of the *Democratic
Review, Godey's Lady's Book* or *Graham's,* for it was all above their
heads anyway. In the attempt to raise the standard of what they
would accept, he was prepared to wear a false nose and be verbally
outrageous like any other clown. His varied and acute criticism was
a crusade for the education of the public as well as a means of
keeping alive.

The crusade did not succeed, and Poe's full intentions were understood by only a few of his contemporaries. But if he had succeeded in founding *The Stylus* in the early 1840s when his mind
was unclouded and his powers undiminished, there can be no doubt
that it would have been one of the memorable magazines in literary
history. The existence of such a periodical would have influenced
a whole generation of American writers. Lowell observed that if
Poe had controlled a magazine he would have been as autocratic

as Christopher North, but added that his criticism would have been far more philosophical and profound. He also commented, in an expressive phrase, that "[Poe] has squared out blocks enough to build an enduring pyramid, but has left them lying carelessly and unclaimed in many different quarries." What Lowell said remains good today. In particular, the handful of essays which treat their subjects at length are almost all of them memorable and permanently valuable. They are the best possible tribute to Logical Poe.

THE POEMS

The Early Poems

POE'S aesthetic theories originated in relation to poetry, although they were extended to prose fiction. He regarded himself as a poet throughout his life. In fact, however, he had published most of his poetry by 1831, when he was twenty-two years old. His fragment of a verse play, *Politian,* was probably written a year or two later, and only a few poems appeared in the following decade. In the last five years of his life, with his critical career almost extinguished, he turned again to poetry. It was in this time that he published "The Raven," "Ulalume," "The Bells," and "Annabel Lee," which are among his most popular poems, although they are not necessarily those most highly regarded. The poems all together do not make a bulky volume.

They fall naturally into two groups. The poems up to and including the 1831 volume are very much in the manner of the English romantic poets of the period. Coleridge is the most marked influence, but Wordsworth, Moore, Shelley and Byron are also often echoed in versification and imagery. The most important of the later poems are still romantic, but in a different way. Their tone is much more gloomy, they are directly concerned with death and personal loss, and they consciously exemplify, as the early poems do not, the theories put forward in *The Rationale of Verse.*

The central figure of the early poems is the standard romantic hero of the period in his loneliness and his melancholy. A typical verse from the 1827 volume runs:

The happiest day—the happiest hour
    My sear'd and blighted heart hath known,
The highest hope of pride, and power,
    I feel hath flown.

The poet feels a tremulous delight in the terror of the lone lake,
his "aching sight" sees the beauty of the girl he loves on her bridal
day, he finds happiness only in dreams, and such dreams belong
to the night so that he has no cheerful prospects in the daytime.
"A waking dream of life and light/Hath left me broken-hearted."
The poem is generally taken to refer to Elmira Royster's marriage,
but its sorrows appear conventional. The lengthy "Tamerlane" is
again based on the end of Poe's affair with Elmira and the abrupt
termination of his university career, but it is the stock figure of
the romantic hero who comes through in the four hundred lines.
The loss of Elmira and the battle with John Allan have been trans-
muted into terms that do not seem deeply felt, only thoroughly
conventional:

I reach'd my home—my home no more—
For all was flown that made it so—
I pass'd from out its mossy door,
In vacant idleness of woe.

There is little to say about the poems up to and including the
1831 volume in a technical sense, except that they are obviously
and uninterestingly derivative. "Tamerlane" and "Al Aaraaf" are
remarkable productions for a young man in his teens, but in the
nineteenth century youthful poets were not exceptional. Kirke
White, who died when he was eighteen, left behind a bigger volume
of poems than Poe, and the American sisters Margaret Miller and
Lucretia Maria Davidson, who both died at sixteen, were much more
prolific. (Margaret wrote a poem of two thousand lines called "Lenore," which attracted Poe's attention.) Among the poems in the
1831 volume, "To Helen" is a famous lyric, and "The City in the
Sea" is perhaps the most effective of Poe's nightmare landscapes,
yet it remains true, as W. H. Auden has said, that the first might
have been written by Landor and the second by Hood. Indeed,
there is hardly a poem of this period which might not easily be
attributed to another poet in terms of diction and rhythm. These
poems are not, in his favorite word, original.

It seems likely that Poe was aware of this. He constantly revised both poems and stories, and his object in revising poems was almost always to make them more musical, more profound, and—since he felt that lack of close definition was in itself a mark of poetic quality—less defined and more ambiguous. The process can be seen at its most successful in "The City in the Sea," which had its origin in the common nineteenth-century theme of a ruined sunken city. If one compares the 1831 version, which was called "The Doomed City," with the final 1845 version, the textually slight changes are all improvements, in the sense that they give us more of what Poe wanted to express in poetry. In the most notable change,

> Up many a melancholy shrine
> Whose entablatures intertwine
> The mask—the viol—and the vine

becomes

> Up many and many a marvellous shrine
> Whose wreathed friezes intertwine
> The viol, the violet, and the vine.

Is that extra alliterative "v" too much? For Poe nothing could be too much, and in this case at least few would disagree with him. Elsewhere in the poem the repetition of two fine lines, "Resignedly beneath the sky/The melancholy waters lie," is peculiarly appropriate to the passive tone. The slightly anodyne last couplet of the original version has been omitted, and single lines have been changed to make them run more smoothly. "Yet tho' no holy rays come down" and "Light from the lurid, deep sea" (a line sufficiently awkward, in its demand that "lurid" shall be given three syllables, to cast doubt on Poe's claim to a perfect ear) are changed to "No rays from the holy heaven come down" and "But light from out the lurid sea." Even changes in single words are helpful, like that from "all alone" to "lying alone" in the second line of the poem.

"The City in the Sea" is the finest of these early poems; if Hood had written it, he would not have brought to the theme the same intensity of feeling, the sense of something important that remains unsaid. Yet even in its final version, the one known to almost all readers, the poem conveys a sensation rather than an experience, and the profundity claimed for it by some critics does not exist.

The successive titles Poe used, "The Doomed City," "The City of Sin," and "The City in the Sea. A Prophecy," make it plain that he had in mind a real city, a kind of watery Gomorrah. To say, as one commentator does, that "it is the symbol of the soul's temporary quiet after death before it begins to sink into oblivion, which is symbolized by the sea," or as others have it, that it is "a picture of the death of the soul, brought on by sin," or "the fact or actuality of the past," is to obscure the reality of the poem.

Such obscurity is almost habitual for critics of Poe, who are more interested in analyzing the symbolism they discover in his work than in discussing the work as it lies on the page. "Al Aaraaf," his longest poem, which was published in the 1829 volume but may have been written two or three years earlier, is a confused, pompous (in its frequent footnotes), and feeble piece of romantic rhetoric about the relationship of God and man, a Coleridgean fag end. Its obscurity, however, has made it a wonderful feeding ground for American critics. They have discovered that it is "the romantic process of the soul's rediscovery of its original being" (Edward H. Davidson), or that the poem's plan "might be illustrated by a chart of the stellar universe, with three slight modifications" (Floyd Stovall, who devotes twenty-odd pages to interpreting the poem), or that it is a fable "about the wholly aesthetic conception of ideality and of an afterlife in which participation in that ideality is possible" (Daniel Hoffman). Any of these views may be right—indeed, all of them may be—but they say nothing about the work as a *poetic* structure, being concerned instead with the ideas moving around in Poe's mind at the time it was written.

"Al Aaraaf" is the first product of Visionary Poe, in its suggestion that human knowledge and indeed human living are incomplete. The great Poe scholar Thomas Ollive Mabbott summed up the ideas behind the poem admirably when he said that for Poe, in "Al Aaraaf": "Beauty is the sole object of poetry. Nesace is Beauty, Ligeia is Harmony, and through them the Will of God, or Truth, is imaginatively communicated to us, who are lacking in the complete knowledge given only to angels." All this was what Poe meant to communicate through the parable of a star which "burst forth, in a moment, with a splendor surpassing that of Jupiter" and then became forever invisible to the human eye. But when we turn from such abstract profundities to the work itself, it is to see them find expression in such mock-Miltonic and mock-romantic terms as

> The Sephalica, budding with young bees,
> Uprear'd its purple stem around her knees:
> And gemmy flower, of Trebizond misnam'd—
> Inmate of highest stars, where erst it sham'd
> All other loveliness: its honied dew
> (The fabled nectar that the heathen knew)
> Deliriously sweet, was dropp'd from Heaven,
> And fell on gardens of the unforgiven
> In Trebizond . . .

Poe the critic would have enjoyed himself in revealing the borrowings here, which are particularly from Coleridge. He would have noticed also the stiffness and feebleness of the verse, and the way in which it seems to be dealing in stage properties rather in anything known and seen. The passage quoted is typical. Elsewhere, within a few lines there are mossy springs, mountain crags, solemn skies, and starry worlds. How can a poem written in such language be taken seriously, no matter what its theme?

And nobody would take it seriously, if Poe had not produced other work. If he had died in 1831, with most of his poems but almost none of his stories or criticism written, he might be represented in a few anthologies by "To Helen" and "The City in the Sea," nothing more.

Originality, Its Perils and Rewards

There must have been times when Poe felt that many of the poems he had written as a young man were not original, that their rhythms were too much in debt particularly to Byron and Moore. In his three important later poems, "The Raven," "Ulalume" and "The Bells," Logical Poe came to the aid of Visionary Poe. His aesthetic beliefs did not change, but the expression of them was ordered by the theories that Logical Poe had worked out. Whatever else may be said about these three later poems, to which "Lenore" and "Annabel Lee" might be added, they are original to Poe in the sense that nobody else could have written them.

He revised these poems with even greater care than he had given to the earlier ones. There are eleven different versions of "Lenore," which was first published in 1843. "The Raven" varies still more, and even "Ulalume" and "The Bells," which were written within a fairly short time of his death, exist in several versions. Some of the versions differ only by a few words, but often the variations are important. Poe experimented continually to try to achieve new effects, and he was interested particularly in the difference made by changing the lengths of lines. There is a short line, or half-line, version of "The Raven," as well as of "Lenore." In his awareness of the importance of the form that lines of poetry take on a page, he was quite alone in his time.

> And, Guy de Vere,
> Hast *thou* no tear?
>   Weep now or nevermore!
> See, on yon drear
> And rigid bier,
>   Low lies thy love Lenore!

is textually identical with the later version, which takes two lines instead of six, but the later one has to be read differently, with a rapid flow replacing the line-end pauses:

> And, Guy de Vere, hast *thou* no tear?—weep now or never more!
> See! on yon drear and rigid bier low lies thy love, Lenore!

These may well be thought two of the most ludicrous lines in English poetry—to an English reader the name "Guy de Vere" is particularly risible—and such determined efforts to be original waver always on the edge of the absurd. Poe was nervously aware from the first that "The Raven" might not be taken seriously, and there is certainly something comic about the feminine internal rhymes and the repeated "Nevermore." "Ulalume" seems similarly an exercise in versification and "The Bells," as Auden says, an excuse for onomatopoeic effects. All attempt to give poetry the quality of music, as Poe conceived music to be. But poems do not survive for more than a century simply as jokes, and their first fame as poems supremely suitable for reading aloud has long since faded. "The Raven" and "Ulalume," at least, triumph over their parodists and over such ingenious critics as Aldous Huxley, who arranged a few lines of Milton as Poe might have written them to show the absurdity of his rhythms.

The thumping rhymes and rhythms add something nightmarish to the effect of these poems. Because they are so theatrical, they

actually convey a feeling of the narrator's passion and pain. It is a
theatrical passion, to be sure, and belongs to a Victorian tradition
of exaggeration; but its strength is undeniable. These are poems
that may be mocked yet they are not forgotten. There seems an
unexplained and overwhelming grief at the heart of both poems,
and it is this that gives them their power.

This is especially true of "Ulalume." When Theodore Watts-Dun-
ton said that the poem properly intoned would have the same effect
whether or not the listener understood English, his remark would
have delighted Poe. This was what he meant by music, something
that could produce an emotion without carrying a specific meaning.
It was his intention literally to produce a sensation in the reader,
a sensation independent of thought. This was Visionary Poe's purpose. Logical Poe devised the way of carrying it out. From this
point of view it does not matter in reading "Ulalume" whether
the dank tarn of Auber takes its name from Jean François Auber
the composer, or whether the ghoul-haunted woodland of Weir refers to the Hudson River landscape painter Robert Walter Weir.
Nor is it important if the title does, or does not, spring from the
Latin verb *ululare,* to wail, plus *lumen,* a light, meaning Light of
Sorrow, or whether Mount Yaanek was derived from an Antarctic
volcano or an Arab phrase. The feeling of the poem is as independent
of these things as of the meanings that commentators have forced
upon it. Yet of course Poe was composing in words, and so the
words must have a relevance, although it is hard to define. Chivers,
whose frightful verses should have served as a warning to Poe of
the perils of originality, had used the meter of "The Raven" two
or three years before that poem was written, in his "To Allegra in
Heaven." After Poe's death Chivers moved on to more and more
grotesque experiments in language. "Lord Uthen's Lament for Ella"
is a mild example:

> On the mild month of October
> Through the fields of Cooly Rauber
> By the great Archangel Huber
> Such sweet songs of love did flow

The fields of Cooly Rauber inhabit the same literally meaningless
world as the dim lake of Auber. They are places that exist only as
sounds. If Chivers's sounds are absurd and Poe's impressive, it is

in some degree because Poe's make more sense, enough to take their places in a believable narrative.

The total of Poe's poetic achievement was not great. The best of the later poems are extraordinary works, and in their own way they have never been matched: but they are remarkable like Hood's "Song of the Shirt," and they bear the same relationship to the best poetry of the period that *Vathek* bears to *David Copperfield*. It would be unreasonably puritanical not to admire their fantastic skill, but wrong to think of them on the same plane as the best of Tennyson. The poetic achievement of Logical Poe, who had the upper hand in these last poems, was technically dazzling; it was also more than a little ridiculous.

Eureka

Eureka: A Prose Poem, the title page of the first edition says, and the subtitle is justified in the brief preface: "It is as a Poem only that I wish this work to be judged after I am dead." A poem in prose, a poem of a hundred-odd pages? Poe has abandoned—or rather waived, in the case of this one work—the theories of poetic composition expounded by Logical Poe, and is prepared to dignify with the name of poem something that attempts to convey a supernal truth, truth combined with beauty. It is this that permits him to call it a poem. *Eureka* is the purest product of Visionary Poe. His intention here is to explain the origin, character and future of the universe, and to show that it is the creation of an imaginative and intuitive artist. The Godhead, acting by Divine Volition, moves always in the direction of unity. Indeed, his artistic intentions are remarkably like these of Edgar Allan Poe.

Eureka is addressed to those who regard dreams as the only realities. And the dream which is the only reality is that of a single individual; the universe is to be found within a single mind. The destruction of the world is envisaged, but so too is its everlasting renewal. *Eureka* may be looked at from two points of view: as a serious account of the creation and nature of the universe based on mathematical and astronomical observations, or as an art product and romance, to use Poe's own terms. It cannot, however, be both, and the many recent commentators on the essay seem to me seriously misleading. They give us their own interpretations rather than

concerning themselves with what Poe actually wrote, and they try
to maintain that *Eureka* is both scientifically interesting and important and also a prose poem. So it is said that *Eureka* demonstrates
the essential unity of truth and beauty, or that it is "the ultimately
depersonalized and mechanical characterization of the psychic
rhythm of existence," or that the astronomical ideas it contains are
near to some modern theories; but such criticism rarely condescends
to details. The case put here is that as a piece of original thought
Eureka is almost valueless, but that it is vitally important as a final
statement of Poe's attitude to art.

Daniel Hoffman, whose piece of gobbledygook is quoted above,
also remarks more sensibly that in *Eureka* Poe uses a mathematical
vocabulary to establish an aesthetic principle. Mathematical and
philosophical, he might have said. The argument is that the universe
was conceived as a work of art, or in Poe's words that "In the Original
Unity of the First Thing lies the Secondary Cause of All Things,
with the Germ of their Inevitable Annihilation." How do you prove
such a philosophical or theosophical idea? Well, of course you can't,
and Poe makes a merit of the impossibility of doing so. We are
told that there is no such thing as mathematical demonstration,
that it does not exist. Intuition is the thing and it is, quite simply,
certain that "All Things and All Thoughts of Things, with their ineffable Multiplicity of Relation, sprang at once into being from the
primordial and irrelative One."

These are the opening statements of *Eureka*. There follow several
pages of clownish joking against those who have advanced the claim
of reason against intuition, including "a Turkish philosopher called
Aries and surnamed Tottle," "one Tuclid, a geometrician," and John
Stuart Mill. These reasoners are condemned for the slowness of their
creeping logic, and also for their rejection of "the Soul which loves
nothing so well as to soar in . . . regions of illimitable intuition."
With logical deduction disposed of, our intuition is free to adopt
as a starting point for discussion the existence of a Godhead, one
who has created a "primordial Particle" which has absolute Unity
yet is capable of infinite divisibility, so that from the Particle are
irradiated spherically "a certain inexpressibly great yet limited number of unimaginably yet not infinitely minute atoms." These atoms
tend to unite, and that is the principle of gravity. They tend also
to repel each other, and that is the principle "which we have been

in the practice of designating now as heat, now as magnetism, now as *electricity.*" Poe moves then into a discussion of astronomy and of the relationship between gravitation and electricity, terms which with a conjurer's sleight of hand are quickly changed to attraction and repulsion. Attraction is the body, repulsion the soul. They are the two principles of the universe, material and spiritual. *"No other principles exist";* these are the sole properties through which we perceive the universe.

At this point, a quarter of the way through *Eureka,* it is time to call a halt and ask why any of these propositions should be taken seriously. Gravitation and electricity are empirically ascertainable facts. The body and soul, in terms of matter and spirit, are metaphysical conceptions. To say that attraction is the body and repulsion the soul is merely a non sequitur, and there is no reason at all why we should believe it. Equally arbitrary are many statements in the latter part of this prose poem. They are based on conjectures about astronomy, in which Poe had read widely, and with his usual facility in grasping and adapting the ideas of others. Some of his material is commonplace, like the several pages given to describing such things as the time it would take a cannonball "flying at the greatest velocity with which such a ball has ever been known to fly" to reach the sun. The nearest modern scientists have come to agreeing with his wilder astronomical conjectures is to say that they are intelligent but amateurish. Poe does not rest on scientific grounds, however, for he has already told us that scientific proof does not exist. His calculations are used throughout to buttress poetic intuition, so that just as the principles of gravitation and electricity are pressed into the service of metaphysics, so speculations about the meaning of the distances between the planets merge into the vision of "a *revolution* of all the orbs of the Galaxy about some gigantic globe which we take to be the central pivot of the whole . . . some orb, let us rather say, of infinite sublimity endlessly multiplied by the infinitely sublime." When the End, the final catastrophe, comes, it will be because final Unity has been attained, so that nothing remains but God. Yet the End will not be the end. There will be "another creation and irradiation . . . another action and reaction of the Divine Will," so that "the processes we have here ventured to contemplate will be renewed forever, and forever, and forever." The universe will swell into existence and then subside at every throb of the Heart Divine. "And now—this Heart Divine—what is it? *It is our own.*" In a revision of the manuscript the solipsistic circle is made perfect. "That God may be all in all, *each* must become God."

In recounting this vision the poet is as impervious to logic as he is to what he calls the "conventional World-Reason"; or rather, he maintains that intuition is a sort of super-logic. It is the expression of "inductions or deductions of which the processes are so shadowy as to escape our consciousness, elude our reason, or defy our capacity of expression." So there is no arguing with him on conventional World-Reasonable grounds, because he will simply say that our inductive or deductive processes are inadequate to grasp the truth. The right way to view *Eureka* is to discard the science with its occasional brilliant guesses (like the suggestion of atomic fission) emerging from a sea of nonsense, and to regard it as a vision. A vision of some grandeur, with its glimpses of worlds uniting and dissolving for ever, and an aesthetically daring one too, for Poe is saying both that God is a conscious artist and that any conscious artist may become God. The supernal loveliness that the artist must look for, he suggests in a strange passage near the end, lies somewhere in the dreams of another existence, and these in truth are not dreams but memories of a time when we were nearer to God, and so nearer to the perfection of art. It is not surprising that when he had finished *Eureka*, Poe felt he had nothing more to say.

THE STORIES

The Beginnings: Tales of the Folio Club

POE wrote in all about seventy stories, and by his middle twenties had produced a considerable body of work. He did not, however, take these early stories seriously in comparison to his poetry. His approach in writing the *Tales of the Folio Club* has already been suggested. They were stories written for money, as distinct from the poems written for love. They had their origins in the popular fiction of the time: the Gothic horror story as it was practiced both in England and in Germany, stories of exploration in strange lands and of scientific marvels recently discovered or imagined, and pawkily humorous tales of a kind indigenous to the United States. The extent of Poe's borrowings was remarkable. One source of his work was material he found in newspapers—stories about ballooning, extraordinary voyages, mesmeric trances, premature burial, and the pestilence. Another was the British magazines, in which humorous tales and stories about hoaxes were common. Similar tales appeared in American journals, but some of Poe's titles indicate that he took much more from Britain than from his own country. His admiration for *Blackwood's* and its editor was so great that this was his primary source.

What Poe borrowed he transformed, infusing it particularly with the detached, frigid sadism that runs through so much of his work, and also with a boyish or adolescent sense of wonder at mechanical and scientific marvels, and at strange practices in distant lands. He described his own procedure very well when he wrote in an early letter of the fearful being colored into the horrible, the ludicrous and the witty becoming grotesques and burlesques, and the singular turning into the mystical. This is what he did with the material he borrowed wholesale, and the compelling power of his best stories, in his own time and in ours, springs from his expression of personal obsessions which articulate universal fears and horrors.

All this becomes fully apparent as, in the last decade of his life, the story replaces the poem as his primary interest. In the *Tales of the Folio Club* one can find every sort of Poe story represented except the tales of detection, but the emphasis is upon mostly trivial comic tales. Pieces like *The Duc de l'Omelette,* in which a comic aristocrat escapes from the devil after a hand at cards, or the parodic view of dueling called *Mystification,* are no more than magazine articles. *A Tale of Jerusalem* and *Lionizing* are unusual only insofar as they exploit a vein of coarseness very unusual in Poe, through excretory and sexual innuendoes. Two of the early comic stories are, however, of interest both in themselves and because of the way in which they show how he turned the ludicrous not only into the grotesque but into the horrific.

King Pest, which is set in London during a plague year, tells how two drunken seamen find their way into a forbidden area. In "the stronghold of the pestilence" they enter a wine cellar beneath an undertaker's, where a variety of decayed figures sit around drinking on coffin trestles. The description of these people is clearly meant to show them as comic, but it is a strange kind of comedy. The president, who calls himself King Pest the First, wears a black velvet pall and has sable hearse plumes stuck in his hair. His forehead is "so unusually and hideously lofty as to have the appearance of a bonnet or crown of flesh superadded upon the natural head," and he holds a human thigh bone in his hand. Each of the party has a feature as distorted as King Pest's forehead—a mouth that, "commencing at the right ear . . . swept with a terrific chasm to the left," a nose that is "long, thin, sinuous, flexible, and pimpled," and hangs down far below the under lip, a jaw tied up by muslin, and so on. These figures like circus freaks call themselves His Grace the Archduke Pest-Iferous, Her Serene Highness the Archduchess Ana-Pest, and so on. They drink from skulls and use charcoal in a skeleton for a light. The story hardly exists—it was designed as a burlesque of a scene in Disraeli's *Vivian Grey*—but the impression left by the freaks is vivid far beyond the modest intention.

Four Beasts in One, or the Homo-Camelopard is a satirical fantasy of a more interesting order, in the form of a historical anecdote about a King of Antioch who, dressed as a "camelopard," roams the streets demanding and receiving the worship of the people. The vulgarity and stupidity of the "idiots and madmen" who acclaim him is contrasted with the dignity of the lions, tigers and leopards who have been trained to act as valets to the unworthy humans. The appearance of the camelopard, however, is too much for them. They revolt, eat some of their masters, and chase the King back to the hippodrome where he finds safety, and is given the wreath of victory in the foot-race. The narration is cast in the continuous present, which adds force to its contemptuous geniality, and the flavor is reminiscent of Carlyle. This neglected story about the decency of beasts and the ignorant cruelty of men (two of the King's amusements are destroying temples and burning Jews) deserves a place in any selection of Poe's works.

Four of these early stories are tales of horror, important chiefly as precursors of the better things to come, but still of some interest in themselves. The brief *Shadow* is a prose poem about the Pestilence (in fact, in the papers of the time, the cholera), and an unavailing attempt by a few people to shut themselves away from it. The story is a precursor of *The Masque of the Red Death*. The other stories, *Berenice, Morella,* and *The Visionary* (later called *The Assignation*) are typical of the many stories in which Poe seems to be suggesting more than he is able or dares to say. The characters, both men and women, are doomed to a fate that they are unable to avoid. Berenice is at first healthy, but becomes eventually so emaciated that "not one vestige of the former being lurked in any line of the contour." She is epileptic. Morella is a woman of profound erudition, who introduces the narrator to "forbidden pages" of literary works, and whose musical voice conveys a melody "tainted with terror." She, like Berenice, pines away to death. The Marchesa Mentoni, in *The Visionary,* fulfills a pact with her lover to take poison.

Beautiful women have little chance of survival in Poe. They are often seen both as the victims of men and as a cause of destruction. The narrator of *Berenice* is her cousin, and his sickness and ill-health is contrasted at first with her "gorgeous, yet fantastic beauty." He is a monomaniac, who is bound to concentrate upon some "invariably frivolous" object his whole attention. When Berenice becomes ill,

he speaks to her of marriage "in an evil moment." After their marriage, as she becomes more and more sickly, he is obsessed by her
teeth. During her final illness he can think of nothing else, and
after her death he raids the grave and extracts her teeth with the
aid of "some instruments of dental surgery." Or rather, after her
apparent death, for the last turn of the screw here is the revelation
that she was buried alive. The idea of premature burial greatly absorbed Poe. It occurs in several stories, and one is actually called
The Premature Burial. The narrator in *Morella* also marries her,
and she bears his child even though the fires that burn in him are
"not of Eros, and bitter and tormenting to my spirit was the gradual
conviction that I could in no manner define their unusual meaning."
He longs for her death, but after this takes place she is replaced
by her child, who is also named Morella. When the child also dies,
"I laughed with a long and bitter laugh as I found no traces of
the first, in the charnel where I laid the second, Morella."

The Visionary, a piece of melodrama derived fairly directly from
E. T. A. Hoffmann, is much less distinctive, but the two other stories
leave a reader asking questions. What is the origin of the narrator's
monomania in *Berenice,* why does he marry a woman he apparently
doesn't love, what is the *meaning* of the relationship between them?
And in *Morella,* what was the lure of those forbidden pages, what
was the nature of the snare Morella set through them; why was
her death desired?

Such questions, however sensible, are irrelevant to Poe's concerns. Indeed, one could go further and say that the lack of background for the monomania is essential to his intention. In *The Imp
of the Perverse,* published in 1845, he suggests that phrenology should
have admitted among its various bumps one conveying "a paradoxi-
cal something which we may call perverseness . . . a *mobile* without
motive, a motive not *motiviat,*" which for some could take the form
of an "overwhelming tendency to do wrong for the wrong's sake."
This, in the form of an irresistible impulse, was what the narrator
felt in *Berenice.* And in *Morella* the idea of death being both supreme
and erotically desirable, blended with the idea of reincarnation,
was what absorbed him. If Morella was to be reincarnated in her
child, was it not natural that she should be learned and wise? These
stories were the work of Visionary Poe, and no rational logic is to
be found in them.

The third group among these early stories contains work both real and super-real, pieces which are meant to deceive readers by a mass of apparently genuine documentation, and pieces which hardly touch reality at any point. The prize-winning *MS. Found in a Bottle* and *The Unparalleled Adventure of One Hans Pfaall* are of the first kind, *Metzengerstein* and the short prose poem *Silence* of the second. There are times when the two kinds merge into each other, as in the narrator's feeling in *MS. Found in a Bottle* that "we are hurrying onwards to some exciting knowledge—some never-to-be-imparted secret, whose attainment is destruction." Here, however, there is little doubt that one is reading a story, a piece of fiction, even though many of the descriptive touches are remarkably convincing. *Hans Pfaall* is full of fascinating detail about gases, one of which has a "density about 37.4 times *less than that of hydrogen*," as well as intelligent and ingenious calculations about the journey itself. It was designed as a burlesque of current tales of the kind, and so contains names like Von Underduk and Rubadub, and other features that make belief impossible. Had such jokes been omitted it might, like some of Poe's other near-documentary pieces, have been regarded as true. *Metzengerstein* is one of the most derivative of the super-real stories, a highly Germanic tale (on its first appearance it bore a subtitle saying "In Imitation of the German") of a wilful young aristocrat who is joined indissolubly to a horse that steps out of a tapestry.

Of these stories only *Berenice, Morella,* and *Four Beasts in One* might find a place in a fairly generous selection from Poe; yet the other pieces cannot be called prentice work. As a writer of fiction Poe had nothing to learn, because his serious stories contain nobody except himself. Morella and Berenice—and later Ligeia, Madeline Usher, Eleonora—have no existence as characters, but are no more than beautiful or horrific shadows existing only in the mind of the narrator. To say this is not to assess the quality of the stories, but to suggest what they attempt to do. In such stories, as in the poems, Visionary Poe was concerned with the nature of art, with man's relationship to God, with the connection between beauty and death. Logical Poe was given the task of making a living, playing jokes, evolving hoaxes, creating and solving puzzles and cryptograms, and in the end creating the detective story. The visionary stories make their appeal to primitive feelings, not to knowledge of the world or of people. One cannot look for any line of development in them, as one might in the stories of Chekhov, because development in that sense was not possible. What Poe had to offer in his later stories was a deeper anguish, a more naked—although always histrionic— account of his suffering heart, described through his still lucid mind.

Tales of Humor

Poe is sometimes accused of lacking a sense of humor. This is true if one confines the idea of humor to the self-deprecating, self-conscious comedy regarded, not without justification, as characteristically English. That he had a feeling for the grotesque and for raw, often crude joking, is made clear by his consistent publication of comic stories. These were in part derived from an American tradition that was both coarse and vulgar. He tells them in a buttonholing, this-will-amaze-you style that was in tune with the approach made in many current magazines, and he uses an abundance of appalling puns. *The Devil in the Belfry* is set in the Dutch borough of Vondervotteimitiss, *The Thousand-and-Second Tale of Scheherazade* is supposed to come from the book *Tellmenow Isitsöornot.* These are two of many examples that seem now something less than side-splitting. Often the stories are no more than anecdotes. When the devil gets into the belfry, he makes the clock strike thirteen and play on a fiddle "Judy O'Flannagan and Paddy O'Rafferty." *X-ing a Paragrab* tells what happens to a paragraph when "x" is substituted for "o" because the vowel is missing in a printing office. *Diddling Considered as One of the Exact Sciences* strings together accounts of a few simple frauds. The long-winded *Literary Life of Thingum Bob, Esq.* is a heavy-handed joke at the expense of magazine editors, all of whom reject lines from Shakespeare and Dante but print the most egregious rubbish written by contributors who flatter them.

In several stories there exists in the comedy an element of unconscious sadism. The Signora Psyche Zenobia is no doubt a tiresome woman, but is it funny that her head should be cut off by a clock hand? Poe thinks so, and elaborates zestfully upon the body's inability to take snuff. It throws down the snuffbox to the cut-off head, which takes a pinch and afterwards makes a speech "which I could hear but indistinctly without ears." In *The Man That Was Used Up,* which may have given Nathanael West the idea for *A Cool*

Million, the impressive Brevet Brigadier General John A. B. C. Smith, who has a marvelous head of hair, tremendous shoulders, perfect arms and legs, and a sonorous voice, is revealed as being in fact no more than an "exceedingly odd looking bundle of something" which the narrator, who does not recognize the bundle's identity, kicks out of the way. The General, a victim of the Kickapoo Indians, has only one leg, arm and eye, his teeth, shoulders and hair are false, and even his palate is not his own. "D--n the vagabonds," he says in his rich melodious voice when the palate has been put in. "They not only knocked in the roof of my mouth, but took the trouble to cut off at least seven-eighths of my tongue."

This story and one or two others, like *Loss of Breath,* remind us of that observation about the ludicrous being heightened into the grotesque. *The System of Doctor Tarr and Professor Fether* (1845) turns the ludicrous into the horrific. The idea of an asylum run by the lunatics did not originate with Poe, but he brings to it a zest peculiarly disturbing because of its own irrational flavor. In one of the "extreme southern provinces of France" the narrator visits a private madhouse, "a fantastic château, much dilapidated and indeed scarcely tenable through age and neglect" (Poe perhaps did not care to set such a place in America), and meets Monsieur Meillard, who formerly ran the place upon "the soothing system" by which the patients were allowed to do what they liked. (The reference is to the battle between advocates of the silent system" and the "separate system" of imprisonment which was going on at the time.) Meillard has replaced the soothing system by the ideas of the celebrated Doctor Tarr and Professor Fether. And what are they? The narrator is more and more surprised when the people introduced by Meillard as his assistants show all the signs of obsessional insanity. The keepers have in fact been tarred, feathered, and locked up by Meillard, who is now himself a lunatic.

The mechanical nature of the story is exemplified in the obsessions, which go no further than the lunatics thinking themselves a teetotum, a frog, or a cheese, but it has in part the frantic imaginative energy of Poe's serious writing. Nothing that he produced with the deliberate intention of being funny ranks with his major achievements, but some of the effects achieved when he was carried away by his own pitiless view of emotional and physical inadequacy are very strange.

Tales of Horror

More than half of Poe's seventy stories are very little read, except by literary critics and honors students. His reputation as a short story writer rests upon some twenty tales which are famous throughout the world. Apart from the four tales of detection, they are all horrific. Almost all are told in the first person, and in them the narrator sees or suffers some frightful experience. A typical Poe anthology will include *The Fall of the House of Usher, The Masque of the Red Death, The Pit and the Pendulum, The Tell-Tale Heart, The Cask of Amontillado* and *Ligeia.* Add to these a selection from *William Wilson, A Descent into the Maelström, Berenice, Morella, Eleonora, The Black Cat, The Facts in the Case of M. Valdemar, Hop-Frog, The Imp of the Perverse,* plus a couple of the detective stories and three or four of what are called here the tales of reality and super-reality, and you have the standard collection. This rather misrepresents Poe, in the sense that his interests were wider than such a collection suggests. But it is a fact that his fame rests upon a handful of stories and poems, and that among the stories the tales of horror are regarded as supreme.

The qualities that make Poe's horror stories unique in their kind are not to be found in plotting, characterization or style. The plots are often borrowed, characterization does not exist here any more than in the other stories, and the style is only too often rusty or rhetorical Gothic. "The thousand injuries of Fortunato I had borne as I best could, but when he ventured upon insult I vowed revenge," is a typical sentence, and many of these stories take place in Gothic surroundings, decaying castles and houses, crypts and vaults lined with bones, bridal chambers which are like tombs. The lasting power of the stories rests in the feeling one has of a terrible experience being conveyed without any of the subterfuges and evasions commonly used by fiction writers. Poe is spelling out his personal agonies in fictional terms. The obsessions, which were accentuated but not caused by Virginia's illness and death, were concerned with the supreme beauty of death, the association of pleasure and cruelty, the fascination of blood. He offers us in some respects the world of de Sade, but it is a sadism made acceptable to a mass readership by the elimination of any ostensible sexual element.

De Sade describes the pleasures to be obtained through torturing

others. Poe shows us, through the thin veil of his narrators, the
agonies suffered by torturer and victim alike. He shows us also,
more nakedly than any other writer of fiction, his own terror of
madness and of being buried alive. As D. H. Lawrence says, "he
sounded the horror and the warning of his own doom." It is almost
miraculous that Poe was able to impose shape and fictional form
upon material which otherwise might have seemed the shriek of
a man possessed by demons, and even to give it some philosophical
content. The horror stories were written by Visionary Poe, but Logical Poe was always breathing over his shoulder. The obsessions are
repeated throughout the stories, and it is probably more interesting
to categorize them than to consider separately stories that so much
resemble each other in theme.

   Cruelty and Confinement. The word "cruelty" was not one that
Poe would have used in such a context. The nearest he got to it
was the innocuous "perverseness." Like several other stories, *The
Imp of the Perverse* is an essay with a fragment of fiction tagged
on at the end. Poe maintains that there is a human instinct to "do
wrong for the wrong's sake," against our rational wishes. So one
has an uncontrollable longing to engender anger in a person one
wants to please, avoids doing essential work, is irresistibly drawn
to the edge of an abyss with the prospect of plunging over. In the
story's last pages it is revealed that these reflections are being written
in the condemned cell by a man who committed murder by means
of a poisoned candle, but after some years was driven to confession
by the imp of the perverse, thus consigning himself "to the hangman
and to hell."

   The story does not in fact prove the principle, because the wrong-
doing was rational (the murderer killed for an inheritance) and the
"perversity" caused him to admit the truth. But that is by the way.
The idea of doing wrong for the sake of it is powerfully expressed
in other stories. It is "the spirit of PERVERSENESS" that makes the
narrator in *The Black Cat* cut out one of the eyes of the cat Pluto.
He does not hate Pluto—to the contrary, the cat is his pet. He goes
further and kills Pluto by hanging it from a tree, doing so "*because*
I knew that it had loved me, and *because* I felt it had given me
no reason of offense." Pluto is replaced by another black cat, which
by chance has only one eye. This cat terrifies the narrator, who
sees in the white pattern of fur on its breast the shape of the gallows.

The new black cat is indirectly responsible for the narrator's murder of his wife, and also for his undoing. He inadvertently walls up the cat in the cellar with his dead wife, and its howling is heard by the police. The final sentences offer one of his finest theatrical effects:

> The corpse, already greatly decayed and clotted with gore, stood erect before the eyes of the spectators. Upon its head, with red extended mouth and solitary eye of fire, sat the hideous beast whose craft had seduced me into murder, and whose informing voice had consigned me to the hangman.

The extraction of the teeth in *Berenice* is paralleled by an obsession with the eye in *The Tell-Tale Heart*. The murder here is in ordinary terms motiveless, unconnected with passion or profit. The victim's eye is the trouble. "He had the eye of a vulture—a pale blue eye, with a film over it," and murder is committed to get rid of the eye. It involves dismemberment of the body, including cutting off the head. Removal of the head occurs in two or three stories. It can be used for macabre comedy, as in the case of Psyche Zenobia, and *Never Bet the Devil Your Head* in which Toby Dammit's head is cut off as he tries to jump a stile, or as part of a detective tale, as in *The Murders in the Rue Morgue*. In *The Pit and the Pendulum* the whole body is threatened by the razor-sharp pendulum descending on the prisoner. In *Hop-Frog*, the most openly sadistic story, the burning of the King and his seven counsellors is described with relish, to the point where they swing in their chains, "a fetid, blackened, hideous, and indistinguishable mass." The King himself is also a petty sadist. He forces the jester Hop-Frog to drink, and then throws wine in the face of the dwarf's friend Trippetta. *Hop-Frog*, like a number of other stories, has an obvious relationship to Poe's own life. It may well be a parable of the neurotic artist and his patrons, who are also his persecutors, as has been suggested; but the first and best reading is the most literal. It is also the reading that gives the story its most terrifying force.

Confinement within a very small space is linked in Poe stories with premature burial. In *The Cask of Amontillado* Fortunato is buried alive by his friend Montresor, who has the pleasure of knowing that the chained victim understands perfectly what is happening to him. Madeline in *The Fall of the House of Usher* has been put living into the tomb, and so has Berenice. In *The Premature Burial* the idea is used for a sort of comedy. A long essay describing in realistic terms various actual cases of people buried alive is succeeded by the narrator's own experience. He is an epileptic, and wakes from a fit to find that he is unable to move or speak. His jaws are bound up, he lies inside a coffin, and no doubt the coffin has been put "forever, into some ordinary and nameless *grave.*" Poe breaks the spell by revealing that the man is in a very narrow ship's berth, that he had tied up his own head in a handkerchief, and that the laborers who roused him provided in their persons the earthy smell of the grave. In *The Oblong Box,* a man taking his wife's body from Charleston to New York by sea becomes desperate when the body has to be left on the sinking ship. In several other stories, like *The Narrative of Arthur Gordon Pym,* the narrator finds himself very closely confined. Part of the fascination held for Poe by Maelzel's Chess Player, about which he wrote a brilliant article, lay in his conclusion that a man must be concealed within this apparently mechanical figure, and concealed in a remarkably small space.

Madness. How does one explain, how did Poe explain to himself, the nature of people who did such things? The simplest answer was to say that they were mad, and this was in a sense the least disturbing answer possible. To account for such aberrations in detail would have been very distressing for him—all he wanted to do was to set them down on paper. A link with the super-real stories that move out of this world is provided by the suggestion that madness is an aspect of a higher awareness outside literal reality. So *The Tell-Tale Heart* begins: "True!—nervous—very, very dreadfully nervous I had been and am; but why *will* you say that I am mad? . . . I heard all things in the heaven and in the earth. I heard many things in hell. How, then, am I mad?" In the opening paragraph of *Eleonora* the narrator claims that madness may be the mark of the loftiest intelligence, and goes on to describe a division of the mind that seems more applicable to the author than to the narrator:

> We will say, then, that I am mad. I grant, at least, that there are two distinct conditions of my mental existence—the condition of a lucid reason, not to be disputed, and belonging to the memory of events forming the first epoch of my life—and a condition of shadow and doubt, appertaining to the present.

A similar confusion between reality and fantasy marks the narrators of *The Pit and the Pendulum, Berenice,* and several other stories, and in other stories still the narrator is suffering from his "old fever" or is excited "almost to madness" by wine.

Beauty, Life After Death, the Double. Another group of horror stories is not concerned primarily with cruelty, confinement and madness, but with the nature and beauty of death. Linked with such concerns are speculations about the possibility of existence after death. Poe's approach to this was not specifically Christian, although he at all times believed in the existence of a supreme being. He was interested rather in the possibility that individual personality might continue after death, either through an effort of the will or by some extraneous means. *The Facts in the Case of M. Valdemar,* the most extreme example of this interest, begins with a speculation about the effect of mesmerism on a dying man, and concludes that mesmeric power may prolong life, even though such life is a kind of death. In *Ligeia,* which Poe called his finest story, he played with the idea that life might be prolonged also by the power of the will. Morella appears to be reincarnated in her child. Ligeia, who maintains that man need not die "save only through the weakness of his feeble will," dies nevertheless. She is like Morella immensely learned, tall, raven-haired, slender, emaciated, and bloodlessly pale. After death she is replaced in the narrator's affections by "the fair-haired and blue-eyed Lady Rowena Trevanion, of Tremaine," who quickly becomes ill and dies. Or apparently dies: for this again seems to be a case in which death has been announced prematurely. With "the bandages and the draperies of the grave" still on her she revives, but when she does so reveals the raven black hair and the black wild eyes of Ligeia. In this story Poe suggests, more clearly than in any other, that the transference may be a delusion caused by the narrator's indulgence in opium. In the slighter *Eleonora,* the much-loved Eleonora returns after death and forgives the narrator for breaking his vow of faithfulness by contemplating marriage to Ermengarde. The painter in the equally slight *The Oval Portrait* is delighted with the portrait of his bride, and cries "This is Life itself," only to find that the painting's subject is dead. Here again we are told that the narrator (who is not the painter) has been badly wounded, and is in a state of incipient delirium.

The idea of the division of personality also interested Poe. In *The Fall of the House of Usher* Roderick and Madeline are twins, and are probably meant to represent two sides of a personality, and *William Wilson* exploits more successfully than has been granted recently the theme of the *doppelgänger* or double. This must be an important story in any view of Poe's career. He gave Wilson the same birth date as his own—or at least, the same as the false birth date he gave to Griswold. His childhood education is set, with loving care, in the school at Stoke Newington where Poe spent two years of his childhood. And Wilson's career is a kind of parody of Poe's. Sent to Eton, he involves himself in a "vortex of thoughtless folly." At Oxford he adds "no brief appendix to the long catalogue of vices then usual in the most dissolute university of Europe," and leaves after being caught cheating at cards. He is pursued always by his double, his whispering and all too evident conscience, and when he kills the other William Wilson sees in a mirror his own pale, blood-dabbled features. The story is monstrously overwritten, but it is an instructive essay in self-revelation.

In several of these stories Poe is struggling both to express the compulsions that drove him, and to deny them. Their relationship to his life is not often as close as in *William Wilson,* but it is clearly present. Most of his heroines are dying of tuberculosis, like his mother, his brother Henry, and Virginia. Their bloodlessness, the blue veins showing on their high pale foreheads, the red spots on their cheeks, and the "waxen lure" of their pale fingers tell their own tale, and in one story Poe's fascination with blood is made overt.

The Masque of the Red Death has a sort of bloody thumbprint on it that makes one forget the overrichness of its Gothic trappings and the overripe language in which it is written. "Blood was its Avatar and its seal—the redness and the horror of blood," we are told of the Red Death. "There were sharp pains, and sudden dizziness, and then profuse bleeding at the pores, with dissolution." At Prince Prospero's masked ball the figure of the Red Death appears "dabbled in *blood*" and its features are "besprinkled with the scarlet horror." Remove the blood, make it the Black instead of the Red Death, and this would be a much less haunting story.

To put these tales into separate categories must be a piece of oversimplification. There is a horrific element in some of the humorous stories and those I have called "Tales of Reality and Super-Reality," and there is a gallows humor in *Hop-Frog*. But the categories are useful if they are not taken too precisely, and the tales of horror do stand distinctly apart from the rest of his work. The effects achieved in them are partly conscious and intentional, partly unconscious and compulsive. There is nothing else like them in Western literature.

Tales of Reality and Super-Reality

Poe was fascinated by tales of travel, and also by travelers' tales. Accounts of wonders seen and extraordinary things experienced stirred his imagination. Some of the travelers made facts seem like fiction, so why should one not make fiction look like fact? The prize-winning *MS. Found in a Bottle* is full of apparently factual detail, and so is *Hans Pfaall*. His most celebrated piece of this kind, known as *The Balloon-Hoax*, really did deceive many readers and so, as we have seen, did *M. Valdemar*. The last of the hoaxes, *Von Kempelen and His Discovery*, about the transformation of lead to gold, was meant both to satirize the California gold rush and to persuade readers that it was true. Poe had an endless appetite for literary jokes that would in one way or another deceive the public. The stories in which he tried to do this, and no more than this, have only curiosity value today.

There are other stories, however, in which he attempted much more, using a story that made sense upon the literal level to suggest ideas about the nature of the universe or to suggest his perceptions of a different world that existed in the imagination, into which one might enter like Alice through the looking glass. This other world inspires awe, and the approach to it is often through terror, which is conceived like the dizziness of vertigo. *MS. Found in a Bottle* ends with the ship being caught in a whirlpool:

> The circles rapidly grow small—we are plunging madly within the grasp of the whirlpool—and amid a roaring, and bellowing, and thundering of ocean and tempest, the ship is quivering, oh God!— and—going down.

In a later story, *A Descent into the Maelström*, the narrator in his fishing smack is also caught in a whirlpool, the heart of which is in some extraordinary passages described as being like a gigantic funnel around which the smack revolves at an angle of more than 45 degrees, being maintained by centrifugal force rather like a rider on a Wall of Death at a fair. The descriptions of sea and storm, and of what it is like to be inside the whirlpool, are romantic writing of the highest order. But Poe's finest writing of this kind is undoubtedly that in his longest prose narrative, *The Narrative of Arthur Gordon Pym*.

On the literal level, as Auden says, *Pym* is one of the finest adventure stories ever written. Basing himself on several books he had reviewed, in particular Washington Irving's *Astoria* and J. N. Reynolds's pamphlet about an expedition to the South Seas, Poe produced a sea story crammed with incident. When his friend Augustus is setting off in the brig *Grampus* on a whaling voyage, Arthur Gordon Pym decides to accompany him as a stowaway, with Augustus's connivance. There follow mutiny, a successful revolt against it, the wrecking of the brig in a storm, the discovery of a plague ship, the death of Augustus, deliverance by a trading schooner, a stay on an island inhabited by black savages, betrayal by the blacks who kill most of the ship's party, and final escape in a canoe into "the wide and desolate Antarctic ocean." Stowing away at sea, mutiny, shipwreck, and deliverance—it sounds like a precursor of *Treasure Island*. But Pym is no Jim Hawkins, and the story is marked throughout by Poe's obsession with suffering, confinement, and bodily decay. Pym, because he is a stowaway, agrees to be confined at first in "an ironbound box . . . nearly four feet high, and full six feet long, but very narrow, inside the hold." His much-loved dog Tiger, who has been put into the hold by Augustus with a message tied round his neck, turns into a murderous enemy when maddened by lack of food and drink. In the mutiny up above, twenty-two of the crew have been forced overboard after being hit on their heads with an ax. At a later stage Pym is again in effect entombed alive with a companion, within the fissure of a gorge. After Augustus's death his leg comes off when his body is lifted to be thrown into the sea. Then, "as the mass of putrefaction slipped over the vessel's side," glowing with phosphoric light, it is torn to pieces by sharks. Literally dozens of deaths occur in the story. The shipwrecked sailors resort to cannibalism, with the victim's body being consumed except for head, hands, feet, and entrails. It is like Stevenson seen in a nightmare.

Yet the effect is not merely sensational. Every incident is recounted with such particularity as to compel fascinated attention if not total belief. There are elaborate instructions about the proper stowing of a cargo and the laying to of a vessel, information about the habits and appearance of tortoises on what are called the Gallipagos islands, similar details about penguins and other birds. Much of this came from books, but it appears transformed from ordinary travel writing into scenes powerfully imagined. The story ends not in a whirlpool but in a cataract, through which appears a vision:

> And now we rushed into the embraces of the cataract, where a chasm threw itself open to receive us. But there arose in our pathway a shrouded human figure, very far larger in its proportions than any dweller among men. And the hue of the skin of the figure was of the perfect whiteness of the snow.

What does this ending mean, and are there symbolic messages to be read into the whole course of the narrative? There is no argument about the fact that Poe filled the story with sensational and horrific events in the hope of making money but recent commentators have suggested that *Pym* is interesting as a symbolic rather than a realistic narrative, or at least that the last quarter of the book has strong symbolic intentions. It has been called a satire on illiberal attitudes, and on the contrary a tract in support of slavery (the betrayers on the island of Tsalal are black, and white is the color of goodness or revelation), a symbolic enactment of man's search for logic and meaning, and an account of a specifically American nightmare—or perhaps the nightmare of being a nineteenth-century American. The most high-flown of recent analysts, Harold Beaver, suggests that the whole tale is to be read as a spiritual Odyssey from darkness into light. The ship's hold, Mr. Beaver points out, was totally dark; Pym had to be "reborn to acknowledge all life inverted to mutiny, storm, shipwreck, putrescence," before being ready to "push on and pierce the white wastelands of total, integrated experience."

How much of all this is supported by the story? In the first three-quarters of the book, very little. There is every indication that Poe began with the idea of telling an adventure story, and that his love of puzzles, jokes, tricks, took over near the end. There is no doubt that in the last part of the book he is suggesting meanings beyond or beneath the literal ones of Pym's adventures. Sidney Kaplan, the best commentator on the story, has pointed out that the name of the island, Tsalal, is the Hebrew verb for "To be dark," that its principal town Klock-Klock is Hebrew for "To be dirty," and so on. The whole world of Tsalal is black, from the people to the soil, and this blackness is opposed to, and fears, whiteness. When the black Nu-Nu ("To deny") sees the white figure at the end, he dies of fright.

It seems likely, then, that this part of *Pym* is both satirical and symbolic. Poe detested the antislavery movement, as he made clear in several reviews and comments, and the villainous behavior of the blacks on Tsalal is meant to show what might happen if they ever had any kind of power. The negro was inferior to the white man, Poe said in a review, because "it was the will of God it should be so." And he was concerned with the will of God here in another sense. One can go along with Mr. Beaver so far as to agree that some sort of revelation is implied in the final scene. The "shrouded human figure" may after all be simply an iceberg in human shape, but it certainly seems to Pym the symbol of a new and pure world. It is a vision, one might say, of the eventual state foreseen in *Eureka*, when man has become the Godhead.

Yet when this has been acknowledged, it must be said also that the symbolic side of the book is of comparatively little importance. The concealed bits of Hebrew and Arabic and the occasional biblical references are in their context no more than jokes of a kind made by an ingenious trickster to show his cleverness. When they have been penetrated and analyzed they give no greater depth of meaning to the story, and they are probably what Poe had in mind when he called *Pym* a very silly book in his letter to Burton. The beauty and the power of the image with which the story ends takes its quality, like much else in Poe, from its ambiguity. *Pym* is much superior to anything else of the kind that Poe wrote—to, for instance, the unfinished *Journal of Julius Rodman* that he began shortly afterwards—but its strength lies in the excitement and horror of the narrative. Considered as an allegory or fable of death and rebirth it is trivial, because the symbols are altogether inadequate to the theme.

The stories in this group that have been considered so far are all rooted in reality. Another kind of story written by Poe is altogether super-real, having as its essence a speculation allied to that fully developed in *Eureka. The Colloquy of Monos and Una, Eiros and Charmion, The Power of Words*, represent this vein in his work. A rather different approach to super-reality is made in *The Island of the Fay, The Domain of Arnheim* and *Landor's Cottage*, which all suggest the possibility of a blissful existence in this world rather than another.

These stories have been much, and surely over, praised. *The Colloquy of Monos and Una* is a dialogue that begins by Una saying to Monos: "Born again?" In language often reminiscent in its flabby feebleness of that used at a spiritualist séance ("You are confused and oppressed by the majestic novelty of the Life Eternal"), some of the ideas expressed in *Eureka* are advanced. Imagination is preferable to reason, and true master minds regard "each advance in practical science as a retrogradation in the true utility." There is an outspoken condemnation of "wild attempts at an omni-prevalent Democracy," and a suggestion that after death all perceptions are purely sensual. *Eiros and Charmion* consists of a dialogue placed in the next world, although it is chiefly concerned with the destruction of this one. *The Power of Words* is a conversation about immortality and creation which again at some points anticipates *Eureka*.

The wish-fulfillment stories are more interesting. They are greatly concerned with landscape. There are two kinds of landscape in Poe, the gloomy and the idyllic. A fierce or desolate landscape is found in many of the horror stories, and it goes along with Gothic architecture to produce the impression made upon the narrator in *The Fall of the House of Usher*, who looked upon the house and its surroundings with "an iciness, a sinking, a sickening of the heart—an unredeemed dreariness of thought which no goading of the imagination could torture into aught of the sublime."

The idyllic landscape of the wish-fulfillment stories—although they are less stories than visions of happiness seen in terms of natural beauty—show a different world and a different architecture. *The Island of the Fay* actually gives us both Poe landscapes in a single tale. The western extremity of the small circular island of the title is sunny, there are flowers, the grass is "short, springy, sweet-scented, and asphodel-interspersed," and "everything [has] motion through the gentle sweepings to and fro of innumerable butterflies, that might have been mistaken for tulips with wings." At the eastern end there is "a sombre, yet beautiful and peaceful gloom," the grass wears "the deep tint of the cypress," and hillocks look like graves. The magical Fay moves from light to darkness and back again. *The Landscape Garden,* and its much improved later version called *The Domain of Arnheim,* is about "my friend Ellison" who inherits $450 million (Poe calculates his income at $1541 an hour), decides to become a landscape gardener, and partly discovers and partly creates the perfect landscape, which is described in several pages. The piece is a disquisition on gardens as works of art, and also the realization of a dream on paper. *Landor's Cottage,* subtitled "A Pendant to 'The Domain of Arnheim,'" gives an idealized view of the garden at Fordham, and also of the cottage. The actual size of the cottage is closely followed ("The main building was about twenty-four feet long and sixteen broad. . . . Its total height, from the ground to the apex of the roof, could not have exceeded eighteen feet," etc.), but the little Dutch-style cottage is transformed as though in a fairy tale. "Nothing could well be more simple," and "its marvellous *effect* lay altogether in its artistic arrangement as a *picture.*" When the door opens the figure revealed is Annie Richmond, although she is given only a Christian name.

This search for the perfect garden has been seen as a parable of an artist's search for beauty. The primary interest of these sketches, however, is in the agreeable, rather touching glimpses they give of Poe as a personality.

Tales of Detection

If a single proof were needed of Poe's astonishingly inventive and ingenious mind, it would rest in his creation of the short tale of detection as a literary form. There had been detectives of a kind before him, but no detection. The investigators of crime in Godwin and Lytton are rather pursuers, embodying the wrath of society or of God, than detectives trying to solve puzzles by reason. In this aspect Poe was again, as his shade would be delighted to learn, totally original.

It is usually said that he wrote four detective stories: *The Murders in the Rue Morgue, The Mystery of Marie Rogêt, The Gold-Bug,* and *The Purloined Letter.* To these I would add *"Thou Art the Man,"* a story which shows that the divisions suggested here are not fixed but fluid. *"Thou Art the Man"* is usually called a comic story, but it is also emphatically a tale of detection, including as it does false clues planted by the villain, and the first instance of the marks made by a rifle barrel being used as a clue in solving a crime. There are also fragments of analytical observation in several stories. In *The Man of the Crowd,* long-serving clerks are said to be recognizable by their right ears, which "long used to pen-holding, had an odd habit of standing off on end," and professional gamblers by "a guarded lowness of tone in conversation, and a more than ordinary extension of the thumb in a direction at right angles with the fingers"; and in *Pym,* reconstruction of the message on a piece of paper which has been torn into three pieces is done by a process of analysis.

These tales are the extreme expression of Logical Poe. They are by intention logical exercises, with no more emotion involved in them than in the solution of a cryptogram. Dupin, the central figure in three of them, is an image of Poe himself—aristocratic, arrogant, and apparently omniscient—and he solves crimes by his capacity as a reasoning machine. If the intentions had been completely fulfilled, the stories would be much less interesting than they are. (*The Gold-Bug,* which is nearest to a pure puzzle, seems to me the least gripping of the four.) Dupin in particular is more than the analytical cipher that is all the stories require.

The Chevalier C. Auguste Dupin is "of an illustrious family" but has become so poor that he has abandoned all hope of retrieving his fortunes, and has retired from the world, living upon "a small remnant of his patrimony." He goes out only at night, and at dawn closes the shutters in the "time-eaten and grotesque mansion" in which he lives, settling down with the narrator to reading, writing and conversation. Then, with "the advent of the true Darkness," the two roam the streets, "seeking, amid the wild lights and shadows of the populous city, that infinity of mental excitement which quiet observation can afford." The wish fulfillment in all this is so obvious that one need do little more than remark it, adding that the placing of the stories in Paris rather than in America adds to the element of make-believe. Dupin is given also the powers of analysis which his creator possessed in a high degree. He is able to interpret the thoughts of others from their gestures, to solve crimes by reading newspaper accounts of them, and to identify the likely whereabouts of a missing letter after being told in detail of the unsuccessful police search for it. Such apparently miraculous knowledge based upon rational deduction is at the heart of the detective story. A thousand crime writers since Poe, from Conan Doyle onward and downward, have paid him the compliment of copying one facet or another of his puzzles and their solutions. Doyle gave to Sherlock Holmes many of Dupin's qualities, including the ability to read the thoughts of others and to solve crimes from his armchair. *The Murders in the Rue Morgue* is the first among hundreds of locked-room mysteries, *The Gold-Bug* the first of all those stories dealing in detail with the breaking of a code, *The Mystery of Marie Rogêt* the first story with a documentary air. *The Purloined Letter* uses brilliantly the theme of a totally improbable, because too obvious, hiding place.

It was not Poe's purpose to create a new literary form, and he called these pieces tales of ratiocination, not detective stories. He could hardly have used the latter term, because a Detective Office had not yet been established at Scotland Yard, and few American cities had any force organized for the detection of crime. And it would be misleading to suggest that these stories fit into a self-contained category. *The Murders in the Rue Morgue* is the first locked-room mystery, but it might certainly also be put among the tales of horror. Certainly the details of the murders of Madame L'Espanaye and her daughter are horrific enough. The mother's throat is so entirely cut that "upon an attempt to raise her, the head fell off," and the daughter is pushed up the chimney, "forced up the narrow aperture for a considerable distance." The difference between this story and a characteristic tale of horror is that here Poe has tried for total detachment. Dupin is describing the crime from the newspaper accounts, and has no personal feelings about it. *The Mystery of Marie Rogêt* employs a variation of the near-documentary technique of the hoaxes to obtain an air of reality. Yet these four stories are still something new. They represent, as the Goncourts suggested in their *Journal* not only in reference to the detective stories, "a new literature, the literature of the twentieth century, scientifically miraculous story-telling by A + B, a literature at once monomaniac and mathematical."

Poe himself did not regard these stories very highly in comparison with his other work. "People think them more ingenious than they are," he wrote to a friend in 1846, "on account of their method and *air* of method." Yet he still did his best to make them mechani-

cally perfect. They were revised, like all his work, with the object
of tightening their structure. Even so, the three Dupin stories reveal
flaws that are damaging to them as pieces of pure rational deduction.

The Murders in the Rue Morgue was revised more than once,
partly on a purely grammatical basis, but principally to make the
details of the murder more plausible. The length of the broken
nail in the window frame noticed by Dupin is increased from one-
eighth to one-quarter of an inch, the distance between the house
and the shutter used by the ape is reduced from 4 to 2½ feet,
and it is said that the upper instead of the lower half of the shutter
is "latticed or worked in open trellis," affording a handhold by which
the ape swings into the room. These were all changes designed to
make what happened more plausible, although they do not affect
the objection made by Laura Riding to the effect that it would
have been mechanically impossible for the ape to climb out and
fasten the window by its secret catch.*

This is an error, although not a gross one. There is a comparable
flaw in *The Purloined Letter,* in the fact that Dupin could have
seen only the front or the back of the letter, and therefore could
not have observed simultaneously, as he is made to do, the large
black seal on the back and the address "in a diminutive female
hand" on the front. In *The Mystery of Marie Rogêt,* however, Poe
cheated to make theory conform with fact. He tried here to take
an actual case, the death of a cigar-store girl named Mary Rogers
in New York, and solve it by analyzing the various accounts of the
case in newspapers, changing the scene from New York to Paris,
and of course changing the names of the papers. It was an immensely
ambitious idea, one almost impossible to carry through, and certainly
Poe never really tried to fulfill it. An examination of the actual
New York newspapers with the extracts he is supposed to have
made from them reveals that he added to or subtracted from the
facts when it suited him—inventing, for instance, an empty boat
floating down the Hudson because his theory required it.

But he went further than this. In the course of writing he encountered an unexpected difficulty. His theory was that Mary Rogers
had been murdered by a single person and not, as was at first believed, by a gang. The story was appearing in serial form, however,

* See my remarks on this in *Mortal Consequences* (Harper & Row).

and after publication of the first installment there was news that death had probably been as the result of an abortion, and that the putative abortionist's sons had been arrested. It is possible although not certain that changes were made in the last installment because of this, but no doubt at all that when the story appeared in book form two years later the theory had been shifted to fit the facts. John Walsh, in an exemplary piece of literary detection,* has shown the process at work in detail. To quote Mr. Walsh: "He made fifteen small, almost undetectable, changes in the story, all of which definitely accommodated the possibility of an abortion death . . . and then added detailed footnotes so that it would appear he had been entirely correct from the start." It is barely necessary to add that Poe never subsequently admitted his mistake in describing death from an abortion as a murder.

These stories then are, like their creator, not impeccable. Yet they are extraordinary, and they really are also something new. If they are not the product of pure reason, neither are those of the hundreds of writers who have followed Poe in attempting to write wholly rational puzzle stories. A rigorous examination will find flaws in them all, from Conan Doyle and Gaboriau to Dorothy L. Sayers and John Dickson Carr. Poe's influence on the form of the detective story has been overwhelming. Conan Doyle put it in the right terms: "On this narrow path the writer must walk, and he sees the footmarks of Poe always in front of him. He is happy if he ever finds the means of breaking away and striking out on some little sidetrack of his own."

* *Poe the Detective* by John E. Walsh (Rutgers Univ. Press).

THE PSYCHOANALYTICAL
APPROACH

"NEUROSIS, writes Freud, is the negative of perversion. And so, at times, is art."

This paragraph from Princess Marie Bonaparte's study of Poe suggests an approach that must already have occurred to readers. Any account of Poe's life combined with a study of his work must make it clear that he is a perfect case for psychological study. Victorian critics were content to call him a mad and wicked genius, and Baudelaire's approach was basically very similar, except that he regarded Poe as a dark angel rather than a demon. In this century only one literary critic, Joseph Wood Krutch, has made a serious attempt to meld Poe's psychology with his art. Mr. Krutch, however, is rather simplistic. He makes something of the same division between Visionary Poe and Logical Poe suggested here, but pushes it further than is reasonable, saying positively that Poe was impotent, and suggesting that his logical side was developed to stop himself going mad. This will hardly do. Yet it will not do either to ignore Poe's personality completely, as many modern critics have done. The neglect of Marie Bonaparte's psychoanalytic interpretation is witness to the parochialism of contempotary literary criticism, and also to the insistence of critics nowadays that only the conscious intentions of a writer should be considered. In Poe's case, as we shall see, this has led to some remarkable results.

Princess Marie Bonaparte was a student of Freud—who wrote a brief foreword commending her book. She was also a student and an admirer of Poe, and there is certainly nothing trivial about her work. She gives two hundred pages to an account of Poe's life, which was up to date at the time she wrote it, in the early 1930s (the book was not translated into English until 1949), and another five hundred pages to studies of the stories and an elaborate comparison of Poe with Baudelaire. She explains Poe's personality in terms of the traumas he suffered in childhood, the death of his mother and the departure of his father. He became absorbed by death, and in particular by the death of beautiful women, because he was re-creating again and again a moment in which he would be reunited in death with his mother. He was also, however, drawn irresistibly to behave like his father. "Given the early ripening of his Oedipus complex, as often happens with clever children [he] would, at an early age, identify himself with the father and indeed, at eighteen months he did take his father's place when, in a final 'fugue,' David Poe deserted his children and their mother." Hence his drinking— David Poe was also a heavy drinker—which was a mark "as is generally the case, of a latent homosexuality." The sexual act appeared to him as a kind of danger, something that would release his sado-necrophilic tendencies, and that could be held in check only by permanent chastity. "That Poe was a potential sado-necrophilist all his work shows and only his most purely literary devotees would deny it."

To subsume into a paragraph arguments that go over many pages is inevitably to do them less than justice. Whether or not we accept Marie Bonaparte's analysis, her conclusion about Poe's psychological makeup seems irrefutable. Sadism and necrophilia are the motive power behind most of the powerful stories, and the repression of these instincts seems the most reasonable explanation of Poe's attitude toward sex. She suggests that at first he would have made the excuse to himself that Virginia was too young, and then that she was too ill, so that what had been "respect" became duty. This is conjecture, but Poe's whole behavior toward women shows a refusal to contemplate them as sexually desirable. Whether or not he was physically impotent, he flinched psychologically—of course for reasons which he did not understand—from the sexual act.

Art is the negative of perversion, Marie Bonaparte claims in the sentence with which this section began, and in her view art's sublimatory healing power stopped Poe from expressing his sadism openly. After a lengthy examination of Baudelaire's life and art, she concludes that the sadism in Poe made a profound effect on the French writer. She suggests also that necrophilia does not always mean a desire to have intercourse with the dead. There is a necrophilia of fidelity also, which involves no more than the desire to lie beside a loved one after death, something that is expressed again and again in Poe's stories. "Among those artists whose function is to bring about, in others, the *catharsis* of their repressed instincts, a special position must be reserved to those who, at once great writers and latent but confessed sadists, could chart their erotic aggression against that first of all victims, the mother-woman."

Marie Bonaparte is aware of the problems inherent in the application of psychoanalysis to literature. She quotes the witty remark of one analyst: "The aeroplane is a sex-symbol; it can also be used to fly from Munich to Vienna." So when, in relation to *Pym*, she says that the sea is a mother-symbol, she anticipates the objection that it is after all the sea, and that Poe may simply have loved sea, ships, islands (all mother-symbols), and tries to answer it. The gist of what she says is that our attitude to every object in nature is rooted in the unconscious, and in "the dim and majestic gods of our infancy which still survive there." She is always reasonable and in manner persuasive, but the practical results of these interesting theories are often not persuasive at all. In the case of *Pym*, since in her view Poe's life was spent in a search for the lost mother, that must be echoed in the story. The unsoundness of the *Grampus* reflects the uncertainty of the child in the womb, and his imprisonment in small spaces is a womb fantasy. Pym's frequent desperate hunger and thirst refer to Poe's own "thirst above all for the failing breast" of his mother, and the mutiny on the brig is the classical Oedipal revolt, even though Pym does not take part in it. The fact that Augustus's leg comes off when it is lifted is an act of symbolic contrition, and the devouring of his body is interpreted as the sea-mother claiming her guilty son, while the teeth of the devourers represent, at a deep level of the unconscious, "those dreadful teeth of the mother which Poe was to fear throughout life." The teeth are "dreadful" because they are thought to be sited in the vagina, it being a frequent unconscious belief of the impotent that the vagina is furnished with teeth that can bite and castrate. The islanders and the island are black, not because of any intended literary symbolic or satirical reason, but because the mother's body would look black if seen from inside the womb, and the fact that the natives' teeth are black "represents a displacement upwards to the mouth of qualities appropriate to the real or, rather, *cloacal* vagina as, for instance, its darkness and absence of *teeth*."

One need not continue, to show that the truths of psychoanalysis are as arbitrary, and as little susceptible of criticism in terms of anything outside themselves, as the truths of religion. But it may be useful to describe briefly Marie Bonaparte's view of *Berenice* and *Morella*, two stories that have already been considered. Here she unhesitatingly identifies Poe with his narrators. Berenice is therefore clearly Virginia, who was Poe's cousin as Berenice was the narrator's, and at the time the story was written was about ten years old, like Berenice when first described. The change in Berenice from health to sickness represents an amalgamation of the healthy Virginia with Elizabeth Poe, "who, likewise, succumbed to what must have seemed to the child Edgar a vague and equally incomprehensible disease." The eyes of Berenice in illness, "lifeless, and lustreless," are those of the dead Elizabeth Arnold in her child's memory. The premature burial of Berenice, and of other women in Poe stories, takes place because "nascent erotic factors had irredeemably crystallized round her at a moment when, so to speak, she was adorned with those appanages of sickness and death." The teeth are drawn in the story because "mouth and vagina are equated in the unconscious," and this is another case of the vagina dentata, the castrating teeth.

In *Morella* Marie Bonaparte finds much the same influences at work. Morella the mother suffers from consumption (like Elizabeth Poe) and when Morella the child is baptized with that name, she is ten years old (like Virginia). "No clearer description of what is known in psycho-analysis as *transference* could be imagined." (Transference means that emotions properly attached to one person become fixed on another.) Morella's forbidden lore is sexual knowledge, and her intellect is gigantic because this is a reflection of Edgar's feeling about his mother. Marie Bonaparte remarks how often Poe repeats the situation "of some ideal woman who sickens and dies, yet does not really die, since she lives on in unearthly radiance, putrescent and ethereal at one and the same time," and she refers this to Elizabeth's agony and death, repeated later by Virginia's illness, agony, and death.

The difference in effectiveness between the application of psychoanalytical ideas to the life and to the work seems to me very great. To put it briefly, Poe's life gives corroboration for many of Marie Bonaparte's ideas, whereas in relation to the stories it is necessary to accept the dogmas of psychoanalysis in their entirety to find what she says plausible. One can accept her assessment of Poe as a sado-necrophilist without necessarily believing in the importance of his infant traumas, but to regard seriously her explanation of the drawn teeth in *Berenice* it is necessary to have faith in something logically unprovable. Those impotent males she calls into aid in relation to the vagina dentata believe in it unconsciously, so how can the idea carry conviction to the conscious mind? And the ingenious idea about transference in *Morella* is credible only if we accept the infant traumas without question. For a Freudian analyst not only a beheading may represent the fear of castration (and there are beheadings enough in Poe), but also a missing eye, false teeth, the removal of the viscera, a broken nail in a window frame, and a hundred other things. The body rammed up a chimney in *The Murders in the Rue Morgue* refers to the mother's genital regions, and the cellar, tomb, and gaping chimney in *The Black Cat* "recall the dread cloaca of the mother."

Such statements demand belief. For the majority who do not give it, nothing is easier than to ridicule analyses like those made by Marie Bonaparte. The inclination should be resisted, however. The insights given into Poe's work by her study are rarely of direct literary value, but they provide the background to his personality and his achievement. To consider the work, as she does, solely in terms of his unconscious desires and motives is inadequate; but then it is almost equally inadequate to write only about his conscious intentions, as though his personality could be ignored in considering his work. It is the recent critics who assess Poe in terms of his conscious symbolic intentions that we must now consider.

EDGAR POE: A FINE
ACADEMIC PROPERTY

THE attempt to show widespread conscious symbolism in Poe is comparatively new. As late as the mid-1920s Edmund Wilson, while rebuking Americans for their neglect of Poe, was satisfied to call him a typical romantic, to speak of his nightmarish vein of fantasy without particularizing further, and to say that the reality he tried to express was that of (in Baudelaire's phrase) the exception in the moral order. Almost a quarter of a century later Allen Tate, in looking for a "clue" to Poe, felt it sufficient to answer that the character of his work took its shape from the terrible reality of his life. In the last twenty years, however, American scholars have discovered, or think they have discovered, symbolic meanings and subtleties in the stories and poems that had previously gone unremarked. These are to do with Poe's conscious intentions, so that the approach of such critics is quite different from that of Marie Bonaparte.

Poe has become in these twenty years a fine academic property, whose works can be expounded and argued about endlessly in American Studies courses. There is a periodical, *Poe Studies*, devoted to explanation and interpretation of the works, there are essays studying individual stories and discovering new meanings even in the tales of detection. Almost all of this criticism seems to me in varying degrees nonsensical—(that is, mere speculation not supported by the texts or confirmed by the life)—or trivial—(that is, relating to verbal tricks and jokes like those already mentioned in *Pym*), but there is such a quantity of it that a brief examination of its character can hardly be avoided.

The founding father of the new Poe criticism is the respected poet Richard Wilbur, and his lecture *The House of Poe* is one of the most important of the approaches made through symbolism. In speaking of Melville and Hawthorne, Mr. Wilbur says, one has to speak of their symbols. And Poe's prose fiction, too, simply makes no sense unless it is considered "as deliberate and often brilliant allegory." To reject Poe as allegorist is to regard the tales as "nothing more than complicated machines for saying 'boo.' "

Objections arise immediately. The symbolism in *Moby Dick* and *The Confidence Man,* or in a good many Hawthorne short stories, is so evidently *there* that these books and stories truly cannot be read without taking notice of it. That this is not the case with Poe is shown by the fact that critics before Wilbur found no need to look for symbolic meanings in the stories. Did several generations of well-regarded critics make no sense of Poe? Wilbur is committed to saying so. A story like *The Masque of the Red Death* exemplifies the case. This is one of the stories most thoroughly dredged by recent critics in search of its "real" meaning, yet when taken literally it has powerful meaning enough. And to credit Poe's work with "an accessible allegorical meaning" would have seemed no credit at all to a writer who expressed his contempt for allegory not once but many times.

Such objections remain unconsidered by Wilbur. Much of his lecture is given to analyzing Poe's conception of the distinctions between art and life, the poetic soul and the earthly self. In Poe, he says, dream and reality interpenetrate, and imagination is to be identified with dream. Very well. But when, after this slightly analgesic discussion, he slips in the assertions that in *MS. Found in a Bottle* the drowning of the captain and all but one of the crew "represents the growing solitude of reverie," and that when at the end the ship is going down in a whirlpool "we are to understand that the narrator's mind has gone over the brink of sleep and descended into dreams," the question arises: who says so? Not Poe certainly, who gives no hint of such a "meaning." Nobody, in fact, but Mr. Wilbur.

By use of such a method everything can become symbolic—and almost everything does. Taking as in no need of proof his fundamental statement that all scenes and situations in Poe are "concrete representations of states of mind," Wilbur points out that Poe's heroes are rarely to be seen in daylight and that they are often physically enclosed (this means "the isolation of the poetic soul in visionary reverie or trance"); that many of his buildings are desolate or in decay (the poet is retreating into dream and into freedom from the material world); and that most of his rooms are circular (the circle is "an infinite form") or shapeless (freedom of dreaming mind again). The rich furnishings of rooms and the rich people like Ellison must not be regarded as anything so simple as wish fulfillment on the writer's part, but in an allegorical sense. And what is the allegory saying? Why, that his heroes are richly imaginative, what else? Rooms without windows, or with windows blocked and shuttered, indicate that the dreaming soul has its own light; and the frequent cellars and catacombs encountered stand for the irrational part of the mind.

This architectural symbolism, it is said, is used in an especially clear and simple way in *The System of Doctor Tarr and Professor Fether*. The madhouse is a mind. The keepers are its rational, and the inmates its irrational, part. The whole story is a dream. When the keepers open the shuttered windows, they are letting in the light not only of day but of reason. In *The Masque of the Red Death*, the Red Death is the disease of rationalism, Prince Prospero's attempt to escape is "the poetic imagination's flight from temporal and worldly consciousness into dream." The figure of the Red Death who stalks through the rooms is "waking temporal consciousness," Prospero's worldly self, and the meeting of Prospero and the Red Death is like that between William Wilson and his double. And the ebony clock in the story, that makes the dancers flinch when it strikes? By a fine Wilburian touch this is explained by an ascent— or drop—into slang. A clock in slang is a ticker, meaning "the clock of the body," and the dancers (who in any case exist, Wilbur tells us, only in Prospero's imagination) feel the approach of mortality with each stroke.

It is hard to deal seriously with such breathtaking absurdities, but the attempt must be made. The first point to be noted is that these stories do not at all fit Wilbur's postulation that without recourse to allegory no sense can be made of Poe. They make perfectly good sense in their literal readings as a macabre, jocular account of a madhouse, and a picture of universal doom. The *Red Death* has been read in this way for decades, and so, by those who read it at all, has *Tarr and Fether.* Poe was not a man who liked to keep his subtleties to himself. He was very ready to elaborate the meaning of *Eureka* to anybody who would listen; he pointed out to a correspondent that "The Haunted Palace" was that of a human mind; in *William Wilson,* the fact that the stranger is Wilson's other, moral self is made absolutely clear. If he intended some or all of the meanings attributed to him here, why did he never point them out? And why did he give no indication of such meanings in the texts? The writer who wrote of Vondervotteimitiss and of Tellmenow Isitsöornot was not one for this kind of obscurity.

But further than this, a textual examination of the *Red Death* gives no support for the view that the Prince (or the Duke, as he is also carelessly called) is the poetic imagination, which for Poe was the noblest thing imaginable. It does not seem that Poe approves the Prince's behavior. When he is said to be "happy and dauntless and sagacious" in retiring from his half-depopulated dominions with "a thousand hale and light-hearted friends," the note struck seems to be ironic; and when he first sees the Red Death, the Prince's impulse is to flinch from it. If one were going in for symbolism, a better reading—one more in keeping with the tone of the story and with Poe's general thinking—would be one that found in it an extreme determinism, and that stressed the uselessness of trying to avoid the inevitable death of all mankind and the destruction of the world. I am far from suggesting, however, that such a reading is desirable. The overt is to be preferred to the covert, and in this story the literal reading is certainly the best.

The truth is that Wilbur and the many scholars who have followed him do not read Poe so much as they read *into* him. They hardly bother to read the lines because they are so busy reading between them. They make statements that are totally arbitrary, like Wilbur's identification of the Red Death with rationalism, or that turn out often to be commonplace. There is no need to invoke slang about the ticker to agree that the chiming of a clock is likely to disconcert those who know that they may not have long to live. But for the Wilburians Poe has proved a wonderful academic property, a kind of palace of symbolic marvels in which they can roam endlessly, forever making new discoveries. So for one critic the seven rooms in the *Red Death* signify the seven ages of man, for another the Red Death does not exist at all, but is simply man's "fear of his own mistaken concept of death," for a third the clock theme is omnipresent in the stories. The mention of *twelve* islands in *A Descent into the Maelström* thus immediately signifies the clock motif, the raven in the poem signifies the hour hand of a clock, and the devil in *The Devil in the Belfry* signifies the minute hand. Et cetera. The passion for symbolic interpretation has even invaded that province of Logical Poe, the tales of detection. It is said that the *Rue Morgue* is really about "the reintegrated and harmonious consciousness of Dupin," who in the story has used "his genius to detect and restrain the brute in himself, thus exorcising the fiend" (Wilbur), that in *The Purloined Letter* the letter stolen by the Minister D— was a love letter written by Dupin, who is D—'s son (Daniel Hoffman), or that D— is the worldly wicked double of Dupin (Wilbur again). There is no authority in the text for these theories, which are spun entirely from the cloth of fantasy.

One story, *The Fall of the House of Usher,* has been subjected to more examination of this kind than any other. It is by general agreement one of Poe's most powerful works, and is worth detailed examination, both in itself and for what has been said about it. A brief description of the story first. The narrator arrives at the House of Usher (the capital letters are Poe's) on a "dull, dark and soundless day in the autumn of the year." It is a dismal, decaying place, with "a barely perceptible fissure" running down the wall. The image of the house is reflected in "a black and lurid tarn that lay in unruffled lustre by the dwelling." The narrator has come to see his old friend Roderick Usher, who greets him warmly but is evidently ill. He is the victim of "an excessive nervous agitation," and his manner and voice vary in a manner resembling that of "the lost drunkard, or the irreclaimable eater of opium." Usher cannot bear the smell of flowers, his eyes are tortured by light, only some "peculiar sounds . . . from stringed instruments" are endurable to him, and he is struggling with some inexplicable irrational fear. His sister Madeline appears. She too is ill, suffering from some kind of catalepsy, and "a gradual wasting away of the person."

There are no other characters, although a doctor and a servant make momentary appearances. Usher improvises dirges on his guitar, one of which is accompanied by the "rhapsody" of "The Haunted Palace," in which madness is symbolized through verses about a palace which is invaded by "evil things, in robes of sorrow." He paints abstract pictures, one of which is described. It shows "an immensely long and rectangular vault or tunnel," with no outlet and no apparent source of light, but which is yet bathed in light of a "ghastly and inappropriate splendour." One day Usher says that Madeline is dead, and the narrator helps him to bury the body in a small, damp, and long unopened vault. After this Usher becomes manically hilarious and excited. On one stormy night the narrator reads to him from the "Mad Trist" of Sir Launcelot Canning, a story about a conflict between the knight Ethelred and a dragon. The reading is punctuated by cracking and ripping sounds which are the counterpart of sounds described in the story. When another sound comes, again duplicating one in the tale, Usher explains that they have put Madeline living into her tomb. With his preternaturally acute hearing, he has for some days heard her moving in the coffin. He says: "Madman! I tell you that she now stands without the door." There indeed is Madeline. She falls forward upon her brother, and "in her violent and now final death-agonies, bore him to the floor a corpse." The narrator flees. As he leaves the house the crack in the wall rapidly widens, he sees "the mighty walls rushing asunder," and the house collapses into the tarn.

Put down like this the story perhaps seems risible, the material of a Charles Addams cartoon. Yet its impact is disturbing, and the reasons for the effect produced on several generations of readers are not easily analyzable. In a sense it is enough, again, to accept the literal meaning, and not even to question what lies below the surface. This is a tale of horror, and when horrors are explained their power is always lessened. Yet it is true that almost any reader may be left asking questions, and that it is proper to ask—as it is not in a story like *The Masque of the Red Death*—what is this story really *about?*

The title of course refers literally to the house, and also to the Usher line, which we are told will end with Roderick and Madeline. The tarn with which the story begins and ends, and the collapse of the house into it, gives this quite transcendently among the tales the kind of unity Poe demanded in his criticism. The narrator is as nearly as possible a blank, a filter through whom things are seen, but it is indicated that he is a rational person who tries to resist the sickly world in which he finds himself. In the end his resistance to what he calls superstition is overborne, but it seems that he is meant to provide a counterpart, an opposition, to Usher. He represents what is rational, where the Ushers show an iridescence of romantic decay. One can agree with Caroline Gordon and Allen Tate that the fissure in the house is a symbol of Usher's split personality. He is the victim of the oncoming madness which he sings about in "The Haunted Palace," and he knows his doom. Here, as often elsewhere in Poe, man's fate is predetermined.

Usher appears in our terms to be a manic depressive, with a strong element of hysteria in his depression. In the terminology of Poe's day, he is afraid that he is going mad. His abstract painting, which might nowadays seem rather humdrum, is probably meant to indicate both the approach of madness and Usher's fear of it. He is affected, as he admits, by the "form and substance of his family mansion," and also by the illness of his "tenderly beloved sister . . . his sole companion for long years," and in fact his twin. It would seem that Poe had in mind a variation on the *doppelgänger* theme of *William Wilson,* and that Madeline was a part of himself which Roderick felt bound to destroy.

So far, so reasonable. It is quite likely that all of this was in Poe's mind, although it was almost certainly not so clearly formulated. Most modern exegesists, however, go far beyond these modest proposals. (I should make it clear that none of them is original.) They find that Usher's painting foreshadows modern abstract art (Paul Ramsey), that he is "the hypersensitive end-product of civilization itself, driven underground by the pressure of fear" (Harry Levin), that an opposition between Life-Reason and Death-Madness is set up in the story, with the tarn and the painting as expressions of evil, and the miasmas rising from the tarn implying a "sub-natural realm" (Daniel Abel), that Roderick and Madeline's relationship is incestuous (Leo Spitzer and others), that the story is a dream of the narrator's, Roderick part of the narrator's self, the exterior of the house Roderick's body and the interior his mind (Richard Wilbur), that it is "a love story in which incest, murder and necrophilia are inescapable" (Daniel Hoffman). Marie Bonaparte's view that the actual house is a Mother-Mansion, and that the blackness of the vault is an anal symbol suggesting the region from which children "in their infantile sexual theories, imagine themselves to emerge," seems reasonable in comparison with some of these ideas. None of this fine-tooth-combing tries to explain the presence of the servant and the doctor in the story. They have no parts to play but still they appear, and if one makes the assumption that Poe conceived his symbols and allegories with fastidious care, they need to be explained. If, of course, you think like me that Poe was half conscious and half unaware of what he was doing, then they can be accepted as casual additions.

What does seem altogether clear is that such theories—and I have mentioned only a few of them—do not enhance the effect of the story. They do not so much explain it as explain it away. This is partly because vagueness of meaning combined with particularity of detail mark Poe's finest work, and any attempt to clarify that vagueness runs the risk of damaging a story. It is also, however, because Poe knew only partly what he was doing. In the end it is impossible to ignore his life in dealing with his art, because the two were impenetrably interwoven.

CODA: THE PROBLEM
OF EDGAR ALLAN POE

THE problems posed by Poe's life and art have been suggested in the course of this book, but they should perhaps be explicitly stated. We are bound to ask, almost more urgently than of any other creator, how did this life produce this work? And what sort of artist was he? If the ideas that the meanings of his work were almost wholly unconscious (Marie Bonaparte) and almost wholly conscious (modern academic critics) are both unsatisfactory, how should we view what he wrote? Again, the answers are implicit in examination of the life and work, but for the sake of clarity they are summarized here.

The nature of Poe's art was ordered by the psychopathic features of his personality and by the fact that, with the exception of his drinking bouts, these features were kept under control in his life. He emerged into what maturity he reached as a split man, a divided personality. Most of the contradictory things said about him as a writer are true. He was typical of European romanticism, yet his work was rooted in American scenes and manners. He was a poseur who desperately and constantly strove for sincerity, a hack journalist trying to make a living by articles and stories that made frequent use of arcane references and ideas, an opponent of rationalism who fathered a form of literature dependent on the use of reason, an original writer who was also a plagiarist. Almost all of the things said against his work are true, although they are incomplete. D. H. Lawrence is right in calling *The Fall of the House of Usher* an overdone and vulgar fantasy, Allen Tate in saying that his "serious style at its typical worst" is so glutinously embedded in Gothic hyperbole and hysteria that it is difficult to read more than one story at a time, Yvor Winters in remarking that Poe's is an art for servant girls. Indeed, Mallarmé's view that Poe had purified, renewed, and civilized the language of literature through his style is enough in itself to make one skeptical about French assessment of his work.

Yet when the hostile criticism has been understood and accepted something unquestionably remains, and this quotient is the personality of Poe expressed through his art. The two are as nearly as possible identical. He had no subject except himself, and there are no characters in any of his serious stories except the fears, hopes and theories of Edgar Allan Poe. Several stories express his fear of madness, others are inhabited only by Logical Poe. All of the women are specters, idealized images drained of blood. The narrators sometimes embody the point of view of Logical Poe while the action is carried through by Visionary Poe, but there are few stories other than the merely trivial in which he found it possible to dispense with a narrator. As an artist he worked always in the first person, looking again and again at his personality in a glass that often gave back frightening reflections. It showed also upon occasion the features of an extraordinarily clever and ingenious man. Concerned wholly with the depths he discerned in the mirror image, Poe was altogether incapable of imagining what other people felt or believed, and his borrowings must have seemed to him the most natural thing in the world. What did it matter whether he was taking or adapting themes from Lytton or Victor Hugo or Hoffmann, from Moore or Byron? He knew that the final result would be something that belonged totally to Edgar Allan Poe.

He was not mistaken in this knowledge, at least so far as his prose writings are concerned. In part the fascination he has held for generations of readers is to be explained in psychological terms. His various obsessions strike chords of fear and longing in us all, and they do so partly because they are hardly ever explicitly stated. "The Raven" and "Ulalume" succeed in holding the attention because they retain an element of mystery, and among the stories *William Wilson* is an exception in making his fears specific. A more characteristic tale leaves its motivation unexplained, like *The Fall of the House of Usher*. Something frightful must have caused the decay of the Ushers, but what was it? It is easy to say that the answer is incest, but the word is not mentioned in the story, the power of which rests partly in the fact that there is no adequate reason for the terrifying things that happen. So far from being a defect, as some modern commentators have suggested, this phantasmagorical air gives such stories their quality. In tales like *The Black Cat* and *The Tell-Tale Heart* we see only the results of madness, not its origins. About these he was unable or unwilling to write. If he had done so it might have been to produce work like de Sade's, or at least like Swinburne's, in terms that would have alienated his audience. The restraint imposed by his American origins allowed him to make sadism and necrophily respectable. A French Poe would have been a more open, and so less interesting, writer.

The unconscious appeal is strong, but one should not leave it at that. Poe exerts a fascination also over our conscious minds, one based on his unique combination of qualities. Visionary Poe alone might have written critical-metaphysical theses that faintly echoed Coleridge, poems not much less woolly than those of Chivers, stories soaked in the dripping rhetoric of German romanticism. Logical Poe alone might have spent his wonderful cleverness in producing mechanically ingenious crime stories on the level of Gaboriau. It is when the two are fully fused that he is at his most memorable, in the *Rue Morgue* and *Pym*, *Usher* and the *Red Death*. Nobody has written quite like this before or since, and perhaps nobody will do so again, for it took an extraordinary combination of circumstances to produce a literary psychopath of genius like Edgar Allan Poe. To award or deny him greatness seems almost irrelevant when the small body of his finest work has struck so strong a chord in the imaginations of generations of readers in so many countries. It is the final paradox of his career that a writer who borrowed so much from so many of his predecessors and contemporaries should have produced the most original prose fiction of the nineteenth century.

SELECT BIBLIOGRAPHY

This bibliography makes no attempt to list all of the books and other material consulted. I have used no manuscript references because there is very little important Poe material that has not somewhere or other appeared in print, and I have not listed sources like George Gilfillan's *Third Gallery of Literary Portraits* or John Sartain's *Memoirs of a Very Old Man,* each of which provided a fragment of text. It seemed better to give only sources that have been particularly useful to me, or may prove so to readers and students, making brief comments on them. These are listed in chronological order, which again seemed better in this case than the usual alphabetical listing.

WORKS

Complete Works, Virginia edition. Edited by James A. Harrison, 17 vols., New York, 1902. This remains the nearest thing we have to a complete and textually accurate edition of all Poe's writings.

Doings of Gotham. Pottsville, Pennsylvania, 1929. Gives the full texts, not available elsewhere, of Poe's contributions to the *Columbia Spy.*

Poems. Edited by Thomas Ollive Mabbott, Cambridge, Massachusetts, 1969. The first volume of the edition of the works projected by Mabbott, the finest Poe scholar of his generation, and unhappily the only one completed before his death. A model of its kind, giving all the variants of every poem, with very informative notes.

Selected Writings of Edgar Allan Poe. Edited by David Galloway, London, 1967.

Arthur Gordon Pym. Edited by Harold Beaver, London, 1975.

The Science Fiction of Edgar Allan Poe. Edited by Harold Beaver, London, 1976. These three excellent paperbacks are a gesture in the direction of the complete works. The texts are always those finally revised by Poe, and there are comments on earlier variants in the notes.

BIOGRAPHY

Works. With a Memoir by Rufus Wilmot Griswold, 4 vols., New York, 1850–56.

Important because it is the first collection of the works, and also for Griswold's memoir, which began the legend of villainous Poe. Griswold's lies and forgeries should not conceal the fact that he had some critical and biographical perceptions, and said some shrewd things.

Edgar Poe and His Critics. By Sarah Helen Whitman, New York, 1860. Mrs. Whitman's passionate but eccentric, and not very successful, attempt to correct Griswold.

Works. Edited by John H. Ingram, 4 vols., Edinburgh, 1874–75. Ingram's long introduction, and his elaboration of it in the 1880 biography, are the first serious counters to the Griswoldian view.

Works. Edited by R. H. Stoddard, 6 vols., New York, 1884. Interesting for Stoddard's memoir, which offers a return to Griswold, and suggests that Ingram had been altogether too indulgent to Poe.

Complete Works, Virginia edition. Edited by James A. Harrison, 17 vols., New York, 1902. Harrison's biography in the first volume does not dig very deep, but his final volume includes letters written to Poe, some of which have not been printed elsewhere.

Life. By George E. Woodberry, 2 vols., Boston, 1909. This remains much the best written biography. By this time Woodberry had conquered the antipathy to his subject shown in his much shorter 1885 biography, and his research had uncovered many new facts.

Israfel. By Hervey Allen, 2 vols., New York, 1926. Lively and interesting, but also romantic and unreliable, concerned very much with Poe as a legendary culture hero.

Edgar Allan Poe, The Man. By Mary E. Phillips, 2 vols., Philadelphia, 1926. Masses of facts and a great many conjectures, all jumbled together. Some of the facts are important, and not to be found elsewhere.

Poe and the Southern Literary Messenger. By David K. Jackson, Richmond, 1934. Gives the fullest account of this period in literary detail.

Edgar Allan Poe. By Arthur Hobson Quinn, New York, 1941. The standard biography, which in a factual sense is not likely to be superseded. Some additions, but remarkably few corrections, are needed after nearly forty years. Quinn is an apologist almost to the point of being a hero worshipper, and in a critical sense his book hardly exists.

Letters. Edited by John Ward Ostrom, 2 vols., Cambridge, Massachusetts, 1948. An impeccably edited collection of the letters, with voluminous and helpful notes. There are very few post-Ostrom letters of importance, and his texts and dating are both generally reliable. Indispensable for any student of Poe.

Chivers' Life of Poe. New York, 1952. Not really a life, but an account of Chivers's relations with Poe. Interesting, although not reliable.

Poe's Literary Battles. By Sidney P. Moss, Durham, North Carolina, 1963.

A very full account of Poe's journalistic wars, especially those with the New York literati.

Poe's Major Crisis. By Sidney P. Moss, Durham, North Carolina, 1970. Gives all the details of the Poe-English affair.

Building Poe Biography. By John Carl Miller, Baton Rouge, 1977, Contains details of letters collected by Ingram, which give new information on minor points.

CRITICISM

The Mind of Poe. By Killis Campbell, Cambridge, Massachusetts, 1917. A collection of studies, highly original in their time and still valuable today, including an examination of the Poe-Griswold controversy and an account of Poe as seen by his contemporaries.

Edgar Allan Poe. By Joseph Wood Krutch, New York, 1924. A psychological examination of Poe, overshadowed by Princess Marie Bonaparte's work.

The Life and Works of Edgar Allan Poe. By Marie Bonaparte, London, 1949. Overstated, but outstandingly interesting and valuable, interpretation of the life and works from a firmly Freudian viewpoint.

The Histrionic Mr. Poe. By N. Bryllion Fagin, Baltimore, 1949. Interesting book that concentrates almost wholly on the idea of Poe as actor.

Poe. A Critical Study. By Edward H. Davidson, Cambridge, Massachusetts, 1957. Sound and intelligent throughout, particularly good on Poe's philosophical-poetical attitude, and on *Eureka.*

The French Face of Edgar Poe. By Patrick F. Quinn, Carbondale, Illinois, 1957. Far the best of the several books about reactions to Poe in France.

The Recognition of Edgar Allan Poe. Edited by Eric W. Carlson, Ann Arbor, Michigan, 1966. Texts dealing with Poe, from the first reviews through Griswold's "Ludwig" article, Dostoevsky, Shaw, and others, up to recent criticism including that of Auden and Richard Wilbur. Several of the texts are not easily accessible elsewhere.

Poe. Edited by Robert Regan, Englewood Cliffs, N.J., 1967. A collection of "twentieth-century views," including those of Wilbur and Jean-Paul Weber, as well as a fragment of Krutch's book and a brilliant article by Allen Tate.

Poe the Detective. By John E. Walsh, 1968. Fascinating investigation of Poe's twists and turns in dealing with *The Mystery of Marie Rogêt.*

Poe and the British Magazine Tradition. By Michael Allen, New York, 1969. A close, useful examination of Poe's debts to, and links with, the British magazines of his time.

Edgar Poe the Poet. By Floyd Stovall, Charlottesville, Virginia, 1969. Mostly high-flown views about several aspects of Poe's poems. Good on his debt to Coleridge.

The Fall of the House of Usher. Edited by Thomas Woodson, Englewood Cliffs, N.J., 1969. A collection of essays about this story, all recent and almost all highly eccentric.

Discoveries in Poe. By Burton R. Pollin, Notre Dame, Indiana, 1970. New critical discoveries, most of them minor, about Poe's previously undiscovered debts to other writers.

Who Murdered Mary Rogers? By Raymond Paul, 1971. Journalistic account of the actual case on which Poe based *The Mystery of Marie Rogêt*, with a suggested and likely solution.

Poe Poe Poe Poe Poe Poe Poe. By Daniel Hoffman, New York, 1972. Too personal, too egotistical, and marked by appalling conflations like Edgarpoe, but offering many critical ideas about the works, some illuminating, others merely ingenious.

INDEX

Abel, Daniel, 237
academic studies of Poe's work, 237–238
The Adventures of Harry Franco, Briggs, 99
"Al Aaraaf," Poe, 32, 33, 43, 107, 193, 195–196
Al Aaraaf, Tamerlane and Minor Poems, Poe, 32–33
"Second Edition," 43–44
Alexander's Weekly Messenger, 69
Allan, Frances Valentine (Mrs. John Allan), 10, 12
death of, 3, 30, 40
Allan, John, 3, 4, 9, 18, 25, 44
background of, 10
description of Poe by, 15–16
financial difficulties of, 12, 14, 15–16
letters from Poe, 22, 25, 26, 29–30, 32, 34, 36, 38, 39–40, 41, 44–45
marriages of, 3–4, 35
personality of, 10
relationship with Poe, 11, 15–16, 18, 25–27, 29–31, 34, 36–37, 193
final break, 38–41
romantic affairs of, 34
Allan & Ellis, 12
allegory in Poe's works, 232–233
American character of Poe's works, 173, 174, 177, 189
American literature, 19th century, 54–55, 61
compared to English literature, 57, 58
Poe's views of, 181–183
American Notes, Dickens, 35
American Review, 96, 113

American theatre, 19th century, 8–9
American Whig Review, 140
"Annabel Lee," Poe, 122, 143, 146, 168, 192, 196
Anthon, Charles, 95
anti-slavery movement, 219
army career of Poe, 28–31
Arnold, Benedict, Poe as grandson of, 34, 38
Arnold, Elizabeth, 5–7, 8, 9
The Assignation (The Visionary), Poe, 205
Astoria, Irving, 217
Auber, Jean Francois, 198
Auden, W. H., 161, 193, 197, 217
"Autobiography" series, Poe, 55, 58, 61, 84, 113

The Balloon-Hoax, Poe, 88–89, 92, 216
Baltimore *Sun,* 170
Barnaby Rudge, Dickens, 185
Barrett, Elizabeth, 97–98, 183–184, 185–186
accused by Poe of plagiarism, 176
Drama of Exile and Other Poems, 186
"Lady Geraldine's Courtship," 176
Barry, Littleton, pseudonym of Poe, 106
Baudelaire, Charles, 166–167, 226, 227–228, 231
Beaver, Harold, 218, 219
beetroot, cultivation of, 69
"The Bells," Poe, 126–127, 146, 192, 196, 197